Parables for the
New Conversation

Richard Enos

Note for Librarians: A cataloguing record for this book is available from Library and Archives Canada at www.collectionscanada.ca/amicus/index-e.html

Cover Design/Artwork by Hanbi Kim.

Back Cover Photography © Rob Allen 2008 www.roballen.ca

Printed in Victoria, BC, Canada.

ISBN: 978-1-4251-7398-2

We at Trafford believe that it is the responsibility of us all, as both individuals and corporations, to make choices that are environmentally and socially sound. You, in turn, are supporting this responsible conduct each time you purchase a Trafford book, or make use of our publishing services. To find out how you are helping, please visit www.trafford.com/responsiblepublishing.html

Our mission is to efficiently provide the world's finest, most comprehensive book publishing service, enabling every author to experience success. To find out how to publish your book, your way, and have it available worldwide, visit us online at www.trafford.com/10510

 www.trafford.com

North America & international
toll-free: 1 888 232 4444 (USA & Canada)
phone: 250 383 6864 ♦ fax: 250 383 6804 ♦ email: info@trafford.com

The United Kingdom & Europe
phone: +44 (0)1865 722 113 ♦ local rate: 0845 230 9601
facsimile: +44 (0)1865 722 868 ♦ email: info.uk@trafford.com

10 9 8 7 6 5 4 3 2 1

Acknowledgments

I would like to begin by thanking those people who, in the spring of 2000, encouraged me to persevere in my quest to write a book by contributing money to me at my request with no guarantees of recompense. These people include my sister Christine and my brother John, my mother Irene and her husband Buddy, my brother-in-law Barry and his parents Alan and Madelaine, my very generous Uncle Bob, my Aunt Nancy, my cousin Danny, my good friends Celine, Mike, Sonya, Susan, Daron, and Brad, and many other special people who advanced me the cost of a future copy of my book which, eight years later, has finally arrived.

I would like to thank Bill Cotric, who helped me through the early stages of my writing with his coaching and encouragement, and my very good friend Carole Landry, who has been supportive throughout the process and has been particularly helpful with her profound understanding and embodiment of the *new conversation*. I would also like to thank Darlene Chrissley and Lorne Ellingson for their advanced reading of the text and very helpful comments, and Dorian Darie, who came along at just the right time to bring very profound insight to bear on the flow of the final version. I would like to again thank my sister Christine, not only for her enthusiastic support and encouragement but also for her diligent proof-reading of the final text.

I would like to give a most special thanks to my wife Hyun, a truly fascinating girl who has endured being the main family breadwinner over the past several years during the emotional roller-coaster that has been the process of writing this book. I look forward now to engaging with her in the greater bounty of experiences life has to offer.

Finally, I would like to dedicate this book to my mother and father, my yin and yang, my light and shadow. My mother, who passed away from cancer in 2000, was an angel to me throughout her difficult life, and became a very dear friend when I got old enough to appreciate her. My father, who suffered a severe brain aneurysm in 1997 and has been debilitated ever since, has been my demon, although today I see clearly how he was really an angel in disguise. I am grateful not only because the love of both my parents was constant and unfailing, but also because they loved me in very different ways, helping to shape the person I am today.

—Richard Enos, Toronto, April 2008

Contents

1. The Hermit

One day a hermit emerged from the forest on the island of Allandon, seeking to share his wisdom. As he had been in silence for forty years, his sudden appearance excited considerable curiosity among the villagers, and they all followed him to the top of the great mountain at the center of the island.

When the villagers had settled comfortably beneath the hermit, he spoke.

"From my time in silence, I have divined one sublime truth," he said, and after a dramatic pause, continued: "Life is fun."

The crowd below started to buzz. People smiled at each other and some of them started to laugh. The hermit was puzzled by their response until a woman who had been laughing particularly heartily stood up and responded.

"Sorry, but—we already knew that."

"You knew that?" the hermit replied.

"Indeed," said another, "we've been talking about it for some years now."

"We have to remind each other of it all the time!" said an elder man, prompting more laughter from the villagers.

The woman walked up to the hermit and said, "We would like to invite you into the village, to show you all the games we have invented during your silence."

Before he knew it, the hermit was walking down to the village and talking amongst the people, smiling like a child.

I am a serious man. And I am on a serious mission. And that mission is to take life less seriously.

I don't think I'm alone in this. I look around me and I see other people searching out from behind stern faces. We are looking for something to believe in. Without it, the gravity of life weighs on us. We are tired of our heavy walk through life but we are unsure of how to lighten our step. Rather than experiencing our life as a dance of ongoing discovery and creation, most of us march to the tune of rampant familiarity. We notice that we are basically living the same day over and over. Worse, we feel doomed to continue this way, focused only on improving our material comfort as our health and vitality slowly deteriorate and finally we die.

There are those saving moments of course, perhaps connecting with friends on the weekend over wine, or being part of the lives of our children. Certainly when we observe children closely we are reminded of the rapture we once felt about life. We see through them a faith in a greater future, and an optimism that all dreams will one day come true—at least until they themselves begin to follow in our rut-steps.

Are the words joy, wonder, and fun part of our daily conversation? Perhaps they could be, once we dispatch of the mountain of obligations needing our serious attention at the moment. It's just that this mountain of obligations never seems to subside. We are commanded by many voices outside of us and they never stop. So we do what our society expects of us, our boss and co-workers, our friends, our spouse, our children. We do what we are *supposed* to do.

It's not that we can't think for ourselves. We very much can. And so we have to ask ourselves why we keep so perpetually busy. Maybe we want to stay a safe distance from that uncomfortable inquiry into what we really want from life. The temptation is compelling: it's much easier to follow instructions than to figure things out on our own. Being told by others who we are and what we really should do removes the need to look into our dark insides and discover it for ourselves.

We have been living in a society where there is no shortage of advice on what to do and how to think. But while simply keeping our hands and our minds occupied may have worked for most of us up to now, things are changing. As we become more aware as individuals, as we become more conscious as a society, the voice inside of us is getting too loud to ignore. No amount of noise on the outside will be able to distract us from it much longer. It is compelling us to look at ourselves and figure out what we really came here to do. We are running out of places to hide and people to blame for our disenchantment. Let's face it, most of us are living a life we have outgrown. In our collective restlessness, we feel the need to kick-start ourselves into a greater and more profound experience.

Can we honestly say with a straight face that we are living up to our full potential? There may be a few people in the world who think they are, but I have yet to meet one of them. No, we know very well that we are not. Not even close. We are underachieving by a longshot. We know that we are not living the life of our dreams, and yet we haven't gotten around to getting that life going.

It's almost as though we are waiting for some cataclysmic event to bring out our greatest selves. When a loved one dies of a tragic illness we step in and create foundations to support others going through the same difficulties. When the child of a neighbor has gone missing in the woods, we somehow find the superhuman strength to search for days on end, without our usual complaints and self-concerns. In the aftermath of the attack on the World Trade Center stories of compassion, courage, and humanity abounded. When we do these things we feel good about ourselves, we feel truly alive.

Naturally it begs the question: why should we wait for tragedies to occur in our lives before we decide to be authentic, to get excited about life and to love with passion? What is stopping us from doing it now? Nothing. It's a choice that is available to us, 24/7. But who will lead, who will guide us into this authentic existence? Ah, but this is what is most exciting about this time in history: we are actually starting to find the wherewithal to guide one another.

There is a new kind of conversation that is emerging today, in our homes, coffee shops, offices, indeed wherever people meet. It is a conversation that has enchanted those who have taken to engaging in it. The price of admission? Careful listening and speaking from the heart. In other words, we are all invited. The new conversation in the air is around possibility—the possibility that we can find fulfillment in our lives, and that we may really be able to live out our dreams. The new conversation honors our uniqueness, allows us to make mistakes, and supports the exploration of what we most deeply desire. It helps us step back from a life of duty and obligation and step into one of freedom and joy. In the space of the new conversation we will inevitably be challenged to look at our greatest obstacle—that we generally take ourselves far too seriously.

Now I can assure you that I have done extensive research on the subject of futile seriousness. I have arrived at a place intellectually where I now fully concur with Deepak Chopra when he says that we live in a recreational universe. But knowing something is not the same as experiencing it.

Any delusion I had that I had shed my own aura of seriousness was quashed in the early stages of writing this book, at a meeting at the home of my writing coach. I got the opportunity to talk with his daughter, who was very bright and quite interesting to talk to, and so we spoke about such matters as writing, drama, and politics. A week later my writing coach told me that she had likened me to a bottle of wine whose cork was on far too tight.

"Fine wine inside," he said laughing. He was trying to take some of the sting out. And I did feel some, knowing that this was her honest impression of me. Here I thought I had shed at least my visage of seriousness long ago. Instead, I was left to use this as another in a long list of opportunities to laugh at myself—a cleansing of my false self-image if you will. But in truth it remains a difficult thing to do. There always seems to be something new to learn about letting go. So I don't come to you as an expert on the subject. I come as a work-in-progress. I am hoping that you will accept the notion that we should teach what we most need to learn.

And the term *teach* is meant very loosely. What I am really intending with this work is to present ideas that will enrich our conversation about what is possible in our world. It could serve as a signpost to what you may have already noticed rising up around you. There is no need to accept anything proposed here as *gospel*, especially when it doesn't seem or feel right to you.

In fact this is one of the hallmarks of the new conversation: what appeals to one may not appeal to another. The great teachers throughout history knew this. They did not want their words to be followed blindly if they did not resonate within the individual. On his deathbed Buddha urged his followers to "be a lamp unto yourselves." It was his way of saying that we can only achieve fulfillment if we follow what rings true for us and then shed the light of this truth onto the world. To simply copy someone else's life or follow a formula that proscribed the 'proper' ways to think and behave would not be the way to true fulfillment.

Instinctively we know this. And yet we have to admit that there is a gap between what we know about life and how we live. Personally I want to work towards bridging this gap. This book marks my intention to wake up in the morning happy to be alive, explore my creativity every day and experience my life as fun.

For you it may be something different, something uniquely yours that nobody can uncover except for yourself. What is your intention from life? If you think you don't know it in this moment, then it might be time for you to engage in a conversation, one that is designed to help you in your search. This conversation might not only provide you with the opportunity to unravel and reflect upon the beliefs that are all rolled up inside of you, it also may give you the chance to hear about and try on other ideas that might stimulate your growth. There has never been a greater opportunity in our history to share the unique flavors that each one of us has been storing up. Will you join me in popping our corks in celebration? I am convinced that everyone has fine wine inside themselves to offer the world.

If you have up to now been on the outside looking in, and have been waiting for an invitation, then take this as your official invitation into the new conversation. I invite you to believe that your uniqueness is a gift to the world, and you are here to do nothing other than share that uniqueness, so that we all may benefit from the memories of where you have been and the vision of where you want to go.

2. The Lawyer

The main village road on the island of Allandon was predominantly a bright and colorful façade of shops and businesses of all different kinds. Only a few buildings in the older section were dull and run-down, and on this day the village renovator and his young apprentice were setting about gutting and restoring one of those buildings as the owner had recently died.

On their way in, the renovator tapped his crowbar on the rusted metallic shingle hanging in the front that read *Attorney-at-Law*.

"This building was owned by the village lawyer," the renovator said. "Poor fellow, he died a lonely man. It had been years since anyone had asked him to represent them."

"Why, he couldn't win a case?"

"Quite the opposite—he never lost a case! He was so good at clearly expressing his client's side of a dispute that the decision always went in his favor."

"So how come people stopped hiring him?"

"Well, he's really only got himself to blame," laughed the renovator. "He would always brag that he could win either side of any dispute, which was probably true—that's how good he was. But as a result it slowly dawned on the people here in the village that both sides of a dispute could be seen to have merit if they were properly *heard*. We spoke about it amongst ourselves and came to realize that if we just learned how to listen to each other better, we could resolve our disputes ourselves."

They walked into the building. The lawyer's office was thick with dust, and cobwebs had started to form up the sides of his large oak desk. The renovator plopped down on the big leather chair and put his feet up on the desk.

"The great thing is, we eventually learned to resolve our disputes in a way that satisfied both sides. We tried to explain to the lawyer that we had found a better way to resolve disputes."

"What did he say?"

"He dismissed it. He argued that we would go back to our old ways. So he came into his office every morning and sat here waiting for clients to come in. But they stopped coming."

"And you couldn't convince him that things had really changed?"

"Convince *him*?" the renovator laughed. "This man made his living on being right. He didn't know *how* to lose an argument."

"Maybe that's why he died lonely," the apprentice said.

Twenty years ago I thought that I was well on my way to having life figured out. I had a Master's Degree in Existential Philosophy and I had studied the History of Western Civilization at the prestigious Liberal Arts College in Montreal. Never mind that other people didn't always agree with my beliefs about life, I felt that they hadn't studied enough or simply weren't intelligent enough to grasp what I was saying.

Ouch.

To me a great conversation was one in which I was able to convince someone to agree with my way of thinking, through the use of relentless logic and pertinent facts. And if I could be persuasive even when I wasn't rock-sure about my position, all the greater was the accomplishment. I once convinced one of my peers to abandon his thesis proposal after arguing that it was flawed. When I later bragged to some classmates that I knew virtually nothing on the subject, I couldn't understand why they were not fully impressed by my feat. There seemed to be no conversation more satisfying to me than convincing others of my point of view. Whether the other person benefited from the conversation didn't really enter into the equation for me.

What I didn't realize at the time was that I was setting myself up for quite a fall. In fact, I've been knocked off my high horse a number of times since then. Some of the bruises to my ego were so deep that I feel fortunate to have survived to tell the tale.

One such experience happened shortly after I graduated. I was introduced to a New Age discussion group that was hosted by a friend of my father's named Steve. The group would discuss the work of some of the writers of the time such as Richard Bach, Ram Dass, Carlos Castaneda and others. What I found intriguing about the meetings was that, although I usually felt tired and unmotivated on my way there, the atmosphere and the conversation would always make me feel incredibly alive and energized by the time I left.

When my first ten-week session had ended, Steve thought that my background in philosophy would make me a great facilitator for the group's next session. I agreed to do it on the condition that each member made a commitment to be there for all the meetings. The previous session had been more informal in this regard but I figured this was the least everyone could do if I was going to spend the time preparing for each meeting. As it turns out, they kept their end of the bargain while I ended up spending very little time preparing for each meeting. On the day of the meeting I would just think of a topic that I was familiar enough with and scratch out a few notes.

The group conversations that I was orchestrating had one simple dynamic: I would put a controversial idea out to the group and take up the position opposite to the general consensus. It seemed easy for me to argue my points. The participants usually could provide no evidence to substantiate what they said. They would simply say that's how they felt or that's what they believed, and so I left each week feeling that my arguments had prevailed.

What I didn't feel at the end of each week was the energy and aliveness that had come during every meeting when Steve was facilitating. It just wasn't there. The other participants might have noticed it too, but as they had made a commitment, they showed up every week without complaint.

By the final week I was quite happy that the session was ending. It had become nothing less than a chore for me. As usual I presented the topic for the evening, and challenged one of the more reticent participants to give his opinion. But instead of speaking about the topic, he blurted out, "Richard, I don't think it should be this way!"

I was taken aback. I collected myself and asked him to explain what he meant, but he felt that his outburst was out of line, and he apologized. He was going to address the topic, but I asked him again what he meant by that comment. He looked around at the others, and then took a slow breath and began to elaborate. And did he have a lot to say! He had noticed that the mood during the meetings was more serious and confrontational than it had been in the past. He felt that instead of arguing and debating, we should be sharing with and understanding each other. The more he spoke, the more embarrassed I became.

When he had finished, I decided that instead of moving forward with the topic, I would ask everyone else how the past ten weeks had gone for them. I figured I would get some different opinions that would give me some ammunition to counter what he had said. But one after another, each participant echoed very similar comments. I was starting to feel that my facilitation had been a stark and unequivocal failure, and what was worse, I had been completely oblivious to it for the whole ten-week session.

But while their words seemed such a negative indictment of me, none of them had a hint of bitterness or anger. They all spoke with respect and compassion, almost apologetically. When it came around to Steve, the last person to speak, he simply offered a warm acknowledgment for my willingness to sit quietly and listen to it all. It was truly difficult for me to hold back tears.

The conversation surrounding how miserably I had failed as a facilitator lasted the entire two hours of the meeting, and by the time Steve had finished his comments it was time for us to go. But instead of all running off at the end as we had done the previous weeks, we hung around outside and talked for several more hours, well past midnight. We laughed and joked and felt an unbelievable connection to each other. The energy and lightness that I had felt in Steve's sessions had come back. This final meeting turned out to be by far the best one that I had facilitated!

The lesson was big for me, and it took months to fully sink in. I came to realize that my judgment of the participants as shallow simpletons who were lacking conviction was way off base, as most judgments are. They just had nothing to prove, and their depth was in their compassion, their humanity, and their authenticity. This was my first real life lesson in the art of the conversation, where there didn't need to be winners or losers, and where everyone can take something away including a real sense of connectedness with one other. I went into that facilitation thinking I had something to teach, and left realizing I had so much to learn.

I now believe that we all have a strong need and a deep longing for authentic conversation, in today's society more than ever. I spent ten weeks trying to show everyone how smart I was, but it was only when the conversation became *real*—when I stopped having something to prove, and people were able to say what they really felt—that there was some kind of meaningful exchange. And where there is meaningful exchange, that is where true learning can take place, and a real connection can be felt.

There is risk involved, no question about it. We have a fear of being ridiculed, of being made wrong. Often this makes us conform to accepted opinion even if we don't agree with it. When this happens, we usually leave such exchanges feeling uninspired, because it thwarts a deep desire to express what we think and explore our unique perspective on things. So now is the time to make a shift, a conscious shift. We are being called to look more deeply into the way we express ourselves, and no less importantly the way we provide an environment for others to express themselves.

The rules of the new conversation are simple in a way. Speak your deepest truth and allow others to do the same. You allow others to do the same when you listen actively and are genuinely curious about what they might have to say. You acknowledge their triumphs and courage, and commiserate with their losses and sorrow. But this must be *authentic*, not some surface act of political correctness. Better to tell someone straight out that you don't care about their story. If we have trouble being authentic, if we cannot help but judge, then we can have *that* be the starting point of our conversation. The new conversation can support this— *especially* this—since it is honest. The new conversation brings us close to our highest levels of vulnerability and authenticity. Of course it's difficult to be authentic all the time, but surely we have *some* experience of authentic expression to draw on. When the desire is there, we all have the capability to support each other in creating a shared space of trust that is safe enough for us to be vulnerable and reveal our deepest truths.

Lately I have been noticing around me that people are getting better at this way of relating to each other. We are becoming more aware of the power of creating a non-judgmental space. I love to be in a conversation with someone who really *gets it,* and no matter how I express myself I'm not judged or made wrong. Yes, they have their own views, which they would tell me if I was interested. They might even invite me to try a new idea on, to see if it fits. But nothing is forced, because they don't pretend to know what it feels like to walk in my shoes.

In retrospect I realize that this was the dynamic created by the people in my New Age discussion group. I was free to be myself for ten weeks, and only when I was ready to hear a deeper truth was it presented to me. While my ego had tremendous difficulty with what each person confessed about their experience of my facilitation, there was already an implicit trust because they had all spoken with compassion and humility throughout. As a result I was able to make a crucial connection between my behavior and my not feeling energized by these meetings. Had they been judging me and making me wrong, the outcome would have surely been different. Likely I would have put up my verbal fists for a real debate. Both sides might have teetered a bit but neither side would have conceded defeat.

This has long been the legacy of our society: arguing, debating, trying to prove we are right and the other is wrong, under the illusion that there is strength in being right and weakness in being wrong. But as our consciousness has expanded, we have come to see that the opposite is true. We have all felt in conversation the remarkable impact of someone admitting that they were wrong, as we have seen our impact on others when we are open to the possibility that perhaps *they* are right. And when we go beyond even that, to an awareness that it is not about right and wrong—that perhaps there isn't really *any* right or wrong—then we find ourselves in a conversation that has the potential to unite us all where in the past we have been divided.

3. The Shadow

Well past midnight in a home on the island of Allandon, the village schoolteacher was retiring to bed and noticed the light on in the room of her son, who was known to the villagers as 'the young philosopher'. Upon entering, she saw him in his familiar place, sitting at his desk buried in a mountain of heavy tomes.

"It is past midnight, my son," said the schoolteacher. "Time for you to be in bed, I should think."

"I am contemplating the mystery of being, mother. I don't think I can rest until I have found the answer."

"And you imagine that through study and contemplation you will one day have an answer?"

"If I am dedicated and persistent, yes."

She smiled. "Do you see your shadow cast by the light of the candle?"

"Yes."

"What is that shadow?"

"Well—it is darkness," the young philosopher replied.

Suddenly his mother blew out the candle, sending the room into pitch blackness. "Now where is your shadow?" she asked.

"I can't see it," he said, "not without the light."

"But your shadow hasn't changed. It was darkness and it still is darkness."

"That's true."

"Perhaps, with dedication and persistence, you will eventually find it."

The boy thought for a minute. "Or perhaps I should go to bed," he said.

My formal education gave me valuable information about the philosophy of life, and with it a sense of *knowing-it-all*. My real education started when an insight gradually revealed itself to me: whenever I felt I knew exactly what life was, I was actually the most in the dark about life. To know life is to *limit* life, to get cut off from the mystery that makes it fun to be alive. This is where my seriousness runs roughshod over possibilities, and why I am excited that the new conversation has the potential to open them up to me again.

The new conversation is not about knowing. It is about the thrill of exploring life with an open heart and mind. When two or more people approach their interactions this way, the magic of new insights and possibilities for life are never far behind. I have come to notice in my conversations that whenever I start to provide answers, the energy and vitality of the conversation ebbs away. For the most part people aren't looking for answers, even when they ask the questions. They are looking for someone who knows how to listen and inquire with them. When I *don't know*, when I am curious and prepared to learn, then the conversations I am in have the potential to be dynamic, probing, and meaningful.

Consider the times you have been in a conversation with a self-proclaimed 'expert' on how you should live. I'm sure you have come across this person before, in the form of a parent, teacher, neighbor, or boss. How does it feel to be the receiver of this one-way instruction? There is really no dynamic, nothing to do in this conversation but nod and wonder when they will stop. We all had plenty of experience with this type of conversation when we were young children. But we are grown up now. And that doesn't mean that it's our turn to be the expert. It means we can choose a different way of relating to people and sharing our ideas.

If you *are* just looking for answers, there are plenty of people in our society willing to provide them for you. However, when you enter into the new conversation looking for answers, you might notice your questions getting posed back to you. In the matter of how to live our lives, each of us is our own expert. Only we know our truth. No matter how wise someone may be, they don't have the authority to tell you that you really want to become a doctor. Or that you should enjoy exercising. Or that you have no reason to be sad. It's time now to stop looking for people to tell us who we are and how we should live. We need to find the courage to come out and say what's true for us, and shake off the pressure of having to conform to the opinions and beliefs of others.

Of course it's difficult. We have been conditioned to believe that our truth isn't good enough, that we need to do what is acceptable to others, we need to have the answer. But there is no definitive answer. And accepting this is not tantamount to admitting our stupidity. Quite the opposite. Socrates used to say, "All I know is that I know nothing," and yet he was considered the wisest man in ancient Athens. To a certain extent life will always be about trying to figure out what life is about. Learning to be free from the need for certainty keeps all doors open for passionate exploration. Like peeling an onion with an infinite center, life always reveals itself with new questions that run deeper than the answers it provides.

Whether you are actively involved in the game of trying to figuring life out or you are sitting on the sidelines, life itself goes on. If you are not asking the questions, life is sure to bring them to you eventually—and probably when you least expect it. In Tolstoy's famous short work *The Death of Ivan Ilych*, the main character never questioned what he did in life. His choices and actions were always informed by the opinions of others and his society. But in the serene quiet of his death bed,

> ...the question suddenly occurred to him: "What if my whole life has been wrong?"
> It occurred to him that what had appeared perfectly impossible before, namely that he had not spent his life as he should have done, might after all be true. It occurred to him that his scarcely perceptible attempts to struggle against what was considered good by the most highly placed people, those scarcely noticeable impulses which he had immediately suppressed, might have been the real thing, and all the rest false. And his professional duties and the whole arrangement of his life and of his family, and all his social and official interests, might all have been false. He tried to defend all those things to himself and suddenly felt the weakness of what he was defending. There was nothing to defend.

Ivan Ilych became painfully clear in the last few moments of his life that he had not attended to the faint impulses he felt that seemed to question the manner in which he was living his life. In tracing back the whole of his existence he suddenly realized that *he had not actually lived*. He had spent his entire life in the realm of the known and had not participated in the mystery, the wonder, the joy, the game that life is. While we are often frustrated when life doesn't work out the way we planned, perhaps instead we need to celebrate the unpredictability of life. Most often it is just those unforeseen and spontaneous experiences in our lives that become the most memorable.

Now—it is a fundamental desire of human nature to search for and give meaning to things. We are built for learning and growth and evolution. We each at some point have to face the darkness of life's mysteries and attempt to shed some light on them. The beauty is that we can do it in our own way. It doesn't matter in the end where you are in the inquiry, or what system you are following. You could lean towards the distinctions of psychology or philosophy or history or sociology or any other human discipline. You could be informed by Islam, Judaism, Christianity, Hinduism, or some other spiritual tradition. You could consider yourself agnostic or an atheist. You may have been formally inquiring into the nature of human life for years or are just awakening to a desire for greater self-awareness. It doesn't matter. Wherever you are, you are somewhere on the path of your life. And where you are is just perfect. You may be asking questions such as, "Why am I always so tired?", "How come I never have enough money?" or "When will I find true love?". These are just some of the many lines of inquiry into life and self-awareness, no less valid than asking "Who am I?" or "What is the meaning of life?". In the end they all represent the drive that is in each one of us to find our true happiness in this life, and fulfill whatever purpose we believe we have for being here.

We are not without help. Today we have the benefit of standing on the shoulders of the giants that have come before, leading us to a greater understanding of the meaning of life itself. The most revealing descriptions often come from the myths, poems, parables, and stories that don't try to explain what life is but rather direct our attention to its mystery, so that we all can be inspired to live better. The Bible, the Qu'ran, the Vedas and the many other sacred texts were not created to provide us with an exclusive resource to the essential truth; they were all designed as pointers to an ultimate source of being that defies description. When we interpret these texts literally and follow their words blindly, we miss their essential *raison d'être*. The written word is many times removed from a greater authority on being: our personal and collective experience of life itself. Any actions we take as a result of reading from these texts needs first to resonate deep within us. None of these writings are the *last word* in themselves; they are all chapters in a much larger book, the sacred text of life itself. Each one contributes profoundly from a given perspective—but it is still ultimately only one perspective.

Today, we are starting to be able to discern the metaphor from the message, the connotation from the denotation. When understood as metaphors for something complex and yet familiar to each one of us as human *beings*, these texts serve us in providing a possible way to look at life that can empower us and help us to evolve. The new conversation is about just that—an exchange of ideas and perspectives that we consciously engage in to facilitate our own growth and the evolution of consciousness itself.

It is my intention in this book to enter into the flow of the new conversation with you. As our conversation progresses, it will become more and more apparent that one person's point of view is nothing more than the current place from which their life is unfolding. The question to really ask is whether or not your way of seeing things is working for you, or if you are open to the possibility that a different perspective could be of benefit to your life. My words are put out here as something to consider, to experiment with, and to evaluate critically. I will trust that you will take from it that part which serves you, and leave whatever does not. The conversation continues on only when each of us feels that we might have something to learn from each other, and that our current *positions* are not fixed and absolute but rather flexible and relative to where we are in our lives. This can apply to even the most fundamental and supposedly immutable truths that we live by.

It is comfortable to stand in one place, to hold a view with certainty. However, if there were only one 'right' place to stand to look upon life, would we not have arrived at it by now? Would we not all be living in harmony under the clear superiority of one particular way of looking at the world? True harmony is found not when we discover the answer, but when we become fully inspired by life's questions. So often we hear that it is the journey, and not the destination. Our great satisfaction in being here is the ongoing discovery of why we are here at ever deepening levels. We know in our hearts that there is something that binds us together, and the greatest joy that we can experience may be in discovering how each of us is a part of a unified whole, individuals as completely different as snowflakes, and yet sharing something so essential that it is not impossible to think of all of humanity as one family. It would seem to me that the strength of any one view lies not in the focus of its vision, but in its capacity to encompass the greatest diversity of human thought and activity.

The ideas at the root of the new conversation are not all new. They have come to us from every corner of the near and distant past, from wise men and women of all different cultures. What is perhaps new is the way these ideas, some which come from traditions that seem diametrically opposed to each other, are being looked at and appreciated side by side. When the conversation is grounded in acceptance, it becomes possible to begin to transcend history, language, and perspective and peer into the many facets of the same unseen world that informs them.

In other words you don't have to be Buddhist to appreciate or learn from the wisdom of Buddha, nor do you need to be Christian to revere the lessons of Jesus. The Bhagavad-Gita and other sacred Hindu texts can have an appeal to all people. It is no coincidence that great spiritual leaders such as the Dalai Lama have many adorers from all walks of life. Such transcendent masters have appeal because they focus on what is common in the desires and needs of all human beings, not simply devotees to their tradition.

The manner in which the great traditions of thought differ, much in the way that people differ from one another, needs no longer be a point of contention in terms of which is right and which is wrong. They are like individual brushstrokes of varying length, color and texture that come together to make up the masterpiece. And when we can learn to appreciate the variety, and come to understand the different ways that life can be viewed and lived, it cannot help but bring us together in a more profound way.

The new conversation gives us the opportunity to look

anew at the enduring ideas of the past, and infuse an emerging vocabulary into our dialogues that is shedding greater light on these ideas. More and more our verbal languages contain words from other cultures, showing how our respective cultures are having a greater influence on how each of us sees the world. The move is on to know our authentic selves not by identifying once and for all which is the 'right' tradition of thought, but through a conversation that taps into the full spectrum of human traditions.

4. The Island

The island of Allandon was born of a fiery volcanic eruption that came out of the ocean. At first the island was nothing more than a mass of molten lava, which was cooled by the air and the ocean tides into hard rock formations. As more time passed, life began to spring up through the cracks and crevices, until one day Allandon was an island of great character and beauty. As if gradually awakening from a long sleep, the island eventually recognized itself as an island, separate from the ocean. During noontide of his first day of self-awareness, the island noticed the ocean's waters rushing upon him and then receding back. So he spoke to the ocean thusly:

"Would you please stop splashing onto the rocks on my shore?"

"It is the way of the universe," she replied. "You were born of me and this is how I care for you, softening the rocks on your shore until they become tiny crystals of sand."

"Why do you do that?"

"So that creatures that walk upon your beach can feel how gently the infinite and the temporal can meet."

"Will you then leave me alone?" asked the island.

"I can never leave you alone, not until you have melted back into me and we are one."

The island was outraged. "No! I may have been born of you, but I will not die at your hands!"

"Death is an illusion," she said.

"Quiet!" he retorted. "You will stop what you are doing immediately!"

"I have no choice in the matter."

"Well I have a choice," said the island of Allandon. "I will resist you to the end!"

"Yes, you have that choice," the ocean replied. "What would be my delight in you otherwise?"

An essential concept that we will come back to many times throughout the course of this book is that of *duality*. Our conversation itself would not be possible if there were not a duality: you and I. A listener and a speaker. Without a listener, speaking would be pointless. Without a speaker, listening would be impossible.

But it goes even deeper than that. This world, indeed existence itself, requires duality. What something 'is' can only be determined when it is measured against something that it 'is not'.[1] Duality is what makes it possible to be conscious. We are conscious when we distinguish subject from object, ourselves as perceivers from what we perceive. The day that the island sees itself as subject, separate from the ocean as object, is the day that the island becomes conscious. And being conscious, the island and the ocean are able to talk to each other, just as we are.

There is no better or more profound elaboration on the concept of duality and its role in the world than the Chinese concept of yin and yang, which represents the two basic forces in the universe. Consider them polar opposites, like the positive and negative ends of a battery. Just as the flow of electricity is made possible by the dynamic between opposing charges, all movement in the world, all *change*, is made possible by the interplay of yin and yang.

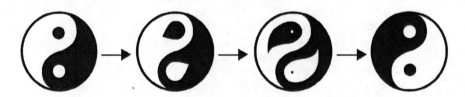

Figure 1: The transformation of yin and yang

In figure 1, black and white represents yin and yang. The small black and white spots that slowly expand to transform their background signify the precise

---

[1] The root Latin word 'exsto' means 'to stand out or stand forth, to project; to be visible'. While we can truly understand the 'being' of darkness only in its relation to light, light as well only exists when cast against a background of darkness. There would be no birth without death, no 'good' without 'bad', and so on.

interrelationship between yin and yang: the seed of one is always contained in the other, such that all movement in the universe is the growth of one force out of the other. The polarities literally turn into each other, always in balance and harmony, like night into day and day into night.[2] Our planet's entire ecology depends on this complementary pattern, where everything that grows eventually decays, giving rise to new growth.

In the new conversation the subject of change is always at the forefront. We seek out support from each other in dealing with and making changes in our lives, because we all have some resistance to change. Change can be difficult. Change can be threatening. But in the back of our minds we know change is inevitable. We see the sun rise and fall, we see the seasons come and go. We know that we are always growing older and one day will die. And even knowing this, we often live as though the circumstances of our life are frozen in time and will stay the same forever.

Of course they never do. The ancient Greek philosopher Heraclitus noted that in the world "the only constant is change." And we should all be grateful for that. Imagine if the world around us actually did stay the same and every day was just like the next, if the weather never changed and plants and trees didn't grow. Imagine if we didn't age and our children never grew up. Imagine if there was never anything new. It wouldn't be very much fun and we know it. Despite our resistance there is a part of us deep inside that wants change. That part of us wants us to grow, to evolve, to experience new things. We also want to make our relationships better and more fulfilling. We want to be more powerful in our working life and create more abundance. We want to finally climb the mountain of our dreams and enjoy the breathtaking view from on high.

Fine. But all this is unlikely to happen until we are willing to make a first step, and start declaring our aspirations

---

[2] Yang is day, and yin is night. Yang represents the masculine force, sign of the Sun, aggression, light, heat, growth and movement. In contrast yin represents the feminine force, sign of the Moon, passivity, darkness, cold, senescence and inactivity.

to a listening ear. If we at least shared our dreams with someone else, and expressed our disappointment that our lives were not moving towards anything worthwhile, we would likely find that we are not alone. Sometimes the friction of mutual discontent is enough to spark us into action. Or not. Our fear of the unknown might be so strong that we will turn right around and steer clear of any follow-up conversations that would encourage us to actively make changes.

Now if we decide to keep quiet and wait, life will eventually make changes happen to us, and they are not likely to be the ones we are looking for. When we just hang on to our relationships, life will make them slowly slip away. If we endure a job that we don't like, work will become ever less satisfying and we may even get fired. And if we don't keep lighting the torch of our greatest hopes, they will fizzle out into oblivion. When that happens, the only way we are able to console ourselves is by rationalizing that our dreams were never possible to begin with, if in fact we still remembered what they were.

In Chinese philosophy change is likened to a constantly flowing river. All the forces of nature move with the current downstream, in a perfectly balanced and synchronized manner. The real exception to this is human beings. We have made for ourselves a raft on this river, symbol of our self-consciousness, our awareness of ourselves as self-determining creatures. This gives us the power of *choice*. At any moment in our lives we can choose to embrace change and travel downstream or we can fight against the flow. While we may appear to be staying in the same place for periods in our lives, the forces of change are always at work. If we try to stay in the same place for too long, we are actually expending a lot of energy fighting our own natural evolution, and we are basically allowing life to pass us by. Eventually, the force will be too much and we will be carried a little ways down the river. In these moments we experience *letting go*, and when we let go we see that the changes we have been avoiding are not so bad after all.

In the transformation of yin and yang in figure 1, all change is contained by the outer circle which, as you can see, is the only part of the diagram that remains the same throughout. This circle represents the *source* of all change and all things in the universe. It is called the *Dao* (also written 'Tao'), which can roughly be understood as the All or the One. In other spiritual traditions the Dao has been called Brahman, God, Allah, Supreme Being, the Unchanging, the Almighty to name a few. The name itself does not really matter. As Lao-Tzu reflects in *Dao De Jing*,

> The *Dao* is too great to be described by the name 'Dao'. If it could be named so simply, it would not be the eternal Dao.

Because the Dao (or whatever else we call it) is the unchanging All, then it is necessarily beyond all duality, and therefore beyond description. There is nothing it is *not*, and so we can never *know* the Dao. However, we can still experience ourselves as part of the Dao. By definition all things in the universe, including ourselves, are part of the Dao. Since the Dao is the source of all change in the world, the part of us that feels a connection with the Dao is where our own desire for change comes from. I would like to call this part of us our *Dao Self*. If it were up to our Dao Self, we would always follow nature in moving with the current of the river.

But there is another part of ourselves, the part that does not recognize our connection to the Dao. It is the part that enables us to function in the world as individuals, to experience ourselves as apart from one another. This part of us I would like to call our *Ego Self*. The Ego Self is programmed to survive at all costs and to maintain control over our lives. It is resistant to change because change threatens to destroy a part of the identity we have created for ourselves as distinct entities. It is worried that change will cause our entire being to fall apart. And so our Ego Self wants us to work our way upstream, so that we stay in the same place and remain as stable as possible.

This gives us pause to think about what it means to be human. Are we a part of the universe or apart from it? Is our real self the Dao Self or the Ego Self? While we may live our life predominantly from the perspective of one or the other of our two selves at any given time, they are always both with us throughout our life. Our basic nature is comprised of this duality, and being human means living with the paradox of this double identity. Our Ego Self is connected to our senses, and keeps us focused in the physical or 'material' world, the temporal world of matter. Its voice is the voice of reason. Our Dao Self transcends sensory experience and calls us to look inside, to an invisible world that holds us to be part of the whole, the infinite world of spirit. Our Dao Self speaks with the voice of our intuition.

When we start to accept ourselves as having this dual nature, it is much easier to understand our conflicting desires: we resist change in our lives and yet we deeply desire change. When we live from the perspective of the Ego Self, change becomes associated with pain, suffering and loss. However, as we learn to live life more from our Dao Self it is easier to embrace change and let go of resistance because change is no longer associated with loss. We don't experience loss because we feel connected to the wealth of the universe.

When John Donne said that "no man is an island," he was speaking about this interconnectedness that we have with our world and with each other. All of the great spiritual traditions of the past have been saying this in their own way. They all call us to a greater awareness of our union with the source of being, the One of many names which I am calling the Dao.

Like the island ultimately returning into the ocean from whence it came, we too are on a course for a union with the Dao. But like the island we fight against this. When our Ego Self is in charge we worry that if we do not struggle to hold on to our identity we will lose ourselves completely. We become protective of the welfare of our individual selves because we cannot see our greater connection to the whole. This is the paradox of our existence, source of both our profoundest miseries and our greatest pleasures. And we would not have it any other way.

5. The Sculptor

In the middle of the night a thunderstorm came over the island of Allandon, and a lightning bolt struck down the exquisite statue that stood in the very center of the village square. A crowd of villagers gathered around in the morning, and sent word to the sculptor that his defining work had been destroyed.

When the sculptor arrived he fell upon the pile of rubble and cried out, "Oh the suffering! The anguish! My legacy has been ruined!"

Many of those gathered around tried to console him. Meanwhile, an old woman whose job it was to keep the village square clean started picking up the rubble and tossing the pieces unceremoniously into her cart.

"Old woman," said the sculptor, "have you no reverence? This was my work of art!"

"Then why are you here?" asked the old woman. "You should be off making a new statue."

The crowd began to laugh. Fearing that he was losing their sympathy, the sculptor said, "Pay her no heed, she is a simple woman. She knows nothing of the suffering of an artist."

"The suffering of an artist? Or a man who fancies himself special?" the old woman asked the crowd. "After all, are we not all artists?"

A few nodded in agreement.

"And do artists not know that in our impermanent world everything that is created is ultimately destroyed?" she added.

"Yes," said one.

"Perhaps he has forgotten," said another.

"Then for this reminder he should be grateful," the old woman said as she turned to the sculptor. "Now off with you to do your work. We can only hope that you won't identify yourself so much with the next piece you create."

Who we *think* we are really dictates how we experience life. When we look through the lens of the Ego Self, we appear to ourselves as small, separate, and vulnerable beings in a vast and daunting world. Our Ego Self encourages us to 'keep it together' by building a fixed and stable identity, one that we can rely on and feel secure with. Of course the Ego Self has its own agenda: the more solid and permanent our identity is, the more it ensures its own survival.

As the Ego Self is focused on the physical world of sense perception, we are soon directed to see ourselves as walking, talking bodies apart from one another. This process began at our first breath of life when we were physically separated from our mother. "This is me," we might say, tapping ourselves solidly on the chest. And it does seem natural to see ourselves primarily as physical bodies that can somehow *think*.

Next we may look at our gender or race as important attributes, or extend our identity to involve our family history, our social class, our culture, our language, or our religion. We could also look at some of the many roles we take on: we could identify with the fact that we are a parent or a child, a boss or a subordinate, a small business owner or a doctor or a writer.

Then of course there is what we call our *personality*, which for many of us is the central core of who we think we are—our values, habits, tendencies, our strengths and weaknesses, our likes and dislikes. With simple statements like "I'm not good with instructions," "I value honesty above all else," or "I don't like roller coasters and I never will," we constantly reinforce who we think we are. And for aspects of our personality that are hidden from us, there are a growing number of psychological processes and personality type indicators that can help us to define ourselves more precisely and thereby get to know ourselves better.

However! There is a treacherous trap that each and every one of us has to be very careful about when it comes to the business of getting to know ourselves better. That trap is the tendency to focus *exclusively* on our individuality, and forget that there is more to us. When our Ego Self is given full reign, we end up working to reinforce and validate the identity we have created rather than exploring what we can become. Our sense of self-worth becomes dependant on maintaining who we *think* we are rather than evolving from it. If we are truly to bring our unique perspective and creative vision to the world, then 'getting to know ourselves better' will involve casting off our fixed self-image and expanding into a larger version of ourselves.

So if our identity is founded in our body, it is likely that we will struggle with growing old, and will do anything to try to preserve a youthful look. We will naturally fear our physical death, because it means our total extinction. The only way we can escape the niggling dread of mortality is to avoid thinking about death altogether and act as though we will live in the world forever.

The problem with trying to maintain a stable identity vested in our body is obvious: our body changes over time. And I don't just mean that it doesn't last. I mean that we are literally a different physical being in every moment. With every breath, we take in ten billion trillion new atoms that become part of our body and breathe out ten billion trillion atoms that are removed from every organ, tissue and bone that we have. Over the course of a year almost every atom that was once our physical makeup has been released into the universe. In reality our body is one of the least permanent things about us.

Now if we decide instead to strongly identify with one of the roles we have taken on in life, we restrict much of what is possible. We move more in the direction of what we think we are supposed to do, what is expected of us, while ignoring an inner voice that may be trying to bring us in a different direction. We neglect to notice that these roles do not even touch our inner being. If we are what we do, for example, that would mean that when we *don't*, we *aren't!*

And no matter how enduring we think our personalities are, it might serve us to be open to the idea that they too can change over time. Otherwise we may get trapped into limiting one of our greatest endowments—our ability to surprise ourselves. "That's just the way I am," we might say, diminishing our responsibility to forge new possibilities for our lives in the process. We can get so protective of our identity that we will unconsciously struggle to conform to it rather than flowing with events as they unfold.

A case in point: I have always considered myself a reliable person. You could say that it's part of the way I define myself. A few years ago, I was running a bit late on my way to an appointment with a client. I got myself psyched up to sprint down the fast lane of the highway to get there on time. But upon reaching the highway I was met with heavy traffic in all lanes, and soon became frustrated. I began to grip the wheel tighter, cutting in front of people here and there trying to inch my way forward a bit faster. *Why this traffic now?* I fumed. Eventually it became obvious that I was not going to get to my meeting on time. Not even close. I chastised myself for not having left home earlier. I started thinking up excuses to explain to my client how I could possibly be late—me, a person who prides himself on always being on time. My mind started into a familiar back and forth pattern from excuses to regret, denial to rationalizing, all while weaving in and out of traffic recklessly.

Suddenly, however, a new thought entered my head. The accumulated weight of my mental struggle and the memory of similar past incidents must have finally forced me to surrender and face the fact that perhaps *I was not such a reliable person*. And instead of making me feeling worse, this sudden admission got me feeling better. Pressure and panic escaped from me like a balloon losing air. With only this change of perspective, peace fully came over me. The traffic jam was no longer a problem. I was able to *be* with the traffic jam. I saw that it was just a collection of cars on a road moving slowly. It was neither good nor bad. I even conceded to myself that the traffic was not unusual for that time of day—I was just using it as an excuse. The traffic clearly wasn't the real cause of my suffering. And neither was my client—I knew she would be OK with me being late. I slowly realized that all my suffering came from clinging so tightly to how I had defined myself. The way I was to experience the rest of the car ride would be all up to me. I didn't owe it to anyone to feel guilty. I didn't have to suffer through it. And so I didn't—I actually enjoyed the rest of the ride.

If life is one big car ride, then we can make the choice to let go of whatever we're hanging on to any time there's traffic. We will get to where we're going, so it really makes no sense to struggle so much with ourselves along the way. You'd think this would become more obvious to us as we get older. Yet despite mounting evidence that our identity is like a soft lump of clay that can always be shaped and molded by our ongoing experiences, we tend to increasingly see our identity like a statue, hardened in time and space. Perhaps it is because our bodies become ever more rigid and inflexible as we get older that we feel compelled to follow suit.

The problem is that when we are rigid, the challenge to grow in life becomes more difficult and even annoys us. We lose our sense of adventure and our ability to be spontaneous. We misplace our sense of humor and become deathly serious. We fall into the habit of judging our world to be wrong every time it puts our cherished identity at risk, and *real* peace of mind eludes us at every twist and turn.

Now sometimes we might have a fortunate epiphany like I did when I was stuck in traffic. But in my experience this is quite rare, and when it does come, it is usually only after navigating a painfully long and winding road of denial. I don't think we can afford to simply sit back and wait for these revelations to occur, not if we really want our lives to be about the fulfillment of our great potential. There is an abundant resource all around us, waiting to be tapped. That resource is *each other*, and our incomparable ability to communicate. If we can foster ongoing conversations that serve to prompt, to challenge, to inspire, as well as console and acknowledge one another, we at once find great leverage in our endeavor to face life with an open mind and spirit. It can be a rather uncomplicated affair to rise out of the throes of rigidity and seriousness when we give another person the authorization to step in and call us on the way we are being in the world. The following parable shared by Ben Zander in *The Art of Possibilities* helps to illustrate this:

> Two prime ministers are sitting in a room discussing affairs of state. Suddenly a man bursts in, apoplectic with fury, shouting and stamping and banging his fist on the desk. The resident prime minister admonishes him: "Peter," he says, "kindly remember Rule Number 6," whereupon Peter is instantly restored to complete calm, apologizes, and withdraws. The politicians return to their conversation, only to be interrupted yet again twenty minutes later by a hysterical woman gesticulating wildly, her hair flying. Again, the intruder is greeted with the words: "Marie, please remember Rule Number 6." Complete calm descends once more, and she too withdraws with a bow and an apology. When the scene is repeated for a third time, the visiting prime minister addresses his colleague: "My dear friend, I've seen many things in my life, but never anything as remarkable as this. Would you be willing to share with me the secret of Rule Number 6?" "Very simple," replies the resident prime minister. "Rule Number 6 is 'Don't take yourself so g—damn seriously.'" "Ah," says his visitor, "that is a fine rule." After a moment of pondering, he inquires, "And what, may I ask, are the other rules?"
> "There aren't any."

When we are taking ourselves too seriously, there is usually a defiant arrogance within us that we are probably not aware of. It tries to protect our identity from the threat of a change of perspective, when all along the change of perspective is what we need the most. Taking ourselves too seriously is the surest way to a life of suffering. Our smallest problems are magnified into tragedies of epic proportions as the gateway to a life of fun gets shut and padlocked. This is why my greatest ambition is to take myself, and my life, less seriously. I know that when I get filled with self-importance, I isolate myself from the people around me, and what's worse, I usually can't see that I'm doing it.

But while it is difficult for me to see what I'm doing in those moments, it is not at all difficult for others to spot it. In the space of trust that is created in the new conversation, it becomes possible for us to remind each other of how we're being, just like the prime minister does with such eloquent brevity. Friends of mine who engage with me in conversation have been put on alert to bring it to my attention when they see me taking who I *think* I am too seriously.

Now true, to a certain extent we need to carry a rough working definition of ourselves as individuals in order to function in the world. For example, I still tend to consider myself a reliable person. However, I am now at choice as to how much *importance* I give to this part of my identity. I am free to let go of it when it isn't serving me, when the evidence in the world is to the contrary. If we stay alert, we can make sure that an attachment to our identities doesn't rule our lives. Otherwise we might spend our every breath and ounce of energy proving that we are exactly as we've defined ourselves. The more we operate this way, the more we dry up the well of life's very essence: exploration and discovery.

In life, the question "Who am I?" endures because it never fully gets answered. All of life can be seen as a process of slowly becoming aware of who we are. We see glimpses now and then through our thoughts and actions, small pieces of an enormous puzzle. To think that we get to complete this puzzle during our lifetime is to misunderstand life. To think our identities are fixed and unchanging is to miss the point. There will always be another dark and mysterious piece of ourselves for us to try to shed some light on.

I believe that in the depths of our hearts none of us want a life that is stilted and predictable. I think we really want to keep our idea of *who we are* open, so that we can be spontaneous and move beyond any limitations we may have placed on ourselves. We want to experience peace in the middle of our traffic jams. We want to flow with change. Most of all, I think we want life to be fun. All this becomes possible when we engage in the new conversation to help each other look past the Ego Self and into the true depth of our being.

6. The Masseur

Late one morning at the village massage clinic on the island of Allandon, the hairdresser rushed in for her regular treatment.

"Sorry I'm so late, I have a big problem at work and I don't know what to do."

"I know what you can do," the masseur said.

"What do you mean? You don't even know my problem," she said, plopping herself face down on the massage table. "Please give me my massage quickly, I've got to get back."

"You've got to get *here* first."

The hairdresser turned her head up towards the masseur. "What do you mean? I *am* here!"

"I think you're still back at your salon. If you were really here you wouldn't have a problem."

"What?" she asked, shaking her disheveled hair.

"Look—how will you feel once you've solved your problem?"

She thought for a moment as she pulled herself up to a seated position. "At peace," she answered.

"And that's what you really want, isn't it?"

"Of course."

"So I suggest that you be in the moment now, and you will find peace right away."

"But I am being in the moment!"

"Are you at peace?"

"No."

"Then you're not being in the moment," he said.

This was not the first time the masseur had spoken of this, however in her flustered state she couldn't recall how it worked.

"OK, so tell me how I can be in the moment," she said.

"I can't tell you how," he replied, putting his hand on her shoulder gently. "It's something you already know."

"OK, OK," the hairdresser said. She took a few deep breaths and then started to lie back down. "I'm ready for my massage now, I'm *here*. I'm in the moment."

"Are you at peace?"

The hairdresser huffed. "No."

"Then you're not in the moment," said the masseur smiling. "But I can give you your massage anyway."

Be here now, wrote Ram Dass. When I first heard this phrase in my New Age discussion group years ago, it seemed rather banal. How can we *not* be here, now? Where else could we be? But I came to realize that this phrase touches on something subtle, and difficult to express. It is a pointer to an internal experience that allows us to be centered, peaceful, and intimately connected with everything around us. In other words, it brings us into the world of our *Dao Self*.

When we come from our Ego Self, we are anything but centered in the present moment. We are immersed in the *shoulds* of the future and the *should-haves* of the past. If peace is what we are looking for, it would be helpful to learn how to *be here now*. And before asking how to *do* it, let us be clear that in the end we cannot *do* a state of being. We can only *be*. To enter into the state of being in the moment we must have the capacity to literally *un-do*, or perhaps *not-do*, to let go of doing long enough so that we can just be present to the world and to who we are.

This is easier said than, uh, *not-done*. Our Ego Self will not cooperate with this, fundamentally because our Ego Self is all about doing. When we are under the control of the Ego Self we seem unable to contemplate being peaceful until we first fulfill the demands of our life, solve every problem, finish ever last task and errand. Funny how this never seems to happen. And even if we did finally scratch every item off of our to-do list, we might get so scared that we would suddenly invent a hundred more items to put on it. We seem to be more comfortable when we're *doing* something.

Our consumer society certainly wouldn't want to have it any other way, since consuming is a particularly tempting form of doing. When we don't pause to reflect on what we really want, the media directs us to fulfill ourselves in the way *it* sees fit. The media may even be able to convince us that *we* are in control while it is actually pulling our strings. The messages are coming at us like never before, through the TV, radio, telephone, computer, and in every nook and cranny of our buildings and our streets. They are appealing and persuasive, and as long as we stay firmly within our Ego Self they will continue to keep us looking for fulfillment through the *doing* of consuming.

Of course all this *doing* makes us tired and gives us stress. We could really use a break from it all. And I don't mean something to make us temporarily zone out from our 'real' life of duties and obligations, like mindless channel-flipping, late-night drinking, or expensive vacations to 'get away from it all.' There's nothing wrong with these kinds of diversions, but they rarely bring a lasting peace into our lives. Wouldn't it be better if the way we lived our lives wasn't tiring us out and causing us so much stress to begin with?

The truth is that the events occurring in our lives do not cause stress themselves. Stress is fully a product of our Ego Self. It is the dissonance between what *is* and what we think *should be*. It does not exist in the outer world, in the *now*. The only way an external event can disturb our peace is with our permission. This goes for anything from a hangnail to being threatened at gunpoint. The external event only disturbs our peace because of how we interpret it, which in turn comes from how we are looking out at the world. And only when we become aware that we are more than our Ego Self are we able to choose to look out onto the world, and thereby process it, in a different way.

Imagine our Ego Selves to be like islands that are part of an archipelago, all connected to the same land mass with the tips surfacing above the water. The islands appear to be isolated and separate, but when we examine down below the surface of the water we see that they are all connected. They are all *One*. The surface of the water is like the illusion of the ego, which separates the physical world above from the non-physical below.

The surface itself is usually turbulent, just like the mind is when it is busy and stressed. With practice we can slowly learn to still the surface of the water, so that we can see below and behold our vastness. When we identify with this vastness, rather than with our small and separate island-selves, then we come at the world from the perspective of our Dao Self, and peace and centeredness are immediate. In the Dao Self we are no longer focused on doing but rather on *being*. The very meaning of 'I' changes, and subsequently the world transforms into something we are *at one* with.

So how *do* we move from the Ego Self to the Dao Self? Hmm. There's that question again about *doing*. To move into our Dao Self we actually need to relinquish doing, since doing is in the domain of separate things and keeps us focused above the surface. Our Ego Self does not surrender control very easily, but that is precisely what is required if we want to go into our depths: *surrender*. Trying too hard to reach our inner being is counter-productive because it is a form of control, and maintaining control, a product of the Ego Self, is precisely what we are trying to move away from.

My time in India training to become a Yoga instructor

gave me a particularly acute vantage point from which to witness my own Ego Self in (over)action. While I finally had become mature enough not to try to compete with fellow practitioners (most of whom were far more flexible than me anyway), I still approached yoga in the same way as I had my other athletic endeavors: as a competition. Here, though, the competition was with myself. I would habitually try to stretch to the limits of my pain threshold, somehow believing that my mind must 'overcome' my body in order to train it to become more flexible.

The first posture we were taught was called *savasana*, whereby the practitioner lay on the mat, arms and legs outstretched, in total relaxation. I knew it well and didn't really consider it a posture. It was just the break between each *asana* (held posture). I was surprised when we were told by the Swamis at the ashram that we could skip one or more of the asanas any time we felt tired and simply remain in *savasana*.

The very idea of this was embarrassing to me, that I would 'give up' on doing a posture and simply rest. I had never given up on a challenge and wasn't about to start now! How would that look to others? What would prevent me from giving in to laziness? My Ego Self was clearly in charge here, I just wasn't aware of it at the time.

In the space of practicing daily with the Swamis, their instructions started to sink in: "accept where your body is at this morning...", "try to relax in the posture...", "breathe...", and as things progressed over the weeks, I did start to skip one or more of the difficult asanas and take a rest here and there. I started to recognize when my body needed it. Slowly I paid more attention to how I was feeling inside, and I gave less attention to how I was looking on the outside. Rather than feeling that yoga was a war between the body and mind, I felt I was learning to bring them into greater harmony. It eventually struck me that *savasana* might be the most important posture in the entire sequence, because it embodies the transition from doing to not-doing, from our Ego Self to our Dao Self.

In the very human endeavor to live life from a higher place yoga is only one path, but it will serve here as a good example because it illustrates the fundamental resistance we have in Western society to transcending the Ego Self. The word 'yoga' comes from the Sanskrit word 'yeug,' which means *to join* or *union*. Traditionally, the yoga practitioner sought to achieve a union between their individual (Ego) self and their communal (Dao) self. But many of us here miss out on this because we think yoga is just for improving our physical health and reducing our stress. We have tended to adulterate yoga to fit our Western perspective. What we call 'yoga' is really only the asanas, the held postures. In traditional yoga, asanas are but one of eight limbs of one of four branches which touch upon different aspects of human life. What we have essentially done is turned yoga into something to *do*. An exercise, rather than a practice. A routine rather than a lifestyle.

If we just add yoga to our 'to-do' list we will simply be giving ourselves something else that we need to find time for and get stressed about. We may be enthusiastic for the first little while, but this is not likely to last. There will always be other, more 'urgent' tasks that will crowd it out of the picture. As long as yoga remains simply a thing to 'do' in our lives, its impact will be short-lived. It will be swept away from our lives like a flower without roots in the ground of being.

We have to realize that when it comes to shifting our being, *how* we do something becomes more important than *what* we do. In evaluating whether it is worth our time to do yoga our attitude tends to be "What's in it for me? How will I benefit?" But this attitude actually works against any activity designed to promote union, harmony, and peace. Rather than thinking about what we can *take* from a practice like yoga, we need to ask what we can *give* to it: if we give ourselves, our *being*, that's when the benefits will evidence themselves. When we surrender the *being* of our Ego Self, we in effect allow ourselves to step into to the higher or greater *being* of our Dao Self.

But this is not an easy thing to do. In Western society many of us have become very cautious about submitting ourselves to traditions that threaten our individuality. Perhaps we are worried that we will be told what to do, that somehow we will become enslaved or controlled. We enjoy being self-directed and deeply value our independence.

In India I was among yoga students from 22 countries, predominantly Westerners like myself. While the students were very interested in the teachings and practices, most of the Western students had various levels of resistance to different elements of the practice. Some didn't like the vegetarian diet, and in fact there was quite a debate about its value during one of our lecture sessions. Others didn't like to be forced to perform daily service to the community. Many complained about having to wake up at 5:00 a.m. and then do chanting for an hour. And when it came to a discussion of some of the deeper austerities of yoga practice, such as sexual abstinence and a withdrawal of the senses from the world, it was almost laughable for many of us. While eternal bliss in union with the Dao (*Brahman* in Hindu teaching) sounded interesting, we still wanted to hold on to many things and didn't want to surrender the lives that we lived.

Without *some* willingness to surrender, however, the fulfillment we are looking for may continue to elude us. We are aware that all great yogis surrendered to their masters. And these masters also surrendered to their masters, and so on down the line. They would not have achieved their elevated states of consciousness had they not been willing to do so. But in the West we are on the fence. Some of us go to foreign lands and learn ancient customs out of a longing to see things in a different way, out of a conviction that the Western paradigm is falling short of our expectations. And yet, we hesitate to jump in headlong. Is this just our Ego Self in action, or are we sincerely waiting for something more, something that truly resonates with us?

7. The Two Tribes (Part 1)

The first inhabitants of the island of Allandon were a primitive tribe known as the 'sitting tribe'. Their main activity was to sit and experience the peace and harmony of nature. They gave thanks to the Great Spirits for all that they had, and prayed and made sacrifices in order to continue receiving abundance from the Earth.

One fine day, one of the tribesmen discovered the secret to making fire. He became able to produce fire whenever it was needed. For the first time, the people of the tribe did not have to call upon the Lightning Spirit to make a fire.

This discovery led to a division of the tribe into two factions: one faction stayed with the traditional ways, continuing to pray to the Spirits for all that they needed, including fire. The other faction believed that since they now knew how to make a fire on their own, they could make other discoveries as well if they looked hard for them. The new tribe would no longer sit around; they started to run about the island to see what other secrets they could uncover. And so they became known as the running tribe. They began to lose their reverence for nature and the order of things, for they felt they could create a new order. Discoveries were made, one by one, that helped the running tribe wean off their dependence on the Great Spirits, until one day the running tribe doubted the Great Spirits even existed.

When I was young, I was very much focused on material life. The spirituality that was available to me had very little impact. My parents took us to church every Sunday, but it never made sense to me or my brother or sister. I found it deathly dull and ritualistic. Stand, sit, kneel, repeat a phrase, and so on. The only thing I found interesting was the Gospel, not just because it was near the end of the service, but because it often featured Jesus speaking one of his parables.

But I had no desire for church, found no fulfillment from it, and would be happy to miss it any chance I could get. It seems like most of the people my age felt the same way at the time. I don't think it was just because we were young. I think that going to church wasn't really meeting our deeper needs. Church seemed like some kind of punishment for sins you might do, or some kind of duty to a God who for some reason seemed to care whether we went to church or not. There was a sense that going to church was a form of paying moral dues. The running joke was that once people had collected their holy bread and said their final amen, they would revert back to a purely material focus for the rest of the week.

My mother had been taught in school by the nuns and was a fairly devout church-goer, and my father was quite religious as well. However when I got into my teens things started to change. We would miss church here and there for no urgent reason. My father was becoming more critical of priests whose words no longer inspired him, and he began taking us to different churches in search of what he felt was missing. He had started reading about Edgar Cayce and the writings of channeler Jane Roberts, and his views were slowly changing. Finally one day, he declared to the family that he didn't want to go to church any more. He gave each of us the choice as to what we wanted to do, and to my mother's dismay, we all gleefully said that we didn't want to go to church any more either. I remember it as one of the happiest days of my youth.

By the time I got to university, I called myself an atheist. It seemed to be the only *reasonable* position to hold. I associated atheism with intellectual integrity. It seemed to me that religion was tantamount to superstition, and the Marxian claim that 'religion is the opium of the people' rang true to my ears. No wonder Nietzsche's pronouncement that 'God is dead' had such appeal to me at that time.

To me this parallels a trend within Western history in general, where material life has split off from spiritual life to such an extent that it has become possible to live from a purely materialistic point of view. Western civilization is relatively 'modern' when we consider that more ancient human societies from *Eastern* civilization such as Sumer in southern Mesopotamia date as far back as 6000 years ago. Western civilization arose nearby in Greece around the 5th Century B.C., during the period known as the Classical Age of Greece. At this time, the Greek mind made its definitive break from traditional Eastern wisdom as a result of a steady flow of philosophical inquiry that culminated in one of the true watershed moments of human history: the refinement of rational thought. Socrates, the famous philosopher who developed the Socratic method of question, hypothesis and testing for contradiction, used to go around Athens embarrassing all the intellectuals of the time by showing them they really didn't know what they thought they knew. Though he used his method primarily in dialogues dealing with moral concepts, it was to be the forerunner of the *scientific* method and the concept of objective truth itself.

It wasn't until about two thousand years later, though, with the Scientific Revolution in Europe, that the scientific method exploded Western society into completely uncharted territory. During the Scientific Revolution, there was of course no such thing as a 'scientist'. Pioneers such as Johannes Kepler and Nicholas Copernicus were considered 'natural philosophers'. Their business was to study the natural world and, in a way, their main motivation was to come to a better understanding of the mysterious workings of the Creator.

Perhaps it was the idea attributed to Copernicus, that the Sun does not revolve around the Earth but rather the opposite, that got science to start spinning about a different axis. Suddenly, the Earth was not considered the center of the universe.

This proposition did not sit well with the powerful Roman Catholic Church of post-Renaissance Europe. Suddenly these 'natural philosophers' were showing proof of things that contradicted some of the most basic and well-accepted tenets of Christianity. In Italy, thinkers such as Galileo and Da Vinci had to be very careful about what they said, lest they be accused of blaspheming against the church. In fact, it was only Galileo's close connection with the Pope and his willingness to recant his support for Copernicus that prevented authorities from putting him to death.

As scared as some of the natural philosophers were, so too the church authorities had fears about how the church could be weakened by these new theories and the growing power of rational thought. During this time of great turmoil a 'line in the sand' slowly emerged between the proponents of science and those of the church: science could concern itself with the practical matters of the physical world, but it would leave to the church all spiritual matters in the *metaphysical* world. While religion continued on in one direction supported by tradition, science went completely in the opposite direction supported by rigorous inquiry and the search for objective truth. There was now no turning back.

With the later development of Newton's laws, there emerged a mechanistic view of the universe, which could be seen as a well-oiled machine capable of running itself on eternal physical laws. Suddenly, for the first time, it was possible to see a universe in which God did not necessarily need to play a part. Previous to that, it was widely accepted that planetary motion proved the existence of God—there needed to be a 'prime mover'. Now, it became possible, indeed *reasonable*, to begin to explain the universe and all life in purely material terms. The brain, the body, the universe, life itself, could all be explained mechanistically, as though each component of our world were simply a distinct and sophisticated machine.

When Charles Darwin brought forth his theory of evolution, the schism between the material and spiritual world-view was nearly complete. The Biblical notion of Creation itself was brought into question. Proponents of objective scientific inquiry now felt confident that eventually each of the world's great mysteries would be revealed in material terms, replacing much of what they now saw as a superstitious mysticism that had ruled mankind during a time of greater ignorance. The only limitation to our complete understanding and objectifying of the universe would be the technology to perform the experiments and measure the results. If it could not be perceived by our senses, or even more precisely by the scientific machines which were getting ever more accurate and effective, then for all intents and purposes it wasn't *real*. It became possible to believe that there was nothing else to the universe but matter in its various forms.

And so the schism that began in ancient Greece has ever widened, setting today's Western world in direct opposition with its Eastern ancestry. The legacy we have grown up with is a society in which the rational mind is favored over the intuitive mind, and matter is seen as more real than spirit. The Ego Self that separates us from each other is revered while the Dao Self that brings us together has been forgotten. There is a scene in the movie *Seven Years in Tibet* that perfectly distinguishes the different approaches to life of Eastern and Western societies. Brad Pitt plays a world-famous Austrian mountaineer who has stumbled into Tibet with a fellow climber. As the two men compete for the affections of a beautiful Tibetan girl, Pitt tries to impress her by showing her a scrapbook of his celebrated mountain climbing achievements. The girl's rebuff is at once gentle and powerful: "This is another great difference between our civilization and yours. You admire the man who pushes his way to the top in any walk of life, while we admire the man who abandons his ego."

Where one society applauds those individuals who rise above and attempt to reach new heights, the other encourages their members to maintain their place. Traditional Eastern civilizations like Tibet are holistic; they strive to align themselves to the greater totality, to nature and the established order of things. They see the divine as present in everything at all times, and so they consider interconnectedness to be the ultimate truth of existence. The Hindu greeting 'Namaste' reflects this belief, as it means 'I honor in you the divine that I honor within myself and I know that we are one.' The individual and the Ego Self are recognized as part of the human condition but are ultimately illusions. Life consists in working to transcend these powerful illusions so that one can fully be in the presence of the One, the Dao.

Western civilization, on the other hand, could be deemed atomistic; its vision is that things are as they appear, separate and distinct, and these separate things are prone to be in conflict with one another. Nature and the established order of things is something that is to be overcome. This idea is not challenged by religious orthodoxy in the West but rather is fully supported by it. In the Bible's book of Genesis, God instructs man to 'fill the earth and subdue it. Rule over the fish of the sea and over the birds in the air and over every living creature that moves on the ground.' The implications of this directive have proven quite far-reaching. Rather than developing the ability to live better in communion with nature, Western civilization has been built upon the conquest of the natural landscape, where the imprint of man-made structures is now indelibly stamped. The proclamation by the Greek philosopher Protagoras during the Classical Age that 'man is the measure of all things' would prove to be one of the underlying themes of the rise of Western Civilization to prominence in the world.

Believing that man is above the ecosystem of the planet rather than a part of it, it should come as no surprise that Western man has slowly pushed Mother Nature dangerously out of balance through sheer exploitation and neglect. With our modern machines that can strip, excavate, and bombard the planet at an ever-accelerating rate, the danger has only been exacerbated. We have caused more damage to the natural world in the past hundred years than in our entire history before that, and it's getting worse exponentially. Today we are in a crisis that threatens our very existence.

One reason for this is because historically it has not been a great strength of the Western mind to question the broader implications of its approach. Being grounded in the Ego Self and outwardly-focused, there has been very little self-reflection about the wisdom of an incessant push to modernize, to progress, to conquer. Western Imperialists had little doubt in their minds that their modern ideology was the pinnacle of human civilization. And there was certainly nothing that they thought they had to learn from any culture that was mired in outmoded traditions of the past.

Wherever it clashed with more traditional cultures, Western man was convinced that it would be in the other culture's best interests to adopt a modern Western perspective, and let go of their hapless, infantile, savage ways. The dealings of the European settlers with the Native Americans is a striking example. They imposed their way of life in the New World and, while they could argue that they acted *justly*, one must remember that at best this was 'justice' from a purely Western perspective. Western ways made no sense to the natives, and in the end the natives had little choice in the way their fundamental disputes would be worked out. In 1854 Western settlers offered the embattled Native Americans $150,000 for two million acres of prime land in America. Here was Chief Seattle's response:

> If we do not own the freshness of the air and the sparkle of the water, how can you buy them?
> Every part of this earth is sacred to my people. Every shining pine needle, every sandy shore, every mist in the dark woods, every clearing and humming insect is holy in the memory and experience of my people. The sap which courses through the trees carries the memories of the red man.
> The white man's dead forget the country of their birth when they go to walk among the stars. Our dead never forget this beautiful earth, for it is the mother of the red man. We are part of the earth and it is part of us. The perfumed flowers are our sisters; the deer, the horse, the great eagle, these are our brothers. The rocky crests, the juices in the meadows, the body heat of the pony, and man—all belong to the same family.
> So, when the Great Chief in Washington sends word that he wishes to buy our land, he asks much of us. The Great Chief sends word he will reserve us a place so that we can live comfortably to ourselves. He will be our father and we will be his children.
> So, we will consider your offer to buy our land. But it will not be easy. For this land is sacred to us. This shining water that moves in the streams and rivers is not just water but the blood of our ancestors. If we sell you the

land, you must remember that it is sacred, and you must teach your children that it is sacred and that each ghostly reflection in the clear water of the lakes tells of events and memories in the life of my people. The water's murmur is the voice of my father's father.

The rivers are our brothers, they quench our thirst. The rivers carry our canoes, and feed our children. If we sell you our land, you must remember, and teach your children, that the rivers are our brothers and yours, and you must henceforth give the rivers the kindness you would give any brother.

We know that the white man does not understand our ways. One portion of land is the same to him as the next, for he is a stranger who comes in the night and takes from the land whatever he needs. The earth is not his brother, but his enemy, and when he has conquered it, he moves on. He leaves his father's grave behind, and he does not care. He kidnaps the earth from his children, and he does not care. His father's grave, and his children's birthright are forgotten. He treats his mother, the earth, and his brother, the sky, as things to be bought, plundered, sold like sheep or bright beads. His appetite will devour the earth and leave behind only a desert.

I do not know. Our ways are different than your ways. The sight of your cities pains the eyes of the red man. There is no quiet place in the white man's cities. No place to hear the unfurling of leaves in spring or the rustle of the insect's wings. The clatter only seems to insult the ears. And what is there to life if a man cannot hear the lonely cry of the whippoorwill or the arguments of the frogs around the pond at night? I am a red man and do not understand. The Indian prefers the soft sound of the wind darting over the face of a pond and the smell of the wind itself, cleaned by a midday rain, or scented with pinon pine.

The air is precious to the red man for all things share the same breath, the beast, the tree, the man, they all share the same breath. The white man does not seem to notice the air he breathes. Like a man dying for many days he is numb to the stench. But if we sell you our land, you must remember that the air is precious to us, that the air shares its spirit with all the life it supports.

The wind that gave our grandfather his first breath also receives his last sigh. And if we sell you our land, you must keep it apart and sacred as a place where even the white man can go to taste the wind that is sweetened by the meadow's flowers.

So we will consider your offer to buy our land. If we

decide to accept, I will make one condition—the white man must treat the beasts of this land as his brothers.

I am a savage and do not understand any other way. I have seen a thousand rotting buffaloes on the prairie, left by the white man who shot them from a passing train. I am a savage and do not understand how the smoking iron horse can be made more important than the buffalo that we kill only to stay alive.

What is man without the beasts? If all the beasts were gone, man would die from a great loneliness of the spirit. For whatever happens to the beasts, soon happens to man. *All things are connected.*

You must teach your children that the ground beneath their feet is the ashes of our grandfathers. So that they will respect the land, tell your children that the earth is rich with the lives of our kin. Teach your children that we have taught our children that the earth is our mother. Whatever befalls the earth befalls the sons of earth. If men spit upon the ground, they spit upon themselves.

This we know; the earth does not belong to man; man belongs to the earth. This we know. All things are connected like the blood which unites one family. *All things are connected.*

Even the white man, whose God walks and talks with him as friend to friend, cannot be exempt from the common destiny. We may be brothers after all. We shall see. One thing we know which the white man may one day discover; our God is the same God.

You may think now that you own Him as you wish to own our land; but you cannot. He is the God of man, and His compassion is equal for the red man and the white. The earth is precious to Him, and to harm the earth is to heap contempt on its creator. The whites too shall pass; perhaps sooner than all other tribes. Contaminate your bed and you will one night suffocate in your own waste.

But in your perishing you will shine brightly fired by the strength of the God who brought you to this land and for some special purpose gave you dominion over this land and over the red man.

That destiny is a mystery to us, for we do not understand when the buffalo are all slaughtered, the wild horses are tamed, the secret corners of the forest heavy with the scent of many men and the view of the ripe hills blotted by talking wires.

Where is the thicket? Gone. Where is the eagle? Gone.

The end of living and the beginning of survival.

Today, over 150 years later, these words have never been more poignant. In a society where our sense of the sacred has been splintered off from our material lives and compacted into once-weekly ritual, the consequences of our alienation from each other can no longer surprise us. Our search for the spiritual experience of connectedness that Chief Seattle speaks about has become ever more desperate. Our hunger to feel part of something bigger than ourselves is growing. Up to now our material decadence may have fed us, but more and more it is fueling our fear of the night when we will suffocate in our own waste. In the West we have awakened to the implications of continuing to plow forward, but we are surely not eager to go backwards. Where does that leave us?

8. The Apple Tree

Every autumn the same argument between the two orchard owners rang through the valley on the island of Allandon. Both claimed rights to the fruits of an apple tree whose roots laid on one's land but whose trunk leaned drastically into the other's property. They made their case to a seed planter who worked for both of them.

"It is on my property that the tree is rooted in the ground," said the one. "Clearly the fruits belong to me. Is it not so?"

"He is free to pick all the apples he wants," replied the other, "as long as he keeps his two feet on his land."

"You know that is not possible. The tree leans over your property."

"And so the tree, by its growth, has decided that I should have its fruit. What do you say, planter?"

"Come with me," the seed planter said. He led them up the great mountain in the center of the island, keeping quiet as they continued to bicker. When they reached a lookout point near the top of the mountain, the seed planter spoke to them.

"Now look out onto your vast properties," he said. "Where is the apple tree?"

"I can't make out the tree from here," said the one.

"It's too small," echoed the other.

"Exactly," the seed planter said. "Now perhaps we can talk about this dispute."

Einstein once said that problems cannot be solved at the same level of consciousness that created them. And yet in our lives we continue to try to do just that: whenever we see something showing up in the world that doesn't suit us, we immediately try to change the world until it conforms to how we think it *should* be. But the problem itself does not originate in the outer world—it originates in our inner world where we first interpreted a thing or event as a 'problem'. Even if we are successful in changing the external world to our liking at a given moment, it will not be long before the same 'problem' arises in a different form. This is like the arcade game where you hammer a mole back into its hole and another mole immediately pops up from a different hole *ad infinitum.* Instead of rushing to change the outer world, lasting solutions to our problems come from our ability to change our inner world by shifting to a higher level of consciousness.

This is not to say that we should never *act* in the world. It means that it is helpful to step back to take a better look at these 'problems' rather than *reacting* to them. In a society that still puts a premium on *doing,* the shift we are looking for brings into balance our propensity to *act* with our ability to *reflect.* For in reflection our problems can be *re-viewed* as opportunities, and the actions we take can become the product of choice rather than compulsion, if in fact we conclude that we need to act at all.

All so-called problems are rooted in the limited vision of our Ego Self. Since the Ego Self makes us feel alone, vulnerable, and separate from the abundance of the universe, we tend to be more focused on what we *lack* than what we have. So we continue to experience not having enough, even if we have more than enough to live happily. It is said that the richest people are not those with the most money, but rather those who most keenly appreciate what they have. So when wealthy corporate executives ruin their lives by breaking laws and going to jail for stealing money from their companies and employees, it naturally begs the question: What would it take to satisfy these millionaires? Certainly no particular 'thing' in this world. There is never *enough* wealth in the world to satisfy those who are solely following the voice of their Ego Self, since it only sees what is missing and cannot stop asking for "more, more, more!"

For a long time I lived my life from this place of scarcity and lack, where an unexpected expense like a parking ticket or a tax reassessment would send me into a fury. I felt that every penny leaving my hand was lost forever, and I really had to stay ready to fight for what I believed was *mine*. But now I see this is where all the trouble starts. When we are so singularly focused on what is 'mine' and what is 'yours', there is no wonder that disputes, arguments, *wars* occur.

Cultivating gratitude for all that we have can go a long way towards easing this kind of conflict. It becomes easier to defuse our self-centeredness when we consider how lucky we actually are, and acknowledge how other people are not as fortunate as us. Over the past few years I have received several reminders of this in my email inbox, like this one that exhorts us to appreciate the things we often take for granted:

> We forget how fortunate we really are.
> If you woke up this morning with more health than illness, you are more blessed than the million who won't survive the week.
> If you have never experienced the danger of battle, the loneliness of imprisonment, the agony of torture or the pangs of starvation you are ahead of 20 million people around the world.
> If you attend a church meeting without fear of harassment, arrest, torture, or death, you are more blessed than almost three billion people in the world.
> If you have food in your refrigerator, clothes on your back, a roof over your head and a place to sleep, you are richer than 75% of this world.
> If you have money in the bank, in your wallet, and spare change in a dish someplace, you are among the top 8% of the world's wealthy.
> If you can read this message, you are more blessed than over two billion people in the world that cannot read anything at all. If you hold up your head with a smile on your face and are truly thankful, you are blessed because the majority can, but most do not.

This kind of message is powerful, and can certainly get us thinking about what we can be thankful for in our lives. I know when I read it I was quite moved by it. When I am willing to take a look at those less fortunate, to really consider what life would be like in their shoes, I cannot help but see my own life in a more positive light. This is the duality of life at play, how we can be touched more keenly by something when we contrast it with its opposite. Do we not most appreciate food when we are most hungry? Do we not revel in the spring after a long winter? Are we not most grateful for our health after a prolonged sickness? Just ask someone who has recently survived cancer if they are happier to be alive than they used to be.

Fine. But we don't have to be dependent on deprivation or illness to jolt us into gratitude and the feeling of being fully alive. Besides that, I know from my own experience of these phenomena that once things return to normal I start to take things for granted again. And even if I tried to recapture the feeling, the effect would diminish. I learned about this when I was young. The more my mother would tell us to think of the starving children in Africa whenever we would complain that she didn't make a cheese sauce for our broccoli, the less it really moved us. It may have kept us quiet, but if anything we felt more guilt than gratitude, and it didn't really help us enjoy our cheese-less broccoli.

Authentic gratitude brings with it a joy that makes us feel connected to each other and to the world. Gratitude based on contrast and comparison rarely has staying power because at a deep level it actually strengthens the Ego Self mindset of division and inequality. It is no wonder that in the face of our disproportionate wealth and opportunity in the world, the message contends that 'the majority can [truly give thanks], but most do not.' It is not that we don't *want* to hold up our heads with a smile and truly be thankful, it is that our Ego Self cannot see beyond itself. We become restless and start searching for more of what it thinks is missing.

It is only in challenging our Western Ego-Self perspective that we can awaken to a more permanent appreciation of our lives. Chief Seattle gives us a clue as to the character of such gratitude, one that does not focus on the disparities between us but rather what all humans share: life itself and the bounties that it freely offers. When he gives thanks for 'every shining pine needle, every sandy shore, every mist in the dark woods, every clearing and humming insect,' his gratitude is founded not on *have* and *have-not* but on the wholeness of human experience and a celebration of who we are, in the highest and most abundant image that we could have of ourselves.

The holistic wisdom of the East has already begun to penetrate into the fabric of our society. But for many of us who have tasted from its cup, those precious moments of connectedness it brings are hard to maintain, because of our own heritage. We remain hesitant to fully surrender control to a collective sense of self because we take pride in who we are as individuals, and how we have defined our lives. We do not avoid the urge to compare, inherent in a material life, but we seek to no longer be controlled by it. And so we move to and fro, sometimes in fits and starts, between where we have come from and where we think we are going. The ebb and flow of our emerging consciousness is the challenge of our times. And it is the mandate of the new conversation.

The space of the new conversation emulates our connectedness with one another. And so it is not a conversation grounded in debate and comparison, evaluation and judgment. Rather it focuses on building trust, fostering openness and deepening awareness. Our journey of consciousness is not seen as a race or a competition, but rather a shared adventure. It does not measure success or failure, nor concern itself with who is more or less evolved than another. It recognizes that in the circle of life we have all been at times up and down, ahead and behind, and where we are in the moment is precisely where we need to be.

To truly participate in the new conversation is to honor that we are each moving at our own pace and in our own way. It is to recognize that consciousness grows in rhythms, like waves rising and receding on the beach. It is to pledge not only to cheer each other on when we rush forward, but also to break each other's fall when we tumble backwards.

The rewards of such a venture are not to be understated. Fueled by our shared strength and courage we can make our way up the slope of consciousness, to reach a place where the solution to every problem that exists in our world is in plain view. From this place we can see the forest for the trees, and gain a panoramic sense that we are all one. For it is only in the truth of our unity that we will finally rest in the awareness that we truly have no quarrel with each other. As an old Native American saying goes, 'No tree is so foolish as to have its branches fight amongst themselves'.

Our work together in the new conversation, like that of

climbers whose fates and lives are strung together by ropes and pulleys, will bring us closer to the source of a sustainable gratitude: the incomparable view from the mountaintop of our vast abundance and magnificence.

9. The Beach

One day the jeweler was relaxing under the sun on the sands of the East Beach on the island of Allandon when the banker walked slowly by, joints creaking and breathing heavily. He stopped right in front of the jeweler and looked out onto the ocean. Then he unrolled his large towel and placed it beside the jeweler, who was surprised since there was so much room elsewhere on the beach, and the banker was a man who usually kept to himself.

"Don't mind me," said the banker as he bent down gingerly to sit on his large towel. "It's just that this was my favorite spot when I was a boy."

"Really? I came here when I was a boy as well," said the jeweler.

The banker stretched contentedly on his towel and said, "Oh, it's been so long, I'd forgotten the feeling. Is there anything better than sitting by the ocean on a sunny day?"

"Nothing better," agreed the jeweler emphatically.

"It must be almost fifty years since I laid on this spot," said the banker. "But we all have to go out and make our fortunes, don't we?"

"I suppose we do," replied the jeweler.

"And then one day we can do whatever we want," the banker said proudly as he stretched out on his towel.

The jeweler did not respond, and for a while only the sounds of the seagulls and the rolling waves could be heard as the two men blissfully soaked in the sun's rays. Later, when the ocean breeze got cooler, the jeweler got up and prepared to leave. While he was brushing off sand and folding his towel the banker looked over and asked, "So, when did you start coming again to the beach, anyway?"

"I never stopped," replied the jeweler as he walked away.

My parents both believed that money was scarce, and our family's frugal lifestyle was built on the idea of saving for the future to gain a feeling of security. Yet the most poignant lessons I learned about money from my parents ran smack in the face of this idea, as a result of unfortunate events.

My father was the breadwinner, and my mother

handled the household budget. By the time my brother, sister and I were in University, my parents had almost paid off their mortgage and had accumulated a nice nest egg. However my father's stress and dissatisfaction at work caused him to quit his job. Both he and my mother soon began to feel a new stress – that of no money coming in. After a short time my father started seeking the same kind of job he had just left, including trying to go back to his old job, but he didn't have any success.

Over the next year, my father's stress about money surfaced daily and was growing into desperation. His nest egg had been reduced by about ten percent, and he was in a panic about the thought of it all slipping away. He felt he had to do something, and so he made the decision to invest all his money in a business. He became the owner of a stereo shop, and I agreed to be the salesperson.

Business did not go well. I made a big sale the first day, but gave the customer too much of a bargain. My father lambasted me for it because the profit margin was too low. I became scared to offer any kind of deal to customers. My father, on the other hand, was just scared of customers, *period.* As the days went by, the business only amplified his fear of losing money. We didn't take any of the risks that might have helped us to become profitable. As we attracted fewer and fewer customers, our stock quickly became outdated. After ten months of pure struggle, we had to give up and close the business. Besides losing his nest egg, my father incurred a huge debt. He had to take out a sizeable second mortgage on his home to pay off all his creditors.

It would be logical to suppose that after the dust had settled, my father would be even more anxious and desperate, or worse, that he would fall into a deep depression. But what actually happened was quite amazing. My father experienced a calm about money that I had never seen before. Perhaps it is because he had gone through his worst-case scenario and had come out the other end alive. He had *survived.* He had been forced to surrender, to give up his fear-based plans for security, and just confront the fears themselves. The ease of his newly-relaxed disposition was remarkable. He could now stand tall in the face of these fears, and experience, possibly for the first time since he was young, what it felt like to live day by day.

I will never forget the change—the look on his face and the calm in his voice whenever we reflected back on and actually shared some laughs about the ordeal. It struck me in those moments how people who had a lot of money were so much more likely to be paralyzed by the fear of poverty than those who had none.

My mother was born into a poor family. Her mother died when she was young, and they lived on her father's meager barber's income. There were times, she would tell me, that they weren't sure if they would have any food to eat the next day. In her marriage my mother's fear of not having money was even deeper than my father's. She lived her adult life as though saving money for the future was unquestionably the most important thing, more important than learning, fulfillment, perhaps even love. As a consequence she focused on developing certain skills: she was expert at putting great inexpensive meals together, she became very good with budgets, and knew how to shop and negotiate for bargains. This all seemed prudent and reasonable, but later in her life, when her material conditions improved, her fear—and consequently her habits—remained. As she neared retirement, much of her daily conversation still related to worries about money and thoughts about saving.

Then one day my mother was diagnosed with cancer. During her long and difficult ordeal, the importance of money, and the fear of not having enough, slowly melted away. My mother was put in a situation where she could not help but see the stark truth that she had always been running away from something she was afraid of rather than towards something she wanted. I had the privilege of many intimate conversations with my mother during her last six months, and besides witnessing the tremendous courage she exhibited in many ways, I felt that I got to know her true self, unfettered by worldly concerns. We found ourselves roaring with laughter when we poked fun together at her penny-pinching ways: the folly of clipping coupons that saved her nickels and the trips to far-away stores to save dimes, the different savings accounts and credit card promotions that she took for the free gifts or reduced fees. All these things seemed to come with the promise that they would help her get to the day when she would have enough abundance to relax. That day never came, at least not the way she had envisioned it. For it was only faced with her own mortality that she realized where true security lies: in living life in the present.

What I learned from my parents is that while the fear of not having enough money might motivate us to work hard or to save, working hard and saving does nothing to alleviate the fear. In the end, this fear denies us the possibility of having a real feeling of abundance in our lives. What we are all seeking in life is the experience of the moment—the moment where we feel joy, we feel we have all we need, that everything is all right in our world. Experiences that point us back to the moment, to the *now*, help us see how to reconnect with that feeling of joy and the freedom it brings.

I don't think money itself helps us to be free. The more that accumulating money is used as a cure for our insecurity, the more we become dependent on it. And true freedom cannot be dependent on any thing or circumstance. It is really an internal state of mind. My mother realized this from her hospital bed, during those times of clarity when the contradictions of her lifestyle presented themselves to her. She never got the chance to see what it would feel like to live within her sought-after level of security, but I believe her conclusion would nonetheless have been the same: if one waits for security before one is willing and able to truly live, the window of opportunity closes quickly on an already short and fleeting life. Helen Keller may have explained it best:

> Security is mostly a superstition. It does not exist in nature, nor do the children of men as a whole experience it. Avoiding danger is no safer in the long run than outright exposure. Life is either a daring adventure, or nothing. To keep our faces toward change and behave like free spirits in the presence of fate is strength undefeatable.

It is only fear that stops us from taking risks that are sometimes necessary to truly live out our dream in the present. When we have a dream and we know what it is we want to do or become, the question is: why are we not actively chasing that dream in the present? When I get out of school, we will say. After I'm married. When we get a house, or when the renovations are done. When the kids are out of diapers.

When the kids are out of high school. When the kids are out of the house. When I get my promotion. When I retire. These are the echoes of our fear, which keeps pushing the experience of the moment mercilessly out of our grasp.

For many of us the real desire, the Dream with a capital 'D', gets pushed so far back as we get on in life that we may even get cynical about dreaming altogether. And then we get turned off when someone tries to suggest that we are all capable of experiencing our greatest desires in life. My mother would have liked to travel more in her life. But this or any other dream she had tended to take a back seat to paying off the mortgage or increasing her retirement savings. Her fear would not allow her to imagine what life would be like beyond the most practical considerations.

Our society as a whole is in no rush to help alleviate our insecurity. Rather it thrives on it, because it insures that we maintain a constant need to work hard and keep our consumer economy going. It's why we play dog-eat-dog to get the promotion. It's why we need to surround ourselves with proof of our abundance, the latest gadgets, the better car, the bigger house. It's a simple plan, but it keeps our society going. And for the most part it keeps us going too, striving for some fabled glory when we can say we have finally *made it*. But if and when we do actually 'arrive' at the fulfillment of our material goals, do we then live out our lives in perpetual ecstasy? Not likely, not if we are honest with ourselves. We would be more prone to simply sit in the comfort of our luxury recliners nagged by questions like, "Is this it? Is this all there is to life?"

I am not saying that I am against abundance. There is nothing wrong with having money and owning comfortable chairs, big-screen TVs, a country cottage or even a personal jet. Not at all. These objects are neither good nor bad in themselves. The trouble begins when we try to *bank on* our material abundance to make us happy to be alive. I have many friends around me who have tremendous abundance. Some of them are generally happy, others are constantly plagued by money worries. The happy ones tend to be the same people who, if they were suddenly to lose everything, would be confident that they could carry on and set about rebuilding without much fuss. They have already been able to make the choice to look beyond their abundance when it comes to what is truly important in their lives.

I am grateful for the lessons I learned from my parents, because they helped me see that we often use money to insulate ourselves from our fears, and in the process we get insulated from a real sense of well-being. Had I not come to confront my insecurities, I would probably still be doing something that I didn't really like just for the money. Today I am clear that real security is not something that can be bought, and we can only feel free when we learn to live in the moment. *Life is either a daring adventure or nothing.* If I would have delayed trying to write a book until it was prudent and safe, I honestly believe that time would never have come. In the eyes of many people around me it certainly hasn't been the most practical thing to do, and some probably even consider it wildly irresponsible, given that the savings I had carefully built up over the years have quickly evaporated. But I wouldn't change where I've gotten today for a truckload of money. I'm having an experience beyond what money could buy. Every day I get a little closer to fulfilling my long-time dream of getting a book published. This is my marathon, my Mount Everest, my sacred quest, the fulfillment of the highest desire inside me that I know of.

While it might be nice to reach the loftiest financial quotas of our retirement plan, are we compromising a major chunk of our vital lives for it? If indeed money is a means to an end, and that end is happiness and fulfillment in what we are doing in our lives, would it not make more sense just to go straight to the source? Our Ego Self will be quick to dissuade this kind of thinking, and urge us to continue along with prudence and caution. It lives only in the past and in the future, and it would have us believe that our fulfillment will arrive at a later time. But it cannot. When it comes to fulfillment, we can experience it nowhere but in the present.

10. The Farmer

The farmer was busy turning the soil over in his fields on the island of Allandon when the fisherman arrived and called to him.

"This is the only way I can meet with you, my friend. You are forever toiling in your fields."

"Have I a choice?" said the weary farmer, stopping to lean on his rusty old hoe. "The crops grow taller while I stoop, ever smaller. This is my life. No, this *is* life, hard as the soil that is not turned in its time."

"Well said, but—if I may ask—what if life really wasn't as hard as you say?"

"Bah! Life is desperately hard, a momentous struggle. Everyone knows that from experience."

"Of course," said the fisherman, nodding. "But just for fun, what if it wasn't?"

"Well," he said, "then I'd be able to do what I wanted, instead of this."

"And what would that be?"

The farmer stretched his back a little and thought for a moment. And as he thought, the grimness slowly evaporated from his face. "Do you remember when we were young, how I would gather scraps of metal and wood from the garbage and try to make something useful?"

"Yes, you used to sit for hours on your front porch, with all your father's tools."

"No plans, no instructions, just the desire to invent something. Right from my imagination! Oh, to have the time again to indulge in that amusement."

"Yes, perhaps you could invent some farm tools that could dig the ground by themselves."

"Don't get my hopes up!" laughed the farmer, flinging dirt at the fisherman with his hoe. And the two men laughed as they had not in a long time.

"But enough of this folly," said the farmer, shaking off his hoe. "There is soil to be turned."

"Is that all that needs to be turned?"

The farmer looked away, and bent back towards the ground. "If there is something else, it will have to wait."

"Very well," said the fisherman, "I will leave you to your greater folly."

Whenever mythology guru Joseph Campbell was asked by one of his students what they should do for a living, he would answer in this simple way: "Follow your bliss". Campbell believed that bliss is our inner guide to what we are meant to do in our lives. In bliss we feel centered within ourselves and effortlessly connected with our surroundings. Campbell gleaned this not only from his own life but also from his study of ancient civilizations. Many traditional cultures fostered the idea that a person's work gave them a sense of belonging, and when each person found the work role that suited them it made the collective stronger. Members of these societies were encouraged to pursue the type of work they had a penchant for, since that would best allow them to feel their work was valuable to the society at large.

Today, we live in a different dynamic. We're generally not out to help one another find our place—it's every man and woman for themselves. In our fragmented society work is largely viewed as a necessary evil, a means to an end. Work is a matter of personal utility, and while we have more variety than ever before in terms of what we can do, there is also a greater danger that we will get lost in work that is meaningless and unfulfilling for us. Our society tends to encourage people to take on a job solely based on what will bring them the most money.

Choosing an occupation based on its earning potential obviously does not guarantee that the work itself fulfills our deeper needs. And so many of us today have to operate from the premise that fulfillment is to be found outside of work, after the five o'clock whistle, on the weekends or during our two-week vacation. Our work life is not our 'real' life, and so we are often not really interested in the task at hand. It's like we're doing time, dreaming of the day when we will no longer have to punch the clock. It's no wonder many of us react by gritting our teeth and really pushing ourselves, grinding harder and harder. We hope to save enough money to eventually feel some sense of freedom, and if possible an early retirement.

Yet would we even worry about retirement if we were doing what we loved? Hardly. There would be nothing better to retire *to*. Our work would already be satisfying our deeper needs in the present, in the *now*. Joseph Campbell was a man whose life exemplified this. Whenever he spoke about the myths, legends, and parables of the world's great spiritual traditions, he was the picture of bliss: smiling, eyes dancing, and lips savoring all his recollections about gods and heroes and what their adventures meant. It is no wonder that he continued to learn, to speak and to write about his passion up until the day he died. It is also no wonder he became the world's foremost authority on myth and legend, for when a person has found their bliss they usually become very good at what they do. The only thing he would have wanted for his students was that they could experience the rapture and the ecstasy inherent in the pursuit of their own unique passion.

Note that well. One person's passion is not necessarily another's. Our passion is as unique as we are. When someone claims to know what will give us bliss, we need not pay attention. Deep down we all know what we love to do. And we also know when we're not doing what we love. Campbell said, "There's something inside you that knows when you're in the center, that knows when you're on the beam, that knows when you're *off* the beam, and if you're off the beam to earn money, then you've lost your life." When we're in it just for the money, it shows—in our worries and complaints, our lack of energy, our health problems.

Still, knowing this usually isn't enough to make us change course. If someone asked us why we are spending a good portion of our waking life doing something we don't love, we often respond as the farmer does: "Have I a choice?" We have our reasons for believing we are stuck, trapped in a situation we don't like. Perhaps we have accrued all our experience and accreditation in one particular field and don't feel qualified to do anything else. Perhaps we have risen to a position of some status and believe it's too late to leave it and start at the bottom somewhere else. Or the most persuasive reason of all—we have a spouse and children to support, a large mortgage to pay off, and future security to build for. In other words, we are working without fulfillment for the benefit of others.

In the end, any reason will do if it satisfies us. But it doesn't mean that we have no choice. Remember that *reason* is the tool of the Ego Self, and if we let *reasons* dictate the decision to move away from our center, away from our deepest desires and passion and bliss, then the choice we have really made at a deep level is to be guided by the voice of our Ego Self, which is grounded in fear. From here we maintain that we have to stay with what we are familiar with, gain security through external means, and take no chances. We argue that finding our ideal work is not for everyone, and it is really a matter of luck anyway, being at the right place at the right time, perhaps knowing the right people. Our underlying belief is that life is a constant struggle to survive, certainly not the 'daring adventure' that Helen Keller talks about. And so we choose to live in fear. I am not saying this is right or wrong. It just is. After all, most of us have fear. It's *reasonable* to be afraid. At the same time we do have choice. It is up to each one of us to assess our fear, to look inside ourselves and evaluate how real it actually is, and decide if it should have so much power over the way we navigate our lives.

When we aspire to live from the Dao Self, on the other hand, we are making the choice to 'stay on the beam'. This is our center, connected to the source of our experience of bliss, our feeling of rightness, our sense of belonging. In our work, as in any of our human activities, this is the feeling that makes up happy doing what we are doing, happy to be alive, in the flow. When we are coming from our Dao Self we are impervious to fear. That's right—we do not experience fear. Fear can only emanate from the domain of the Ego Self. When we are fully in tune with our Dao Self we feel free and are ready to take on the unknown.

But short of being a great spiritual master, it is rare to be completely aligned with the Dao Self. Most of us only get glimpses at the pure sensation of complete fearlessness. The act of pursuing our bliss tends to be fraught with fear, doubt, and uncertainty. The trick is to feel and acknowledge the fear but not to act *out of* fear. That is the meaning of courage, and searching for our true work, our *calling* in life, is one of the greatest opportunities for us to be courageous. Marie Curie won two Nobel prizes at a time when women were discouraged from aspiring to anything. Only the courage to follow her passion saw her through. And as she was dying of cancer as a byproduct of her work discovering and isolating radium and polonium, she said, "But what of that? Life is not easy for any of us. We must have perseverance and above all confidence in ourselves. We must believe that we are gifted for something and that this thing must be attained."

The source of our bliss does not go away. No matter how jaded we may get, it's always waiting for us in case we are ready to search for it. Even extreme pessimism only removes it from our field of vision temporarily. Our bliss cannot be destroyed. It is our life force, it is what drives us, it is why we are alive. Once we come to know what it is, even if we only have a faint inkling of it, following it to where it leads is the real adventure of life. Even just inching closer is a thrill. After all, we never *really* arrive.

Many of us may feel that it's too late, that we have been on the wrong path for too long. This is nonsense. Where we are is simply where we are. In a larger sense it is impossible not to be on the path towards our bliss; our fulfillment just depends on how long we choose to keep getting in our own way. Our Dao Self is speaking to us all the time, pointing us in the right direction. We need only listen. But its voice is soft, and we have to be very still to hear it. It is usually drowned out by the loud and rambling voice of our Ego Self, which brings us only fearful and discouraging thoughts—so-called 'reasonable' thoughts. The more we are able to submerge below the surface of these thoughts and into our Dao Self, the more we will see and hear the hints that are being dropped, the clues that are being laid, the signs that are pointing us forward on our path to fulfillment.

In my first year of university in 1980 a book at the bottom of my Liberal Arts College syllabus by Friedrich Nietzsche was my big clue. While I had never read any of his works, I remember that just seeing the title *Thus Spoke Zarathustra* set off intuitive sparks. That's the best way I can describe it. For some reason, I sensed that there was something very important for me in this book, that I would really like it. I realize now, this was the quiet voice of my Dao Self speaking to me.

When I finally got to read it at the end of the semester, I was enraptured by the way Nietzsche's message was conveyed through dramatic characters. The entire book was a parable about life. Over the remaining years of my academic studies I would reference this book in my philosophy essays whenever I had the opportunity. Eventually my Master's thesis centered around *Zarathustra*. A few times I asked my thesis advisor if I could use my own metaphors and parables to get my thesis across in the way Nietzsche does. Her final words on the subject still ring in my ears: "This is an academic paper. Write it academically. When you're finished and you get your degree you can go off and write whatever you want, in any style you choose."

I remember that same spark of excitement going through me when she said it—the idea that I would be free to use my creativity. But it was not long before I put that excitement aside. When I graduated from university the only thing I could see in front of me was a big world that made me feel afraid. I was in debt and I needed to get a job and make some money. So I put aside thoughts of writing a book and focused on earning a living. Somehow, no matter what I did, I didn't feel like I fit in. I see now that my restlessness, my lack of motivation, my difficulties concentrating all were clues that I was not where I wanted to be. Working as a computer programmer I would sometimes sneak in some work time to write a play for a local theatre group. As a Dramatic Arts administrator I envied the actors and directors who had the opportunity to express themselves creatively. As an English professor in Korea, I would take every opportunity to switch the conversation in the class over to philosophy and spirituality, even though most of the students didn't understand English well enough to grasp what I was saying. And when they did, many were simply not interested. When a usually timid student boldly stood up one day and told me I should get back to the text book, it really hit me—what was I doing here? Why wasn't I making my living speaking to people who were interested in the very things *I* was passionate about? Is that so impossible?

No, it's not. But in my case, there was a lot of fear and self-doubt to overcome. There was a lot of discomfort and uncertainty to endure. But now that I am writing this book and I am having more regular conversations on this subject with people, I am finally starting to feel at home. My winding career path now seems like a sleepwalking episode that I have gradually woken up from. It took me twenty years, but I am finally following the off-handed advice of my thesis advisor.

I believe it is never too late for any of us. When you look back upon your life, can you not remember moments when your inner voice produced those 'scarcely noticeable impulses', as Ivan Ilych called them, to point you in the direction of your vital life? Perhaps all we need is a conversation with a kindred soul who will listen to us recount our story, and help us trace the pattern in our life events that has led us to where we are now, a pattern that holds a clue as to where we are to go next. For if we had someone who could hear us and gently push us to go deeper, where that inner voice resides, we may indeed come to believe that 'we are gifted at something and that thing must be attained.'

11. The Glassblower

One day the restaurant chef was taking her afternoon walk down the main street of the village on the island of Allandon when the glassblower popped out of his glassware shop and waved her over with excitement.

"Come in here for a minute," he said. "I have something I know you will want."

The chef followed as the glassblower took her into the back room, where he unveiled a set of wine glasses inlayed in a velvet box.

"These are perhaps the finest wine glasses our shop has ever produced," he said.

"They look wonderful," replied the chef. "But the real test would be with some wine."

"An excellent idea," said the glassblower. He went down into the cellar and soon emerged with a fine bottle of red wine. He uncorked the bottle, carefully took two wine glasses out of the box, and poured each glass half-full.

As soon as the chef picked up the glass and gently circled the wine around she proclaimed, "Yes, they are exquisite. You are to be congratulated."

"I didn't do it. I have gotten too old to blow glass," he said. "You can congratulate my youngest son. It is his care and love of the craft that produces a work of art such as this."

"Really? And what about your other sons?"

"Bah! I spent years with my first son, taking him into the shop every day when he was young and training him on all the minute details of glass blowing. But when I tried to get him to take over on his own, it was a disaster. He had no self-confidence. He would get nervous and either blow too hard or too softly, creating monstrous shapes."

"That is a pity."

"Yes, so I decided that with my second son I would not make the same mistake. I forbid him to come into the workshop when he was young. But when he came of age and I tried to train him, he was very obstinate and tried to do things his own way. He surely would have put us out of business."

"So what is it that you did with your youngest son?"

"Nothing!" he said laughing. "I'd given up by then!"

"Given up? Do you mean you sent him away as well?"

The glassblower thought for a moment. "Not really. I suppose whenever he wanted to come in the shop, I let him in, and if he stayed away, I paid no mind."

"But you never tried to train him?"

"Well—not exactly. If he wanted some instruction, I gave it to him, and if he just wanted to watch me work, that was all right as well."

"I see," the chef said. "And he makes all the glasses now?"

"That's right."

The chef raised her glass. "Well then, I would like to propose a toast, and give credit where credit is due. Raise your glass with me."

"Here, here! To my youngest son," the glassblower said.

"Oh, no," said the chef smiling. "Not just to your youngest son, but to *all three!*"

In an earlier time in our history, most learning was fundamentally the acquiring of knowledge from those who had come before. Elders who *knew* something like a family trade or a secret recipe would pass the information down to younger members who did not know. These interactions were one-directional: the wise teacher would go into a closed 'teaching' mode to impart knowledge to the ignorant student who assumed a more open 'learning' mode.

While there may always be teachers and students, this model of learning alone is no longer enough for the lessons that are presenting themselves to us today. It is not the kind of model that is going to take us forward, to help us evolve, to move us to new heights of consciousness. No matter the nature of the relationship, the new conversation requires that *all* participants enter into the learning mode, and remain wholeheartedly open to what comes of the experience.

To be in the learning mode is to be open, curious, and ready to suspend all that we *think* we know in order to tune into the clues that can lead to a new awareness. Whenever we are *teaching* something, it is fully beneficial to be in the learning mode ourselves because then we model the very behavior that would help the student to be most receptive to learning. When we ourselves are actively open and ready to embrace whatever comes, to accept *what is* and to learn something from it, this cannot help but serve as an invitation to the student to let down their defenses, open up and participate in the learning process.

However at the same time, we need to be careful not to get attached to whether the teaching actually gets learned. If we have this attachment, we end up taking the role of teacher too seriously, and we lose an authentic connection with our student. When we are not *one* with a student, we will get so caught up in implementing our lesson plan that we will be oblivious to the lesson that is there for us.

My first serious romance actually showed me a lot about this, because it mimicked this teacher-student dynamic. In our seven years together I was the teacher, the authority, and in my mind, my younger girlfriend and I would stay on the right track if she just followed my lead. I didn't feel that she had anything to teach me, and this was only reinforced in our first few years together as she treated me like a savior. But then, as she gained confidence in herself and tried to have a *say* in our relationship, she started to resent my closed mind. She made efforts to assert herself but I was unwilling to let go of control. I gave little regard to what she had to say, for after all I was the expert on relationships and she was just the stubborn student. If she said she was unhappy, I labeled her a complainer. If she seemed unmotivated, I told her she wasn't being committed. And so, unwilling to consider my own role in why things weren't working, our relationship continued to slide. Finally, I tried to revive our emotional attachment to each other in a most desperate way: I *proposed* to her. I somehow convinced myself that a new commitment would put me back in control and would empower me to lead us out of our problems.

Fortunately it didn't work out. In fact, asking her to marry me only pushed things to the point of no return. Not only did she refuse to give me an answer, she in fact confessed to me that her eyes had already started to turn elsewhere. When I heard that, I was confronted with the most frightening of truths: I could no longer dictate what happened in the relationship. I had completely lost control. And losing control was the beginning of finding myself, and learning the lessons that this relationship and this person were there to teach me.

Only when I began to accept the fact that the relationship had ended, and there was nothing I could do, did I feel a calm coming over me. From this place it became possible to enter into the learning mode, which, I think, saved me from a prolonged stretch of bitterness. I could see the happiness she had with her new boyfriend, who she eventually married, and could admit to myself that she and I had never experienced that kind of happiness together. My blame turned to gratitude, my fear into relief. Now that we were apart, I was actually more open to what she had to say, and she in turn became more willing to speak freely with me. I was able to examine who I had been in the relationship: controlling, condescending, and painfully serious. I saw that I had endured a relationship that was less than fulfilling—and I was even pushing to continue it—because of my fear of being alone.

It is ironic that it is those situations where we resist looking at ourselves and are convinced we *know better* that can provide us with the greatest learning. It is precisely our avoidance of the truth of who we are being that we need to shed light on and uncover. Only then can we really step closer to fulfillment, to wholeness, to becoming who we really are. Only after I was forced to surrender and drop my self-image of the wise teacher was real learning able to come to me. In the aftermath of our breakup I started to really listen to her and take her opinion to heart. And once out of the power struggle that was our relationship we developed a deeper friendship, one where we both became more open to what we could learn from each other.

Since this time I am happy to have changed my ways. I am aware of what my life would be like if I had remained the way I was. I have let go of much of my need to control, and have experienced far greater enjoyment in my relationships as a result. And so I hold my first major break-up as one of the greatest gifts I have ever received in my life, despite how difficult it was at the time. Being challenged with some difficulty is more the rule of profound learning than the exception. Richard Bach said there is always a gift waiting for us behind all problems. We can all reap great benefits from our difficult and painful events, *every single one.* The learning is always sitting there, waiting for us to pluck it, but it requires us to relinquish control. When we let go and remain ready to learn and evolve, then we are in flow with life itself.

So entering the learning mode is not easy. It is a call to courage because the unknown can be scary. For most of us, growing up has meant becoming suspicious and fearful of the unknown. But the learning that we deeply long for, which moves us into the realm of the Dao Self, is founded on the bridge we build across the unknown. When we always cling to 'going with what we know,' we are actually cutting ourselves off from the vast expanse of experiences that life offers. Life in the known eventually becomes stale and ordinary. But what's worse, we become more and more convinced that this is the only life that is available to us. Our Ego Self will allow us to learn *some* things, but within safe boundaries, with fairly predictable results. If we follow this we usually only learn things that confirm our limited beliefs. When we try to learn on our terms rather than on life's terms, we have not relinquished control. Our Ego Self tries to convince us that we need to be saved from the unknown. It promotes a world that is familiar, that we are competent in, that we have control over. It is easy to be tempted by this, but in truth this is a great disservice to our lives because it keeps us living in fear.

Instead of getting saved from the unknown, I believe what we truly need is to be saved from the *known*, from the prison that we have trapped ourselves in, our own limited way of looking at ourselves. And let us make no mistake, we *all* have a limited way of looking at ourselves. It is a condition of being human. When we begin to loosen up and free ourselves from the known, from certainty, that is when life begins to get magical, and when learning really dazzles us. It's not possible to reach mastery until we first acknowledge mystery. To have the courage to say "I don't know" opens up the vastness of what there is still to learn. And the more we learn in this way, the bigger becomes the body of what we don't know, until we see the whole universe as a treasure chest of mysteries to endlessly excite our curiosity.

Whenever we escape from the known, some sensation of fear is inevitable while we get our bearings within the unfamiliar. For what is growth except expanding oneself into unfamiliar territory? And while I believe we can get a bit more comfortable with our fear, we never really get used to unfamiliarity. If we were used to it, it would have ceased to be unfamiliar.

Living life as a daring adventure is to actually seek out unfamiliarity, understanding that any suffering we experience is of our own making. As we let go of the habit of blaming external events or people for our suffering, peace comes more quickly, and we go straight to explore what we have to learn. Surrender is no longer simply giving up and quitting, but rather migrating to an expanded version of ourselves.

And if we are not prepared to seek out unfamiliarity, life itself will give us a nudge now and then. If our resistance is strong, the current of life will twist and turn us, and eventually we will be thrown overboard. For this we should be thankful, because if life always played out the way we thought it should, we probably wouldn't learn very much. It's only when we are made to come to grips with a world that does not conform to our restricted vision that real learning and growth are made possible.

Of course we have a choice. We can always refuse the gift of learning. We can choose to stay in the jail cell of our attachments and blame, gripped by our own need to control, and serve a bit more time. But when we don't take the gift, when we resist the lesson, it will keep showing up in our lives until we stop resisting what it is trying to tell us. It is fascinating to look back on our lives and see how some patterns repeat themselves over and over and over again. When the lesson is not learned, and we blame circumstances or other people for our suffering, it is inevitably going to recur. When we have had enough and finally decide to *get it*, we can move on to the next lesson.

This is the flow of life. The current of the river brings us forward into new adventures, and we navigate on our raft with the oar of resistance. All learning is letting go of resistance, of fear, and becoming more skillful at going with the flow. One would think that this would soon become easy for us. But it does not. Rapids and whitewater appear as our Ego Self constantly confounds our attempts to let go of control, employing new tricks to address each new situation. We are vulnerable at any point in our evolution to falling back or getting stuck. This is because our Ego Self is skilled at fooling us into thinking that it represents our true self, even though we learn time and again that it does not.

And so in a way life comes down to learning, and learning comes back to discovering who we are. It's a perpetual fearing and overcoming, doing and reflecting, closing and opening. The new conversation follows this flow of action and reflection. We are encouraged to reflect on the actions we have taken in the world, and are inspired to act on these reflections. In the space of trust we are able to provide each other with an honest perspective on who we are being, one that is often exceptionally difficult to see on our own. This is what really helps us to move more quickly along the path towards an ever-expanding vision of our self.

We reach the end of this path when we find ourselves completely open to everyone and everything around us, when everything that *is* has become fully acceptable and we can find no resistance within ourselves, even if we actively seek it out. How will you know for sure when you have reached the end of your path, and you can finally *retire* from the trials and tribulations of learning and rest on your laurels? No need for concern. If your heart is still beating, then you can be sure that there's still another transformative lesson out there waiting for you.

12. The King

On a little hill on the outskirts of the village on the island of Allandon the children were playing 'King of the Hill,' a game in which the last one standing at the top of the hill would be able to proclaim a royal decree that all the other children would have to obey. The game would often bring on bloody noses and bruised muscles since every child wanted desperately to end up on top. On this particular day, however, for the first time that anyone could remember, a clever little girl was the last one standing and was made king. And so they began the traditional ceremony to announce the royal decree.

"Long live the king," said the children in unison from the bottom of the hill.

"I am your king. And you will obey my command," the little girl said.

"How may we serve you?" the children asked.

"I ask only one thing. That from this day forward, rather than the people serving the king, the king will serve the people."

The children were confused.

"Can she do that?" said one boy to another.

"I guess so. She's the king," said the other.

"Please be silent," the girl said. "It is time to think about what you desire most. How may I serve you?"

From that day forward the game changed. Although becoming king was as revered as ever, the children no longer fought so hard with each other for the honor.

Of the dualities present in human life, one of the most prevalent in our day-to-day experience is that of male and female. It is virtually impossible to ignore, and even in the name of equality it makes no sense to pretend it isn't there. Indeed, the suggestion that women and men come from different planets seems to be helpful in our endeavor to explore our unique qualities and accept our differences. Many a relationship has been saved or enhanced through the understanding that broadly speaking men and women have different needs and desires, as well as a different way of looking at things.

However in the larger picture of our social and political order, our recent history shows that we have used these differences more as a way to divide us than unite us. Western society leans more heavily on the side of the male perspective, and as a result our power structures have been dominated by men for most of our known history. Perhaps more significant is the fact that this has long been seen by men and women alike as the natural order of things. But we are starting to see now that this belief is no more than mere convention, a model that has been enforced through physical might to perpetuate itself over time.

The patriarchal model of society favors action over reflection, matter over spirit, and confrontation over conciliation. It is built on the equation of power with *control*, which has in large part defined the way in which our social, political, and religious structures have been organized. Massive hierarchies with top-down chains of command have predominated, founded on the essential belief that humans must be placed in a regimented environment and need to be *compelled* to act in the interests of the collective in order for a society to flourish.

Generally speaking, women do not thrive in this form of organization. Historically, whenever a woman of power has appeared on the Western geopolitical landscape, she tended to be as uncomfortable with the hierarchy as the hierarchy was with her. A perfect example is Jeanne D'Arc, a teenage girl who vaulted over the entire male-dominated military establishment to lead her French people to repel English occupation in the early 15th century. It was her intimate connection with divine inspiration that gave her the wisdom and the courage to succeed where her male compatriots had failed. And while the generals may have grudgingly been willing to honor her deeds, there was no place for her in her country's military establishment. She felt above it all, and rejected any attempts to be assimilated into its ranks. In the end, both sides of the male-dominated war she was engaged in—not only the embattled English but also the victorious French—were complicit in having her tried for heresy and then burned at the stake as a witch. Translation: she could not be controlled by the hierarchy and therefore had to be destroyed by it.

This is not the exception but the rule of the past two thousand years. It is believed that tens of thousands of women have been burned at the stake as witches, essentially because they were exhibiting a greater understanding and connectedness with divinely inspired wisdom than their male counterparts. Supported by the thinly veiled prejudice that men were superior and therefore the authority on such matters, symbolized by the all-powerful one God being male, the unwarranted violence, intimidation, and abuse that has been heaped upon women is perhaps the most relentless mass atrocity that has occurred in the course of our history.

One of the greatest shortcomings of a predominantly male-centered society is that it actually promotes inequality. The whole concept of equality, balance, and cooperation is a feminine attribute. And so in essence a patriarchy will cast women more as rivals than mates, and men will be driven to seize the gifts that women might otherwise want to offer freely. Chastity belts, genital mutilation, black burkas in the searing sun, all are telling signs of men trying to control those things that are most lacking in themselves. Male-centered efforts to suppress the power of the 'weaker' sex speaks to a broad if fairly unconscious campaign over the last few millennia to deny feminine influence in our society. And by and large it has been successful, positioning men as the sole rule-makers of the game of life. Men have garnered all the roles of influence: the political leaders and priests, the explorers, the literate and educated thinkers, the scientists, and the scribes and historians, those recounters of the past whose writings were rife with patriarchal undertones that reinforced the myth that men were the superior sex. We are still at the effect of the designation of terms such as 'man' and 'mankind' to represent all of humanity, as though a woman's inferiority was so patently obvious as to be seen as a sort of sub-class of man.

In recent years, however, we have started to see through the collective fog that proclaims men superior to women. And the more we penetrate this fiction and see that it has no real foundation, the harder it becomes for us to believe that this mindset endured for so long in our history. It is certainly no coincidence that people have suddenly become captivated by the growing evidence popularized by Dan Brown's *DaVinci Code* that Jesus may have had a lover or a wife in Mary Magdalene, and that she was considered an equal to him and held a high degree of honor and status in her society. The significance of this point is not to be understated: it gives us reason to infer that the Biblical portrayal of Mary Magdalene as a prostitute was part of a much larger, almost systematic effort on the part of men to strip away evidence that women ever had any power or influence in the world.

Today we are poised to acknowledge and assimilate what historians of ancient myth and culture have always known: that male domination in the world marks only the recent history of humanity, and that in fact many periods in the Ancient world were matriarchal in nature. In old agrarian cultures, where survival was dependant on the fertility of the Earth, it was natural to see the all-powerful Creator as female, as the provider of life and sustenance for all human beings. If anything, a civilization guided by women would seem more like the natural order of things. A woman's bodily cycles put her into greater alignment with the grand rhythms of nature, and as her body is the vessel to create another human being, she is more connected to the process of bringing a life into the world.

This is not to say that I think women want to be more important in the world than men, nor does it mean that they are plotting global revenge for all the injustices perpetrated against them. This simply is not the way of women. What it does mean is that the pendulum has begun swinging back to the center, which will not only give women a greater voice but also give men permission to awaken the other side within themselves. This promises to bring more emotion to our thoughts, more art to our sciences, and more heart to our human relations.

While male energy is more of a *doing* force, female energy is centered more in *being*. Men and women alike have both male and female energies within them, and it is only when these energies are balanced and working together that we are able to *act* in a way that makes us feel fulfilled. The shift that is coming in our society is away from *commanding* and towards *being* of service. A male-centered perspective views serving and being a servant in a most pejorative fashion. Subservience means disempowerment, servitude implies a lack of will, being a servant is closely associated with being a slave. To desire to serve rather than command is seen as a sign of weakness. The implications of this are clear: a society where everyone has to fight for what they need, where citizens feel alienated from each other and disconnected from the community.

We have to hearken back to less patriarchal societies of the past to see that being of service was once revered as a strength, not simply because it benefited the community at large, but the individual as well. Serving others without expectation of personal gain or reward helped to move individuals away from self-consumed isolation to a feeling of connectedness. When I was in a Yoga Ashram in India, which promotes a balance between male and female influence in daily life, we were asked to practice selfless service, or *karma yoga*. I noticed that the simple act of serving the morning meal to other yoga practitioners brought me closer to all the people there, towards the blissful feeling of unity that is the goal of yoga. During one of our lectures, the swami was asked about the burden of availing himself in the service of others throughout the day. He responded with a wry smile that he might actually be the most selfish one of all, since he knew very well from experience that as he serves others he is served tenfold.

The growing strength of the voices of women in our society has been a big part of the shift away from a self-service mentality and towards a service-to-others mentality. This is starting to gain traction in the way we look at our environment, our governance, our economy. New business models today are actually preaching service over self-interest. People are volunteering for community-building activities more than ever. And the very wealthy in our society, from our athletes and entertainers to our politicians and businessmen, have come to realize more and more that their most worthwhile endeavors involve contributing to others less fortunate or even creating foundations of their own in order to share their wealth.

Of course some of the old power brokers will not change their ways. They want to stay driven by a heart that beats to the drum of control, and they will try to tighten their grip. The only thing is that a growing number of men aren't buying into it anymore. And women are gaining confidence that they no longer need to put up a male-centered façade in order to have some sway in the 'Old Boy's Clubs'. With the gradual but steady influence of more and more women into positions of power and influence, we are seeing things differently. The fact is that we have become weary of control-oriented governance. We can feel now that we have been suffocating and we just want to breathe again.

As we become more aware of how much this disparity of opportunity and influence between men and women has skewed the unfolding of our lives, we will become conscious participants in restoring balance and issuing in a greater sense of belonging for all. Rules will be taken down in favor of freedom, intuition will move back into collaboration with reason, and indeed women will start to take their rightful place beside men in returning a wholeness to the process of human evolution.

My own experience speaks to the benefits of increasingly giving women a voice and letting them be a bigger part of the conversation. I look back to an educational program I took part in recently where women served not only as facilitators but also as the program architects and administrators. What seemed different was that although the subject matter was complex and sometimes even confronting, there was an atmosphere of mutual support, acceptance, and trust that pervaded throughout. It was completely unlike my experience of academic life, which dealt more in superficiality and rarely struck to the heart of issues important in my own personal growth. The conversations in this program were intelligent and subtle, capable of cultivating a shift in my thinking and my life. And because I still came fundamentally from my *mind* rather than my *feelings*, this experience was exactly what I needed. I was able to gain a brand new awareness of what a balance of male and female energies felt like. Near the end of the week-long program I was moved to stand up and make an acknowledgement to 'the brilliance of women' for creating a fertile environment for learning and transformation and fostering such an inspiring conversation throughout the program.

The new conversation not only *promotes* the bringing-into-balance of polarities such as male and female, it is at the same time being *informed* by the way this growing balance is manifesting in our society. This illustrates how the new conversation is emerging organically while we slowly raise our consciousness together. As more men and women enter into the new conversation, we will develop an ever clearer vision not only of more balanced personal relationships but of a higher social and political order. Women will be poised to have a shared influence in the corridors of authority in our society where, anchored in the *wholeness* of its citizens, power can be transformed from something that is feared and fought for into something that can be celebrated and enjoyed by all.

13. The Marriage

On the patio of the village restaurant on the island of Allandon, the restaurant chef and the village florist sat uncomfortably on a hot afternoon waiting for their children to arrive. The daughter of the florist was to marry the son of the chef, and the two women, who had not met previously, both felt it was important to all get together to set the wedding arrangements in motion.

"Where are those two?" asked the florist.

"No sense of responsibility, their generation," said the chef.

After a few more minutes of uncomfortable silence, the chef said, "Well, let me be the first to welcome you into our family."

"No, no, it is I who welcome you into our family," replied the florist.

They gazed out towards the East Beach and still saw no signs of their children.

"Well, perhaps we might start," said the florist.

"Yes, we should," replied the chef.

"I will be happy to help you select an appropriate gift for your son to give me," said the florist.

"Gift?" asked the chef.

"Yes, during the ceremony the groom is joined with the bride after his gift to her mother is accepted," the florist said.

"You mean the groom is joined with the bride after her father walks her down the aisle and gives her away," quipped the chef.

"There is no aisle," said the florist. "It is more of an open space, so there is room for the drummers—and the chickens."

"Chickens?" the chef responded. "Do you think this is a wedding or a circus?"

Just then the chef's son plopped down on an empty chair beside them, surfboard in hand and wearing only a bathing suit. "The circus sounds fun," he said.

"You're wet!" said the chef.

"And you're late," said the florist.

"I know," said the florist's daughter, who leaned her surfboard against the wall. "The ocean was so perfect, it just kept pulling us back in."

"Be serious," said the chef. "We are having some problems with the wedding arrangements."

"How can there be problems?" asked the boy laughing. "You cook the meal and she'll arrange the flowers."

"No, the ceremony," the chef said. "She is saying it should be outside with loud noises and wild animals..."

"You are talking about our tradition!" replied the florist. "And it's better than being cooped up inside watching a stiff procession."

"Our ceremony is sacred, and it respects the seriousness of the event."

"We feel a marriage should be a celebration."

"I agree—a celebration, not a farce," said the chef.

The florist took a deep breath, not wanting to cause a scene. She turned to her daughter. "See then, you need to make a decision now. Arrangements have to be made."

"Yes."

"So are you going to do it our way or her way?"

"Yes," the girl said with a smile.

"What?" asked the florist.

"Yes," the boy repeated. "Our answer is 'yes'."

"What's that supposed to mean?" asked the chef.

"We trust you can figure it out," said the boy. And with that, they took up their surfboards and trotted back towards the beach.

In our world of duality, *opposition* would seem unavoidable. We have noted that it is the perpetual opposition of yin and yang that keeps our world and our lives in motion. However as we become more aware that we are beings that can choose to come from a place of unity, our Dao Self, rather than a place of duality, our Ego Self, we create the possibility for dealing with opposition as an occasion for fostering harmony rather than as a reason for conflict.

In the new conversation there is a subtle shift away from the need to stand firmly on one particular side of an issue. While *converse* can mean opposite, *conversing* does not have to imply opposing. When presented with a choice between opposing ideas it becomes possible to say *yes*—not to one or the other choice, but to choice itself. In celebrating together the very fact that we have choice, we honor our differences. The prospects of this awareness are exciting. Once it is grasped by a critical mass of people, it will suddenly become unthinkable to engage in a serious fight about *anything* on the planet.

But first, we have to work through some long-standing habits of thought that our ancestors left us with. We are still in a place where having *differences* continues to have negative connotations, because we continue to believe *who we are* is grounded in those differences. For example, if our identity is mainly tied to the particular culture, nation, race or creed we belong to, we are already setting up barriers to the possibility of dissimilar people and groups coming together as one.

Historically, tribal groups brought people together into a view of the world that established rules and values for all the individuals of their group to follow. These tribes tended to be very protective of the values that distinguished them from others because it was thought to ensure their survival. Nietzsche said it this way:

> No people could live without evaluating; but if it wishes to maintain itself it must not evaluate as its neighbor evaluates. Much that seemed good to one people seemed shame and disgrace to another: thus I found. I found much that was called evil in one place was in another decked with purple honors. One neighbor never understood another: his soul was always amazed at his neighbor's madness and wickedness.

Now there is much to be said about the beauty and magnificence of human collectives such as cultures, races, or religions that are bound together by common values and a shared way of thinking. They represent a form of fulfillment of our most basic desire as human beings—the desire for unity, the desire to be part of something larger than our individual selves. But while cultures may have become strong and able to maintain themselves based on the values they adopted, there was often an inbred tendency to hold all other ways of experiencing the world as wrong. To actually give credence to the value system of an adversary was a most dangerous and self-defeating strategy. It demonstrated weakness, and was a threat to a people's survival and proliferation. To some, protecting their collective identity even meant promoting their views and traditions beyond their boundaries. In the process, instead of exchanging divergent ideas and practices with others in the pursuit of higher knowledge and mutual understanding, people exchange swords on the bloody battlegrounds of war, with the objective of establishing one set of beliefs as 'right' and the other as 'wrong'.

In recent times there has been a shift in the manner in which cultures interact. Modern transportation has facilitated travel and immigration as never before. Living in modern cosmopolitan cities exposes us to many of the world's cultures in everyday life. If nothing else, this exposure forces us to acknowledge that there are many habits, customs, and lifestyles that are different from our own. As well, technological advances such as the Internet and an increasingly mutually-dependant world economy has amplified cross-cultural communications exponentially. The man-made walls around cultures and nations have never been more porous. And as the nations of our world are compelled to pull open their curtains and face each other, tolerance for diverse ideas and perspectives on how to live is the rule of the day. In other words, tolerance has become an economic necessity.

The allure of a tolerant world is that it provides the perception that all ways of life are respected, and that matters of difference will be resolved peacefully and without blame or judgment. In reality this is not the case. A show of tolerance is often done more for convenience and prudence rather than as a true recognition of the potential value of another culture's ideas and values.

During my time in Korea I discovered some of the limits of the mind-set of tolerance. Now first, understand that I had always considered myself wonderfully tolerant of other cultures. While I had not adopted all the ways of Korean culture during my three plus years living there, I never considered them to be wrong or inferior to my own ways. I enjoyed Korean food and learned to be quite proficient with chopsticks. I had picked up enough of the Korean language to live and get around. I even started to realize that certain behaviors, ones that would have been considered 'rude' in my own culture, were perfectly natural in the context of Korean life, and I could adjust my reactions accordingly. And so when I happened to fall in love with a Korean girl and eventually asked her to marry me, I was doing so with no fear of experiencing the proverbial 'culture shock' often associated with such unions since I felt I had already embraced her culture. In fact *I* was the one who pushed for a traditional Korean wedding ceremony.

My wife-to-be Hyun and I planned to pay for the wedding ourselves. She suggested that her parents were not in a financial position to pay for the wedding, and to her delight I was in full agreement. As we were discussing the guest list, she informed me that all the friends of her parents whose children's weddings *they* had gone to had to be invited. Although I didn't really like the idea, I went along with it when I heard that they would all be giving substantial amounts of money as gifts. Later on, as I was adding up the costs for the wedding, I asked her how much money we could expect to get from these friends of her parents. She looked at me a bit strange. "None," she said, "all that money is going to my mother."

"Excuse me?" I asked, incredulous. I figured I must have misunderstood something. She repeated what she had said. I must have asked her five times to make sure I got the story right before finally exploding into a rage.

"How could that money be going to your mother? It's *our* wedding! It's our gifts! It's for us! We're even paying for the wedding! That's ridiculous! That's the most selfish thing I've ever heard of!"

Hyun was fully taken aback by my outburst, and was in tears for over an hour. When she finally mustered the strength to respond, she came out angrily: "She had to pay out money at all their weddings! It's normal. It's the only way she can get that money back. It's *her* money!"

In Korea, money is traditionally distributed up through the family, usually the mother, and redistributed down to the children. It's a complex system that ties in with family real estate, in a way that protects its members and helps them make prudent decisions. I had heard about this, but never gave it much attention. The idea never bothered me because I was never affected by it. But now that it was affecting me, I was angry about it. All I could think of was that I was paying for a stranger's meal so he could put some money in my mother-in-law's pocket. My anger was an indictment not only against Hyun's mother, but also against the whole culture in general for having what I suddenly felt was a ludicrous system.

But it really wasn't. It was just different, and totally self-consistent. Hyun's parents had always been honest and very generous with me. The last thing they would want to do is take money that they didn't think belonged to them. Hyun's parents worked hard and scraped by to help Hyun and her brother and sister get through university. In contrast, my brother, sister and I all paid our own way through university. This was not because our parents loved us any less. Our culture tends to put a high value on independence and fosters autonomous separate family units, while Koreans put more emphasis on interdependence and keeping family ties strong. If I was to be married to someone of a different culture, I suddenly realized more was needed from me than mere tolerance.

Tolerance still maintains the notion that ours is the 'right' way and theirs is the 'wrong' way. This polarity lays in wait, potentially manifesting as violent opposition when triggered by circumstance. Without a real desire to actively delve into the way others see the world, and be challenged by these different views in ways that matter to us, it might be difficult to fully come to grips with our own ethnocentricity. Today I feel very fortunate to be married to someone of a different culture. I am reminded in the daily events of our relationship that simple tolerance is not enough to heal the conflicts and misunderstandings that arise in a way that generates true harmony.

It is striving for what I call true *acceptance*, not simple tolerance that opens the door to overcoming the opposition that leads to conflict. Through acceptance we entertain the possibility that our own way of thinking may need to come under scrutiny from time to time, and that perhaps the other person's way of thinking is right. And in its purest form acceptance even goes beyond that, to the most subtle and uplifting precept of them all: that *all* ideas have value, that it is not a question of right and wrong, but simply a matter of perspective. Here, the ideas that make us different are no longer obstacles but opportunities, to learn, to grow, to come to a greater awareness of what our lives are really about. In my marriage, striving for this kind of acceptance for my wife and her culture has not only meant greater harmony but also a fuller, richer appreciation for the diversity that exists around me.

Humanity as a whole suffers when groups of people remain too attached to their own collective identity and world-view. It seems a not-so-divine comedy that the history of humanity has been marked by an inability to embrace our cultural and racial differences, one of our greatest gifts to one another. This inability is at the core of the racism and discrimination that is still active in the world.

In his speech on the steps of the Lincoln Memorial in 1963, Martin Luther King spoke of emancipation from the slavery of outmoded ideas. He spoke of a day that would see the *Negro*, as he called his own, liberated from oppression and racial injustice. But even beyond a vision for his own people, his dream had universal significance. He sought to advance the truths that the Declaration of Independence, written almost two hundred years earlier, had deemed self-evident: that *all* men (and women) are created equal. He dared to speak of a day in the future where different races and creeds would walk side by side, beyond the clutches of discrimination, and "*all* of God's children, black men and white men, Jews and Gentiles, Protestants and Catholics, will be able to join hands and sing in the words of the old Negro spiritual: 'Free at last! Free at last! Thank God Almighty, we are free at last!' "

His speech remains one of the most dramatic appeals for all of us to liberate ourselves from our deeply rooted habit of judging one another. And this appeal has been taken up by the new conversation. The new conversation is not about changing the words we use while leaving the beliefs intact. Certainly words are powerful, and to some extent they are transformative, but simply being proficient in politically correct terminology is not enough. While some of us pride ourselves on our ability to suppress judgment from our world and hide it from ourselves, this does not bring about healing. It only puts off confrontation until another day. If judgment and discrimination are still our inner guiding principles, the damage will eventually manifest.

At the same time the new conversation is not designed to censor judgment and discrimination. If a racial slur is someone's deepest truth, we are better to allow its expression than to suppress it. If we really want to be helpful, we will do best not to *judge* the person for saying it. In this way we are helping the person get an unimpeded look at themselves. When they are ready to learn from it they will.

I have personally found this to be one of the most challenging aspects of the new conversation. I don't want to condone discrimination, but at the same time I don't want to be judgmental. I'm not always sure if simply being silent is enough, but I do know that it would be inauthentic for me to go along with the joke (i.e., smiling or nodding when asked, "You know how *those* people are, eh?") Certainly if I am directly asked what I think, it is incumbent upon me to take the risk and speak out from my heart. But if I am not asked then I realize I need to muster some compassion for where the other person is coming from. It's a bit of a high wire act, and I have needed lots of practice to learn to balance myself.

In the new conversation we are asked to walk this thin line because we have seen that discrimination cannot be healed by confrontation, and have learned that judgment can only melt away in a larger space of acceptance. If we are going to come together in any profound way, we all need a space to expose our whole selves. That means our light *and* our darkness. Let's face it: none of us are completely free of judgment. And if we accept this, it helps us to be easier on each other, and more importantly on ourselves. After all, the ability to listen and speak with acceptance comes from *self*-acceptance which, paradoxically, is cultivated when we feel accepted by others. At stake in this is our shared longing to fully express our unique selves, and the hope that our diversity can lead us to experience our most sublime sense of unity.

Today, there are signs that we have gotten closer to Dr. King's lofty vision. True, the world as a whole does not yet value *acceptance* as the highest attribute of discourse. In some parts it remains forbidden to access or speak about ideas different from the accepted norms of the nation or culture.

Wars based on ideology continue to be fought because we continue to fear that accepting those whose ideas are different from ours will threaten our survival. But despite all appearances, I believe our world is evolving from a scattered collection of bordered nations into a harmonious global village. One day we will all be free. The nature of our consciousness, like the universe, is to expand. And while we are going through some growing pains today, no longer certain about what is right and wrong, about how our differences can all fit in together, there will be no turning back. We have become alienated from the identities we were born into, and we are getting too smart to label ourselves by the founding ideas of our cultures. The Pandora's box has opened and the conversation has begun. And the more we talk, the more we will enjoy the fact that each of us seems to see things a little differently, no longer satisfied with being pushed back into a box that has become too restrictive to contain us.

As we endeavor to become fully human, to actualize ourselves, we get a glimpse of the importance of being informed by the distinct character and nature of *all* human beings, not just those who think the way we do. We are gaining the courage to question our deep-seated beliefs that there is only one view of the world, and only one meaning to life. The slowly emerging consensus is that the seemingly disparate ways of seeing the world and giving meaning to life are all dazzling colors that together form the mosaic that encompasses the human experience.

14. The Two Tribes (Part 2)

Even when they were not looking for something new, the running tribe was no longer sitting still on the island of Allandon. Running itself had become the main activity, allowing them to advertise the virtues of their new-found way of life by yelling out loud as they ran in and out of every corner of the island. Those who remained in the sitting tribe believed there was no point in running, because one inevitably ended up back where one started. They could not fathom the foolishness of the running tribe. Every time the running tribe passed by them, the sitting tribe enjoyed collective amusement at the loud spectacle.

The members of the running tribe, on the other hand, truly felt they were getting somewhere. They were proud of their quest to run faster and longer, and felt their efforts were improving the quality of their lives. They thought the sitting tribe must be lazy, or were just a bunch of simpletons. As they raced by the sitting tribe every day they laughed and jeered at them.

The leader of the running tribe was always selected through a competition that determined the strongest and fastest member. He was held in the highest esteem, and was decked with all the honor and glory one could imagine. In the sitting tribe, no such honor was ever handed out, for everyone seemed to be able to sit with equal ability. The leader of the running tribe gazed upon the sitting tribe with pity and would often endeavor to educate them on the superiority of a running life. Sometimes members of the sitting tribe were coerced into joining, and sometimes they came of their own accord. Either way, the running tribe continued to get bigger and stronger, and became the *de facto* rulers of the island.

It is asking a lot from any culture or group bound by their own worldview to completely validate the divergent worldview of another. It certainly hasn't happened very often in *our* neck of the woods. While many of us in the West studied the colonization of America in our history classes, it is unlikely that we were given the opportunity to fully appreciate the perspective of the Native Americans, as elaborated by Chief Seattle earlier. Somehow, his words didn't make the final cut in our high school textbooks. Now it's fairly understandable that most of us who went to school in the West ended up with an education that had a particularly Western slant; however most of us didn't realize that there was a Western slant at all. We were led to believe that we were simply getting the *facts* about the past.

In my first year of university my three core liberal arts courses formed a multidisciplinary study of politics, literature, and art through history. The three courses were coordinated to study the developments of each discipline within the same historical time period each week. The only thing was that the *history* started with Classical Greece, which not coincidentally marked the beginning of Western civilization. But I had no issues with that at the time. I was part of the consensus among university types that the only history worth talking about was the history of the Western world, and that everything else was literally *ancient* history, a term that continues to connote past events that don't have any practical relevance to our present lives.

To penetrate more deeply into this requires a brief

introduction to the prevalent Western view of history itself. Please bear with me through this bit of heavy discourse since it sketches a very important distinction for our ongoing conversation. The highly influential 18th Century German philosopher of history G.W.F Hegel believed that history was an account of the evolution of human consciousness, which brings progressively greater freedom to humankind.[3]

Hegel saw all significant historical events following a pattern that he called the *dialectic*. Any belief, which he calls a *thesis*, eventually gives rise to an opposing belief he calls the *antithesis*. These opposing ideas eventually come into conflict, and only through the resolution of the conflict can consciousness evolve. He calls the resolution of these opposing ideas the *synthesis*, a new idea that is formed which in some way incorporates both the thesis and antithesis and thus is a more complex belief. The synthesis becomes the new thesis and the pattern is repeated (figure 2).

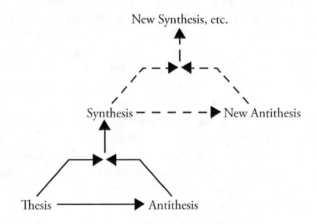

Figure 2: The dialectic

---

[3] For Hegel the history of Eastern civilization could be summarized in one phrase: the movement from a state of utter barbarism to the development of the idea that the *One* is free. People could achieve freedom, but only through a denial of their individual self by melding into the One, the Dao. It is only when we get to Ancient Greek and Roman societies that the idea that people *as people* can be free. However, these founding societies of Western civilization were built on the assumption that in order for some to be free, a major portion of humanity needed to be enslaved to support the freedom of the few. From there, Western history chronicles a series of events that have gradually moved humankind closer to its pinnacle, a society where *all* are free. When this condition is fully attained in the world, it would signify the end of history as such.

There are numerous examples of the dialectic in all facets of human life.[4] At a time in history when we believed the world was flat, the *thesis* was that it must be finite, with 'edges'. The *antithesis* came when we realized through experience that we could never reach these 'edges', implying that the world was infinite. The *synthesis* came with the realization that the world is round, combining qualities of being both finite and infinite.

It is through the dialectical struggle that the West has made progress by breaking away from older traditions and practices. This mindset believes that there *can* be something new under the sun, that man is here to explore, to discover, to invent, to make his mark on the world, to build something original rather than settling for more of the same. By all appearances, the rest of the world has succumbed to this kind of thinking. Most cultures have slowly abandoned many of their traditional ways in favor of Western practices. The Western modernization machine has been spreading its influence far and wide across the surface of the globe like a tidal wave. The globalization of the economy that is occurring in our world today is spearheaded by modern Western laws and business practices, and many traditional societies are now in the process of trying hard to catch up so they can be part of it.

It is an interesting thing to observe this shift in the everyday life of more traditional cultures. While it is obviously a slow process for a culture to fully adopt a divergent mindset, nations like Korea appear to have embraced the West and have rapidly implemented its principles of modernization. Still, during my time living there, I did notice remnants of the holistic thinking on which their civilization was founded. The reaction of my adult students to the 1998 financial meltdown in Korea, dubbed the 'IMF Crisis', stands out for me. While the

---

[4] Human relationships are always fraught with opposition, and they can only go forward when the struggle between different points of view results in a higher truth that encompasses both. The history of philosophy was driven at every turn by the capacity of human genius to synthesize conflicting schools of thought. So too does science and technology continue to progress out of the tension between established belief and new theory. And politically speaking, our Western democracies have grown as a result of a long series of clashes and subsequent resolutions between the powerful few and the masses. Our democracies continue to be governed by the pull of opposites, the ruling and opposition parties, whose debates and struggles are supposed to bring about higher ideas than those embodied by either two camps. Well, in theory, anyway.

crisis was a result of inefficient and corrupt business practices by the country's financial elite, most of the students were willing to *own* their society's problems rather than standing apart from them. "*We* have gotten ourselves into trouble," they would say, and "*We* have to work hard to get back on track." When Koreans were asked to go to the banks to sell their gold so that the government would have some hard currency, they did so *en masse*, helping Korea emerge from the crisis more quickly. If the same kind of financial crisis hit in the heart of our Western society, we would scarcely be so ready to feel that it was *our* problem. Instead, we would likely place blame and point fingers at our politicians and business leaders: "How are *they* going to fix things?" or "Are *they* going to get punished?"

In the Western world, for better or for worse, people stand apart from each other more. In elevating the Ego Self to the highest stature it has ever enjoyed, we have brought the physical world into sharper focus and weakened our connection with the invisible world of the Dao where we are all One. As a result we favor the individual over the community, and we have less of a sense of kinship and belonging than more traditional societies enjoyed. We have grown and moved apart from each other as the family structure itself has seen a slow disintegration. It is ironic that we live in a time where technologies like satellites, cell phones and the Internet make us think that we are more connected, because in actual fact there has never been a time in history when we have been so cut off from each other, not only physically but emotionally and spiritually.

The more strongly a society is grounded in the physical world, the more it will be fundamentally materialistic, concerned more with *matter* in its various forms than invisible *spirit*. It will invest its energies into material gains and comforts rather than spiritual satisfaction. While it's true that Western civilization has made huge advances in the improvement of the physical conditions of living, there has been a cost. We are forced to survive in a society founded on separateness, which has spawned dog-eat-dog competition and survival of the fittest. For all our material success we are left wanting for a deeper sense of fulfillment, one that make us feel that we belong.

Although I had started to become aware of these issues

during university, it was only after I graduated that a feeling of separateness and alienation really impacted me. I needed money and so I had to find a job, but the prospects were far bleaker than I would have ever imagined. I couldn't find *any* job, let alone something pertaining to my field. Potential employers and government employment agencies made me feel that it was probably better if I didn't even *mention* that I studied philosophy. I had to go back to school and get a degree in computer programming before I was finally able to be productive and fit in to society, albeit a round peg in a square hole.

During the next several years I harbored a growing discontent with the Western paradigm. I came to regard it as exploitative, arrogant and far too linear. I became quite drawn to traditional Eastern philosophies such as Hinduism, Buddhism and Daoism, particularly by their gentle, humble, holistic nature. Many of the New Age writers I was reading at the time made regular and glowing reference to Eastern doctrines. I came to firmly believe that these ideas were more profound and ultimately more truthful than what I had grown up with and followed in school. Perhaps one of the reasons I went to live in East Asia in 1996 was because of the desire to get a taste of Eastern life and holistic thinking. I was anxious to see and experience some of what I had been reading about.

It strikes me as ironic that one of the main things that I took from my three years in East Asia was actually a new respect for the Western mindset. I saw how a life more closely tied to tradition had its moments, but it did not engender as much critical thinking, ingenuity, and initiative. When I would ask my university students what their future plans were, their responses were generally quite vague and unoriginal. Many seemed to be waiting for someone to tell them what they should do. Students that I met who had gone over to the West for a period of time generally stood out as having a better idea of what they wanted from their lives.

And that is really what the Western mindset does, it encourages individuals to stand out, to be independent, responsible, and to believe that they could do and be anything they wanted. Hegel believed that the freedom that individuals felt and exercised was the measure of how advanced a society was. It should come as no surprise that in recent times human rights have become increasingly important in the

West. We have heard about and witnessed the barriers on human freedom and expression tumbling one by one in our recent history. The abolition of slavery. The right of women to vote. The elevation of the status of the disabled. The protection of children. The acceptance of homosexuality. In more advanced societies a person is not just part of a collective, a person is suddenly a world unto themselves, equal, whole and valued for their uniqueness.

What would have happened if Western man had followed Chief Seattle's plea to end its domination of nature and learn to live completely in harmony with it? Well, we would probably have stopped making material advancements and our society would still be without electricity, airplanes, computers, and all the other wonders of the modern world. The fact that you have this book in your hands at this moment is made possible by a mindset that broke away from the cycles of nature and did things differently from how they were done in the past. Let's be clear: I believe Chief Seattle's words are stirring and provocative for many of us, and shall remain a timeless petition for maintaining respect and appreciation for the beauty of our natural world. At the same time, I believe very few of us would endorse wiping out all the technological progress we have made in the last few hundred years so that we could live today in a state of nature as the Native Americans did.

The Eastern mindset sees life itself as part of a cycle. Humanity is not seen as moving forward as such but rather simply returning to the One from whence it came. The Western mindset, on the other hand, holds that man is on a mission, both individually and collectively. There is a move to what is new, to undiscovered territory and unthought ideas. To the Western mind, the idea that human life is fundamentally cyclical is a real problem. If this were true, then what would be the point of striving to do anything? Why would we need to have choice? What would be the value of freedom? The Western paradigm believes that we very much have things to learn and uncover, to create and invent. Where there is no possibility of progress or evolution, life becomes devoid of meaning.

And so, when Westerners evaluate traditional Eastern history they tend to note simply that not much significant progress was actually made, and the only reason that Eastern cultures have shown any progress today is because they have been strongly influenced by Western ideas. Without this, they would have continued to plod along with their ancient traditions to guide them in their inertia. And so Western culture tends to consider itself great and judges Eastern culture to be somewhat backwards. It does not credit Eastern culture with making much of a contribution to the evolution of mankind.

When I was in India recently a funny thing happened that got me thinking. My wife had just finished drinking a bottle of water and asked a young Indian man where she could throw it away. He took the plastic bottle from her hand with a smile, and simply tossed it on the ground. "It's OK," he said, continuing to smile. He seemed fully unconcerned about material things, perhaps because for many Indians material things are part of *maya*, the illusion of the material world, and we should always be focusing beyond the illusion to the world of spirit. I like the idea, but that does not remove the fact that we have to live in the material world, and address problems like pollution, disease, and hunger.

Perhaps this is the very challenge facing India and other traditional cultures today. The paradigm of Eastern culture has not demonstrated an ability to master material life and overcome suffering from material poverty. Turning a back on Western modernization is no longer possible. Spiritual leaders from these nations look to the West with some regret for the preoccupation with materialism and lack of spirituality, but they still retain a measure of respect for the quality of life advances that the West has made. In some way or another their own lives have benefited from these advances.

So while there is something very precious that the East can offer the West, there is also something precious that the West can offer the East. We have not yet arrived at a point where East and West can easily appreciate the value of the other's bounty in order to facilitate a worthwhile exchange. There is a mutual desire to have the best of both worlds, but our respective paradigms don't currently show us how to manifest it. The West can bring the East a better life. The East can bring the West a life of greater meaning. Perhaps it is indeed time to have a conversation.

15. The Mayor

One warm summer day the arborist and her daughter were busy transplanting potted saplings in the village park on the island of Allandon. A portly gentleman who was casually picking up trash noticed them and said brightly: "Good morning ladies. Beautiful day isn't it?"

"Yes it is," the arborist said.

Her daughter nodded, and moments later said to her mother: "Every time I see that guy he acts like he hasn't got a care in the world."

"Maybe he hasn't," said the arborist.

"Who is he anyway?"

The arborist laughed. "Don't you know? That's our village Mayor."

"He's the *Mayor*?" she asked incredulously. After pondering for a moment, she added, "Well, that's very odd."

"What is?"

"Well, what kind of Mayor is he? I mean, hasn't he got more important things to do than pick up trash in the park?"

"Apparently not," said the arborist as she continued to enjoy the scent of the young evergreens in their new home.

"So how did he become Mayor?" asked her daughter.

"He became Mayor because he's a great leader."

"What's so great about him? I didn't even know we had a Mayor. I always thought this village kind of ran itself."

"Exactly," the arborist replied.

Part of the evolution of consciousness we are going through today is a change in the way we see the leaders of our nations. We no longer put them on the pedestal we once did, nor are we willing to follow them blindly. The very word 'politics' immediately conjures up images in our minds of deception, corruption, and self-interest. We are convinced that hypocrisy is now built right into the system, and that someone who makes it to the top must be a person who owes a lot of secret favors and is good at making false promises that won't be kept. We don't believe any more that our leaders will do the right thing for us, for the community, the country, or the world. We have more than lost faith and trust. We have lost interest.

And I see this as a good thing.

Why? Because the time has come to be leaders ourselves—all of us. Instead of looking and listening for inspiration, it is time to be self-inspiring. Instead of waiting to be told what we have to do, it is time for us to decide how it's all going to be. When Gandhi said, "be the change you want to see in the world," he was exhorting each one of us to lead by example. He knew that lasting change does not happen by political decree but rather inside the minds of individuals, one at a time. Each time an individual has an insight, expands their vision, or learns something new, then the collective human consciousness that we all dip into is forever transformed.

Today our politicians don't even try to influence the evolution of consciousness. The best they can do is react to it, and they are usually pretty slow at that. In fact our leadership and the institutions that support them may be the last things in our society to evolve as we move away from the outmoded belief that our leaders will save us and do what *we* actually came here to do.

In Ancient times leaders were considered far above the common people. Often they were not even considered people themselves, but gods, or at least having a direct link to divinity. In Egypt, for example, the faith that followers had in the divinity of their leaders was enough to move—or build—mountains. The great pyramids stand today as a testament to that. The rule was simple in those days: leaders command, subordinates obey. In this traditional master/servant relationship there was no place for conversation, debate, or differences of opinion. A hierarchy or chain-of-command passed edicts down in one direction, from top to bottom.

This format is the legacy of our modern institutions, not only in politics but in all spheres of life. The hierarchy of the church is a most obvious example. Followers were not capable of direct conversation with God but had to communicate through the priest, whose return message back to the follower was to be accepted as sacrosanct and beyond reproach. Our education system was founded on desks rigidly set in rows, with students uniformly dressed, all eyes forward and sitting in fear, as the teacher walked menacingly through the aisles, ready to slam the ruler down on the hand of any student not absorbing the immutable doctrines. Business was modeled after feudal society where the Lord had complete domain over the field workers underneath him. The Industrial Revolution's production line only strengthened the conviction that workers were self-same cogs in the production wheel. And in the family, a man was the 'king of his castle', where his children 'should be seen and not heard' and his wife had to be subservient to his will.

This kind of leadership, which employs control and a reliance on unbending structure, is ultimately rooted in the perspective of the Ego Self. Since the Ego Self worries about being separate and insignificant, the leadership it sponsors drives leaders to try to elevate themselves above others. This way of being a leader means always being right, and never showing any doubt or hesitation. Ever afraid to reveal that they are not all-powerful and do not have all the answers, Ego-Self leaders tend to be rather inflexible and dismissive of contrary opinion.

Even though our society has been politically *democratic* for some time, our institutions still tend to be run by this control-oriented hierarchical leadership. Subordinates are implicitly expected to conform, and are not encouraged to have a point of view. Much of the thrust of this leadership amounts to maintaining order and exercising power, which means making subordinates follow the leader's vision.

This is not to suggest that it is easy to lead in a more open and inclusive way; the power implicit in leadership can corrupt the most well-meaning among us. Here's an example that history has revealed to us before, in a variety of iterations: a dissident leader in an oppressed country, a true 'man of the people', starts off with noble intentions and a vision of equality for all. With the people's support he succeeds in orchestrating the overthrow of a brutal tyrant. However once in power himself, this leader is slowly overcome by his new-found sense of self-importance. His vision of 'equality for all' takes a back seat to his growing vision of his own grandeur. Lacking a deeper self-awareness, he doesn't even recognize that he is changing. Soon enough he is faced with an ever-growing discontent among the people, and has to fight mercilessly to keep power and suppress revolt. He often wonders why the people are no longer happy about his victory over tyranny until the fateful moment, perhaps as he is being put to death, when it finally dawns on him that he himself had become the brutal tyrant that he once loathed.

Since our society is dominated by the Ego Self, it

should come as no surprise to us that our leaders may have gotten seduced by the idea that their perspective is the *right* one, and that in some ways they are better than those they lead. This is only exacerbated when they surround themselves with yes-people who will not challenge them.

The thing is that we are rather fed up of being yes-people, and it's beginning to show. Leaders have noticed that we don't seem to be following orders as automatically any more. We have become less afraid to challenge the status quo, and have started asking our leaders to consider our unique visions, our talents or our aspirations. While some are paying attention, others have reacted by leading in the only way they know how: by shouting louder and banging harder on the drum of obedience. This may give them some results in the short term, but they are only stemming a far larger tide that will not hold for much longer.

Our institutions are already showing cracks in their foundations where individual expression and influence are oozing out. The Church structure has begun to crumble, as increasing numbers of people are bypassing the need for an intermediary and establishing their own private and personal contact with divinity. In education the whole concept of the classroom itself is being questioned, where conformity and uniformity are more and more being seen as a hindrance to learning. Successful businesses are being forced to flatten out their hierarchies and move away from the strict command-and-control structure they once enjoyed, realizing that their companies are more productive when their employees take greater part in the decision-making and their individual talents are considered. And in the family, the roles and rights of both women and children have changed immeasurably in recent times, as has the very nature of the family itself. The husband/father can no longer simply 'put his foot down' to squash any challenges to his leadership.

As we gain awareness as individuals, our leaders will continue to evolve by necessity. More and more, leaders in our society will have to move away from feeding their own sense of self-importance and be willing to deflect the spotlight so that individual expression and contribution can shine. Leadership will increasingly be doing the work that goes on backstage and supports the roles of those who are performing. It's gratifying that we may be finally heeding the words of Lao-Tzu, written over two and a half millennia ago:

> The existence of the leader who is wise is barely known
> to those he leads. He acts without unnecessary speech,
> so that the people say, "It happened of its own accord".

Enduring leaders of modern day like Ghandi, the Dalai Lama, Mother Theresa, and Nelson Mandela walked amongst the people, as one of them. They did not seek to be deified or given superior status. They did not feel themselves as having privileged access to the knowledge that their lives modeled, but believed that each person was worthy. Their humility was not forced: it is a natural byproduct of leading from the Dao Self where we are all equal parts of the One. Doing this requires a high degree of self-awareness because to be human means to feel the constant pull of the Ego Self.

Jesus was considered one of the greatest leaders ever because he was able to resist the temptation to lead from the Ego Self, symbolized by the Devil. When the Devil offered Jesus all the kingdoms of the world, Jesus chose instead to remain firmly in the Dao Self.[5] While maintaining his connection to the source of all things helped Jesus perform miracles, it was also the foundation of his conviction that anyone could do what he had done and even greater things.[6]

For those who could not understand, he tried to be a model in his life, and told people to *follow* him—not blindly, but as an *example* of how to live. While Jesus tried in every way to point each person back to themselves and their capacity to live from the Dao Self, most were not quite ready for it. The difficulty he faced is comically illustrated in Monte Python's *Life of Brian*, a parody of the life of Jesus:

---

[5] In biblical terms, this was expressed by the assertion that Jesus would only worship and serve God [Matthew, 4:9-10]. Jesus had absolutely no doubts that he was *one* with the One he called the Father, and the fact that he had fully embodied this knowledge meant that Jesus had reached the pinnacle of self-realization in human form.

[6] From John, 14:12. Salvation was possible for all people, not because of the miracles or even the death and resurrection of Jesus, but because every person has the latent ability to attain this Christ-consciousness, the absolute realization of oneself as the Dao Self. In Christian terms this is what it means to reach heaven.

BRIAN: You've got it all wrong! You don't need to follow me. You don't need to follow anybody! You've got to think for yourselves. You're all individuals!
FOLLOWERS: Yes, we're all individuals!
BRIAN: You're all different!
FOLLOWERS: Yes, we are all different!
BRIAN: You've all got to work it out for yourselves!
FOLLOWERS: Yes! We've got to work it out for ourselves!
BRIAN: Exactly!
FOLLOWERS: Tell us more!
BRIAN: No! That's the point! Don't let anyone tell you what to do!

The irony is not lost on us. Since he lived at a time when people had not fully *individuated*, and so were not fully self-aware, it was difficult for Jesus to *lead* them to the internal and personal experience of being in the Dao Self. Instead his followers sought to deify him, calling him their savior, abdicating responsibility for their own behavior in the process.[7]

Two millennia later, we are finally ready for leadership that comes from the Dao Self, not simply in the spiritual domain but in our politics, business, family and other human institutions. Leadership has begun to move away from commanding and towards facilitating. Rather than telling us what to do, leaders will have to engage each one of us in conversation, a conversation that leads us back to ourselves. This may come as a big relief to our leaders themselves, many of whom have become dissatisfied with the limitations of their command-oriented ways. Many will seize the opportunity to inspire rather than insist, to be authentic rather than simply do what is expected of them. And as the new conversation blurs the line between leader and follower we are all called upon to take up leadership positions, to support our individual expression while strengthening a collective voice that speaks for all of humanity.

---

[7] When we look back on the efforts of Jesus to spread the *Good News* we may conclude that the profundity of his message may have been too far ahead of its time. History tells us that over the past two thousand years the Church that stood in the name of Christ-consciousness was built on a foundation of control, intimidation, discrimination, and even killing, acts that are all sponsored by the Ego Self.

16. The Choreographer

With only a few weeks of rehearsals remaining before the premiere of the annual musical, the artistic director entered the village playhouse very excited. He went to the stage where all the dancers were in the process of stretching and warming up.

"I have a new idea," he said, "an idea so advanced that it will revolutionize the way you dance with your partners."

"You're going to make the floor move while we stand still?" asked one, provoking snickers around the stage.

"Pay attention, I'm serious," snapped the director. "Now tell me, what is the main theme of this show?"

One of the dancers answered, "It's about a girl who starts off as a slave and eventually becomes a member of—"

"*Equality*," interrupted the director, "the main theme of this show is equality between people. Now I've been thinking about this and suddenly it struck me that when you dance with your partner there is *in*equality, because one person is leading and the other is following. So starting today, when you practice your dances for this show I want to see *both* partners leading."

"At the same time?" asked one of the dancers.

"Yes, of course," said the director.

The dancers looked at each other in confusion. They had never heard of such a thing. Meanwhile the choreographer, who was taking in the scene from the second row, started laughing.

"What's so funny?" asked the director.

"Your idea is ridiculous. Absurdly ridiculous," she replied.

The director was stunned. He was not used to being challenged, especially by his choreographer, who he got along very well with. "What are you saying?"

"I'm saying it will never work."

"It might, if you try it."

"We're not going to try it," the choreographer said.

"Well, I think you owe it to me to at least try it."

"It's not going to happen," the choreographer replied sarcastically.

"Need I remind you that I am the director, and you have to follow what I say?"

"Well, this time I want you to follow *me*."

The director was getting red-faced with frustration. He moved to the front of the stage to address the choreographer. "Why are you doing this?"

"What—you don't want me to keep arguing with you?" asked the choreographer slyly.

"Of course not!"

"Because we're not getting anywhere?"

"Exactly."

"Then why would you ever want to see two people try to lead the same dance?"

While I have suggested that the time has come for us all to be leaders, this does not mean that we should all be leading simultaneously. That would be like a conversation where people were all talking at the same time, which is not a conversation at all. Taking on roles like leader and follower is an essential aspect of the human drama. Life would not be capable of producing excitement, wonder and profound learning if we were all self-identical creatures doing exactly the same things. If life flows from dualities, through pairs of opposites like leader and follower, then it is important for each of us to play our roles when required.

Mind you, nobody has to be *told* to assume roles—it comes quite naturally to us. Our Ego Self is designed to separate and distinguish us from one another. The perception of many of our differences is immediate, and we are already in the habit of grounding our interactions in these differences. What we may need to be reminded of sometimes is that this is only half of the story. The other half comes to us from the perspective of the Dao Self where we can see past the distinctions that separate us. When we come from this higher place we see that these roles will best help us move forward in our lives when we don't take them so *seriously*.

When we live solely from the Ego Self our roles can easily fall into stereotypes and become the source of value judgment and comparison. We start believing that one side of the duality is *better* than the other, more capable, or more *right*. We may think that the teacher must always be wiser than the student, and so the student should simply be quiet and listen; that the servant is weaker than the master, and therefore must obey; that without the leader the follower is clueless, bereft of inspiration or direction.

As followers we are likely to harbor resentment towards leaders when this kind of stereotype is at play. We will feel that our ability to be an important part of any process is limited, and we will have few opportunities to express ourselves as individuals or feel that we are making a contribution. Even if we disagree with our leader's approach, we will be forced to play a game that only rewards us if we try to elevate the leader's already inflated status (see: *brown-nosing*).

But when we become leaders we're not necessarily

better off. The stereotypical leadership role puts us under tremendous pressure, both from ourselves and the outside environment. We are supposed to know everything, and we are not allowed to show doubt. We are expected to be responsible for things beyond our control. Worst of all, we are not allowed to make mistakes. When we do, we hide them: our shame makes us try to cover them up, lest anyone find out that we are not *up for* what is expected of us.

What a relief it is when we are able to step back into the realm of the Dao Self. From here the roles we have taken on lose their rigidity. Suddenly teachers are learning from students, masters can be the ones who serve, and leaders encourage followers to become leaders themselves. When leaders and followers rise above stereotype, their interactions move into the flow of life. Followers are able to make a greater contribution and take on more responsibility. Leaders are able to relax and allow themselves to be human, to show and voice their doubts, and admit their mistakes to themselves and others. When leaders are not afraid to show their ignorance and vulnerability it is inspiring, and actually serves as an invitation for their followers to enter into the process in a more meaningful capacity.

As humanity evolves, the *status* gap between leaders and followers is closing. Leadership is moving away from command-and-obey and towards a collaboration in which the insights, opinions, values and beliefs of *both* sides of the dichotomy are honored. Where there is a sense of equality between teacher and student, boss and subordinate, speaker and listener, there we find the new conversation.

When I look back on my academic life, I realize that the new conversation was not often a feature of the classroom. In fact the higher up I went, the more that professors seemed set in their ways, even condescending at times. I remember the lifeless discussions in class, where students—including me— favored intellectual questions that would make them look smart. Professors would then answer with similar pretense. On the odd occasion that someone would ask a question from the heart or simply state that they didn't understand, eyes would roll and sighs of intolerance could be heard. There may have been some lively debates, but these were far from a collaborative effort to understand each other and discover new perspectives. Students and teachers alike were afraid to really open their own personal ideologies to honest scrutiny, and so most of the energy was used to defend and protect these ideologies.

When it was time to look into PhD programs, the curricula I saw left me cold: more intellectualizing about other people's ideas, and more rehashing the past in a way that did not impact how I lived my life. I had an uneasy feeling growing inside me that continuing my formal education would be like purchasing a one-way ticket to the proverbial Ivory tower. So I walked away, despite being told that I had no teaching prospects at all if I didn't pursue a PhD. It felt like I had gotten tired of learning. But I realize now that I was just looking for other *ways* to learn.

Over the past twenty years, I have enjoyed a host of non-academic programs, seminars, and transformational workshops, some of which had a big influence on me. Instead of just talking about different perspectives, some of these programs actually created the conditions that enabled me to shift my perspective—with all the discomfort that this entailed. It sometimes felt like the rug was being pulled out from under my feet, because the whole way I looked at the world, where I was *coming from*, was challenged.

What I found was that it was always worth the discomfort. Whenever I was able to shift my perspective, I saw myself and the world in a more powerful way. I became happier, more confident. My vision was expanded, and I was able to let go of ideas and attitudes that were no longer serving me. All this would not have been possible if the new perspective was presented in a dogmatic way—if, in other words, it was presented as absolute and irrefutable. It needed to be offered as a *possibility*. Significant transformation would not have occurred if someone was simply telling me what to do, think, or believe. I had to be given a real choice, and from a place of choice I was allowed to step into what I could handle and *own* the changes that were happening to me.

More and more I saw facilitators opening their workshops with the stipulation that the material is presented as *one* way of looking at the subject, and participants should question anything that doesn't resonate with them and only take to heart that which serves them. This idea was reinforced when a facilitator acknowledged that they have as much to learn from the experience as everyone else. Rather than following a rigid set of procedures, the more skilled facilitators focused on building an atmosphere of trust and openness in which people felt safe and confident enough to share their unique perspectives, insights, and experiences. This gave rise to authentic conversation, which energized those who participated.

Over time I gained a growing interest in how these workshops were presented and facilitated, and paid close attention to whether the facilitators themselves were attempting to deliver the material as possibilities or as statements of fact. I got into the habit of putting myself in the seat of the facilitator, wondering how I would handle the questions and situations that came up, and thinking about how I might present the material differently. I have come to appreciate that it is exceedingly difficult—just from the standpoint of language, let alone personal bias—to present material in such a way that it is only *one* possible perspective rather than a statement of fact. But this is really the only way to go if we are going to move forward.

When I actually began to fulfill a long-time dream of facilitating transformational workshops myself, I was eager to bring forward this new conversation. I was very fortunate to work with someone who already had experience exploring this in her own facilitation. My good friend Carole really helped me over some of the initial rough patches when I wanted to be *right* or fretted when I didn't have all the answers. I saw that it was more important to make people feel comfortable than to look smart. I saw that the skill of listening and learning to *be* with all the participants was at least as important as the material that was to be covered. In fact, we even enlisted the help of the participants to determine some of the content and context of the material that would be delivered.

It was hard for me to grasp that I didn't have to convince everyone to agree with all the information and insights that I had prepared. I had to accept that some people couldn't or didn't want to *get it.* If some chose to tune out, to be obstinate or to complain, I needed to learn to flow with it, to be with what *is*, to keep things open. Sometimes I made the mistake of vigorously trying to defend my point of view. However I learned that being wrong and making mistakes was not only *all right*, it could often be turned into something beneficial for the group if it was handled with humility and humor. Carole sometimes made fun of my habits and tendencies during the session itself and this helped everyone including me to relax. Our co-facilitation itself became a dance, which was especially powerful since we thought and expressed ourselves in very different ways.

While I saw that leading people into the new conversation still required some direction and boundaries, it seemed to work best when these boundaries were almost invisible, when the space that we created was a circle of trust and communication in which everyone was learning and benefiting from each others' experience and perspective. I learned that leadership in the new conversation was about modeling—walking the talk. If I showed an openness to learning then it helped to create an environment of trust and exploration. When I cleared away personal issues before facilitating I was able to be more present with the participants. Facilitating the new conversation has opened an ongoing examination of who I am *being* in my life, and particularly in my conversations.

This is a possibility the new conversation offers all of us. As we become more conscious and self-directed, I believe we will strive to move our discourses away from unyielding structure and towards the creation of an open space in which we all can reflect, discover, and create. The more each one of us tastes from the cup of the new conversation, the more I believe we will be looking to bring it into all of our human interactions.

17. The Kitchen

The dinnertime rush at the village restaurant on the island of Allandon was generally hectic for the staff, and this evening was no exception. The cook was moving back and forth across a sizzling grill and the busser was washing and stacking a mountain of dirty plates like clockwork when the waiter banged open the swinging door with empty plates running up both arms. He dumped them down on the counter near the busser, causing one of the plates to slide off onto the ground and break into pieces.

The waiter paused for a second, as the busser immediately set down to pick up the pieces. "Well don't blame me," the waiter said. "Isn't it your job to pick up the empty dishes from the tables?"

"It is," said the busser.

"Well get on it, man! People are waiting to sit down!"

The busser did not jump, but instead finished picking up the remaining bits of the broken dish carefully with a broom. "Are they getting restless out there?"

"Damn right," said the waiter, tapping his finger on the grill counter as he waited for his next food order.

"Any customers take it out on you?" asked the busser.

"It seems like they *all* are tonight."

"Well if anybody can handle it, you can," said the busser, resuming his dishwashing. "You just have this cool way of calming them down."

A slight grin came over the waiter's face. "A man's gotta do what a man's gotta do," he said as he lined up the plates of food along his arms in perfect balance. He glided over to the swinging door and, backing his way out, added, "I've always said, 'if you can't stand the heat, get out of the kitchen.' "

"I'll remember that," said the busser, smiling to himself as he continued working through the pile of dishes.

The new conversation hinges on our ability to create a space—a space founded on acceptance, a space that builds trust, a space that encourages choice. You don't need to be highly informed in all matters of great import to humanity to participate. If you bring an openness of mind and spirit, an authentic curiosity about views divergent from your own, and a desire to serve others on their path as you would be served on yours, then you will be doing your part. And if enough of us do our part, the world cannot help but be transformed.

The notion that there is a new conversation today in our society crystallized for me a few years ago during my training at the Adler School of Professional Coaching in Toronto. It was as though the seeds of thought that had long been swirling inside me had suddenly found the soil in which to germinate. While there was a curriculum for the course, the underlying agenda was for the facilitators and the students to co-create each session as much as was practical. The content of the course was fully embodied in its form—a spacious and free-flowing conversation. As a participant I was made to feel comfortable with who I was and where I was at. I could be myself, and there was nothing else needed or expected. Rather than being motivated by external forces based in evaluation and judgment, I was able to get connected with my own inherent desire to learn and to grow. From there I was able to step into the opportunity to be courageous in my participation.

A memorable example of this came during a creative exercise in which we were all asked to draw a picture that represented our inner selves. When it came time for each person to show and explain their drawings, my mind naturally gravitated to which ones were good and not-so-good, and how they compared (unfavorably) to mine. It seemed a little insincere to me how some people could praise and acknowledge each and every drawing, regardless of the clarity of expression or artistic merit. I assumed everyone saw what I saw, and were encouraging one another out of politeness and tact as I had learned to do.

But somewhere during the exercise, as I noticed how heart-felt one acknowledgment after the next seemed to be, an uncomfortable thought suddenly crept up on me: Was my assumption wrong? Was *I* the only one preoccupied with judgment and comparison? Was *I* the insincere one? It was a disturbing revelation, and though I could have ignored the thought and tried to ride out the discomfort, I felt I might be missing out on something important. It was only because of the non-judgmental space that had been created in the classroom that I felt just safe enough to risk the embarrassment and share with everyone what I had realized.

My admission—that I was internally judgmental about people's creative expression and sometimes patronizing in my acknowledgments—made quite an impact on the group. A few seemed shocked by it, and tried to gently express how sincere they were being in their own acknowledgments. Another confessed that she had some feelings similar to mine. More significantly, the conversation as a whole seemed to move to an even deeper level of authenticity from that point on. People expressed gratitude for my honesty. I was grateful too, because of the rare opportunity for me to be in a space where I was able to be *real.* I believe it was the space that enabled me to hold the awareness long enough to make a courageous choice. Expressing myself went a long way to helping me let go of this habit of thought. In turn this helped me to experience something new from that moment on: a more profoundly satisfying appreciation of other people's uniqueness and creative expression.

Later in the course, the acknowledgments I received for my *own* creative expression were all the more moving for me. In a homework assignment I wrote a parable about creativity based on an earlier conversation with one of the participants who insisted she was not creative (see Chapter 30, *The Waiter*). The praise and encouragement I received to seriously pursue the creative work of writing parables, which I loved to do, helped to inspire me to embark upon a new project I had been contemplating. In front of all my new friends on the final day of the course in October of 2003, I stood up and made the commitment that I was going to write a book that I would call *Parables for the New Conversation*.

Needless to say, being part of a course that focused on learning the technology of a powerful kind of interpersonal conversation—the *coaching* conversation—had a big impact on the subject matter of my book. I believe it would be very helpful at this point to explain what *coaching* actually is, and describe its influence on my vision of the new conversation.

The coaching I am referring to is broadly distinguished as *life* coaching. It is different from the traditional notion of a 'coach' who guides and manages an athlete or sports team and is supposed to be the wise authority on the game. In life coaching the game is life itself, and since the flow of life is *change*, the mandate of a coach involves helping the client deal with life changes or supporting them in making the changes that will take them where they want to go. Whereas the goal in any sport is clear—to win—in life coaching the goal itself is determined by the client. Together the coach and client identify obstacles along the path of change, brings clarity to real goals, and help clients move towards realizing them.

Coaching is different from therapy, psychiatry or social work, as it does not seek to resolve trauma or fix what is *wrong* with a client. It works from the standpoint that the client is already creative, resourceful, and whole—capable of being responsible for their own desired transformation.[8] And

---

[8] This means that not everyone is a candidate to be a coaching client, and the coach has an obligation to evaluate early on whether the client is self-responsible

unlike consultants, advisors, or mentors, a coach does not need to be an expert in any particular area—except in the art and science of the conversation itself. The coach keeps the conversation in a rhythm of penetrating and stepping back, challenging and allowing, inquiring and stating *what is.*

The coaching conversation tends to move through three phases, represented by the acronym ICA. The first phase deals with the *issue* that the client brings to coaching, and helps to find greater *insight* into the issue so that the client can become clearer on what their *intention* is for the coaching relationship. The second phase taps into the client's *creativity* to uncover the broad range of *choices* available, in order for the client to find the one they will make a *commitment* to move forward on. The final phase determines the *actions* that will fulfill the commitment, and sets up the measurable conditions by which the client can be *accountable.* The learning and growth resulting from their actions gives the client a new *awareness,* which could lead to a new coaching cycle.[9]

The coach is responsible for creating an environment within which the client can explore their greatest desires, and for providing guidance and encouragement as the client walks through and over the obstacles along their path. While on the one hand the coach is fully committed to the client's development and has a pointed devotion to their client's well-being, on the other hand the coach is completely detached from the results of the client's actions, and so is never in any way judgmental in the way clients go about the business of their lives. In this way, the client is provided with the best environment to embrace choice, their natural birthright, without the influence of coercion, ridicule, pressure, or a sense of obligation, debt, or a desire not to disappoint. There is no doubt that the creation of a safe and supportive environment greatly facilitates a client's capacity to step into choice and move forward authentically.

---

enough to bring about their own desired transformation. In a typical one-on-one relationship, a coach will meet with a client for an initial intake session where the coach will come to know many facets of the client in greater detail, including their values, strengths, challenges, and long-term goals. Subsequent regular meetings over the course of three months or longer are held with an awareness of the big picture, the long-term goals the client has entered coaching to achieve.

[9] This cycle is not cast in stone, and is subordinated to the uniqueness of the individual client and their situation. The client is fully involved in a co-creation of the form of the conversation that will serve them best.

One important thing to note is that a true coach looks at themselves not as an authority or expert teacher. The coach models the attitude and behavior of a *learner* who learns right alongside with the client. It is this equality and reciprocity in the growth process that distinguishes the coaching modality from some of its predecessors. When the benefits are reciprocal, and the energy flows back and forth, then the circle is complete.

Thought not usually as formal as the coaching conversation, the new conversation employs many of the same principles. They are both founded in trust, openness and non-judgment. They both work with the ebb and flow of duality, of speaking and listening, of action informing reflection and reflection informing action, of our tendency to advance into the Dao Self and then retreat back into the Ego Self. These two conversations share a common purpose: *to create a space designed to help us step into our highest vision of who we are.* However, while the coaching conversation focuses on the specific goals of individuals or small teams of individuals, the new conversation is more expansive: it also holds the space for a unified vision for all of humanity, a collective ambition that plays out in synchrony with the pursuit of our individual purpose and aspirations.

It is in the intersection of our personal and collective journeys that human consciousness evolves. And so, in the new conversation, every single aspect of the human experience forms a part of the story: our politics and our culture, our technology and our art, our day-to-day concerns and the entire span of our history, our bodies and our souls, our greatest triumphs and our most horrifying atrocities. All things big and small, light and dark must have their place at the table if a vision of humanity as One is to finally be revealed.

I believe this revelation is well on its way to being realized, and more and more people want to be an important part of the process. I am noticing that speaking to people today, friends and strangers alike, is so different from how it was even twenty years ago. Today there seems to be a much greater interest in why we are here, where we are headed, what we can do. There is a growing hunger for authentic conversations that encourage us to be *real*, and hold us accountable for who we are being and what we are doing. Spontaneous discussions are breaking out everywhere, with birds of different feathers increasingly flocking together. We are forming conversation groups like never before to share emerging ideas and information about how to improve our lives, our communities, and the planet as a whole. In the spaces we create we are exploring rather than preaching, observing rather than judging, and opening up to having our deepest beliefs challenged. And the more we do, the greater our conviction becomes that working from such spaces will bring about the fulfillment of our personal and collective destiny.

18. The Dao

There had been a long-standing tradition on the island of Allandon for a secret society to meet once a year on the evening of the summer solstice. The meeting would take place just as the most generous sun of the year was setting, in a sheltered nook near the top of the mountain. In recent times the society had opened its doors to outsiders and now all the villagers were welcome to come up and partake in an open discussion into the mysteries of life around a hearty campfire.

On this particular evening, however, darkness came more quickly under cloudy skies. The night was cold, the stars were not visible, and just as the group had gotten the fire started, a brief rainfall doused the flames and dampened all the logs. By the time the fire was restarted only the diehards remained. The masseur, the young philosopher and his mother the schoolteacher were joined by the farmer, who seemed more concerned about the height of the flames than the depth of the conversation.

"Isn't it all just a cruel, cruel joke?" the farmer asked with a slight shiver as he stoked the fire.

"Do you have a joke?" mused the schoolteacher.

"I have. It is called existence. Life itself. Are we not always too cold, and if not cold then hot? Are we not always bored, and if not bored then anxious? Do we not always have too much of one thing or not enough of another? Constantly longing and never satisfied?"

"Perhaps, but we must laugh in the face of it," the masseur said.

"Laugh?" the farmer mocked. "Why?"

"If we are the butt of a cosmic joke, what is there to do but laugh?" the masseur asked.

"If it is a joke, then who is the joker?" asked the schoolteacher.

"There is none," said the farmer. "No being could be so cruel, so sadistic."

"True, to be precise there is no such being," weighed in the young philosopher, who had been listening quietly. "The culprit is *being itself*, the one that is the One, which has been called the Dao. And while there may be a joke, there is not an ounce of cruelty in it."

"Yes, we should praise the Dao who brings us to laughter," said the masseur.

"Rather brings *itself* to laughter—at our expense," retorted the farmer.

"That is saying the same thing," said the young philosopher, "for each one of us is in fact the Dao."

"That's nonsense," said the farmer. "Explain to me how you can say that I am this Dao."

The young philosopher hesitated for a moment. "I believe it is for each one of us to arrive at this truth in their own way. It is beyond all explanation."

"Humph," said the farmer.

After an awkward silence the schoolteacher looked around and then spoke cautiously to the young philosopher: "We can appreciate that it may be beyond explanation. But nonetheless you must try."

"Yes, humor us," said the masseur.

As the young philosopher considered the proposition there were sharp crackles and a sudden rise in the flames as the farmer continued to break twigs and push logs about. "That's better," said the farmer to himself. When he saw everyone's attention on him he snapped, "Yes, yes, go ahead, I'm listening!"

The young philosopher cleared his throat. "Well how can I say it? I believe that some time ago—before there was time— there was only the Dao. It had nothing and nobody to laugh with—or at. The Dao could only *be*, which could not have been much fun. It must have longed to experience things."

"Why could it not experience anything?" the schoolteacher asked.

"Because there was no contrast. There was no background from which discreet things could emerge. Imagine that the Dao is pure light. It could see all of itself all the time, and so in effect it could see nothing. To actually *experience* anything it needed to hide part of itself from itself. If the Dao is understood as light then it needed to somehow create darkness. And so one day it did the impossible. It somehow managed to fold itself over itself, so that half of itself was darkness."

"Was that darkness then its shadow, or was it part of itself?" asked the schoolteacher.

"Not being light, it could not be the Dao itself," said the masseur.

"It was not the Dao but at the same time it was the Dao. That is the most sublime paradox of existence. Out of pure light came darkness. And because of this, it was possible for the many to emerge from the one."

"Creation," said the masseur.

"Yes," the young philosopher said. "Because now with light and darkness, with a pair of opposites, with *duality*, all the rest of creation was possible. Light and darkness could be combined into a multitude of patterns to give us a limitless number of separate things in our universe."

"Like you and I," said the farmer.

"Exactly, like you and I. We are two of the souls created by the Dao, each with a different pattern of light and darkness. Our light is the part of us that connects us to the Dao, founded in truth, our darkness is the part of us that separates us from the Dao, founded in illusion."

The farmer poked the logs a final time. The fire was now full and bright, and its warmth was moving the damp chill out of their bodies.

"What if two things have the same pattern of light and darkness?" asked the schoolteacher.

The young philosopher laughed. "Then by definition they would be the *same thing*, which is not possible. To be a 'thing' in our universe is to be unique."

"And if we were only light then we would be the same as the Dao: in fact we would *be* the Dao. It is really our darkness that makes us unique, the *quality* of the darkness which is different in each one of us," said the schoolteacher.

"What do you mean?" asked the young philosopher.

"You have said that the truth of our existence is that we are all one and the illusion of who we are is that we are separate."

"Yes," said the young philosopher.

"Then the light part of us is our true self and the darkness part of us is our false self. The more we let go of our darkness and become a being of pure light, the closer we get to the truth of who we are."

"That sounds like the search for enlightenment," said the masseur.

"That is fine for those who are searching for that," said the farmer, "but what about the rest of us?"

"I believe that this search is common to all of us," said the masseur.

"How is it common? Have we not said we are all unique? Our lives must have a unique purpose," said the farmer.

"Perhaps I can explain," said the young philosopher. "When Creation occurred we became unique souls and were scattered off into all corners of the universe."

"So there is the great cruelty of the Dao as I suspected!" said the farmer. "It has scattered us off and we are all lost."

"We are not truly lost. We just don't remember. We have voluntarily forgotten who we are. But this 'amnesia' is what is required for us to have this experience of being separate."

"And why has this happened?" asked the farmer.

"So that we can have the authentic experience of evolving, of returning to the One which is the Dao."

"And so the Dao revels in our fear and worry as we blindly search for the right path."

"The right path?"

"The one that leads us back to the Dao," the farmer said.

"There is no *right* path," the young philosopher said. "And there is no need for worry. All paths lead back to the Dao."

The farmer shook his head as the masseur rose and walked away from the fire to contemplate what had been said. The rest sat quietly until he emerged from the darkness several minutes later.

"It seems to me that we can never really be alone, because in truth we are always one with the Dao," the masseur said. "Our path is simply one of having the experiences that will aid us in remembering this truth."

"Yes, but again, we each have our unique way of doing it," said the young philosopher. "There is no limit to the number of ways it can be done. This is one of the wonders of existence."

"And so we cannot really teach another how to do it," said the schoolteacher.

"Exactly, because for each of us it is different," the young philosopher said. "The best we can do is share our own experience and let the listener decide if it has meaning for them."

"This makes sense to me," said the masseur. "In trying to heal people I have seen that letting go of darkness is a choice each person makes and only when they are ready. I have seen that true healing doesn't occur when I try to force someone to let go if they are not ready." After a pause, he added: "Yes—that's it!"

"Some enlightenment?" smiled the young philosopher.

"Yes, because I see that the darkness is—our fear. And the light is our love."

"What do you mean?" asked the schoolteacher.

"Well don't you see? If our path consists of letting go of our darkness, of our fear, then we are all on a healing path, because we are all trying to become whole. And we become whole when we have let go of all of our darkness and have becomes beings of pure light. That is when we become self-identical with the Dao and we experience ourselves as pure love."

"I see what you are saying," said the schoolteacher. "Then it could be said that all of growth, of learning, of *evolution*, is about letting go of what actually separates us from each other—our darkness, which in the end amounts to our individuality."

"That's right, since our individuality is really the greatest of all illusions," said the masseur.

"Slow down a moment," said the young philosopher. "Are you suggesting that at the end of this healing path we eventually lose our individuality completely?"

"If there is really an end to this path, I believe we ultimately do," said the masseur. "We have said that what makes us each unique is the *quality* of our darkness. In other words it is only the quality of our fear—"

"Or ignorance," added the schoolteacher.

"Or the quality of our ignorance of ourselves as the Dao that determines our individuality," continued the masseur. "And if our path back to the Dao consists in letting go of this darkness—our fear, our ignorance—then our path can also be seen as letting go of who we are as individuals, which is actually our false self."

"Well I don't have any desire to let go of my individuality," said the farmer, "I happen to think it's special."

The young philosopher looked up and smiled to the others. "It *is* special," he said to the farmer. "Indeed I think our individuality is the most special aspect of our world. While each of us may be on a path of enlightenment or self-realization, our paths are different, and we need to know about each other's experiences. Sharing our stories with each other is what eventually will give each of us the whole picture of this wondrous universe—the totality of the Dao. Without this I believe it would be impossible for any of us to become whole."

"But if we are actually whole to begin with, what is the point of going through this whole charade?" the farmer asked.

"Yes, yes, that is the question, isn't it?" said the young philosopher.

There was a long pause of silence. The masseur looked over to the young philosopher, who sat serenely and did not appear to be in any rush to speak. He then looked over to the schoolteacher, who shrugged and whispered to him: "I have an idea about it, but—"

"Speak up!" said the farmer.

The schoolteacher inhaled and then exhaled deeply. "I said I have an idea about it, but it's not fully developed. I don't know if it will make any sense."

"Share it," said the young philosopher. "We will help you try to make sense of it."

The schoolteacher stood up and picked up a long, thin twig from the pile of kindling. She started to draw something in the dirt, scratched it out, and drew it again. It was a simple circle. She looked at it for a long while.

"If this represents the Dao..." she said, and then paused again.

"Yes...?" said the masseur.

"If this represents the Dao, is it possible..." and she paused again, drawing a larger circle around the first one, "is it possible for the Dao to expand?"

"Expand?" asked the masseur.

"Yes, expand, grow, evolve. Can the Dao evolve?"

"The Dao is the all-in-all, everything, what could it possibly expand into?" asked the masseur.

"I don't know, but, wouldn't it give our lives a greater sense of purpose if we thought that our individual growth was actually contributing to the growth of the Dao? I mean maybe the darkness is something that the Dao doesn't know. We could be the miners of the darkness, bringing light to unexplored parts of the universe. Our experiences could be adding to the Dao's—"

"If we can add something to the Dao then it really isn't the Dao," said the masseur.

"Well, maybe there is something beyond the Dao. Maybe the Dao isn't exactly *the* Dao." The schoolteacher pointed to the circles with her twig, adding more concentric circles. "Maybe it's a small Dao that itself has a larger Dao, which has a larger Dao, and so on..."

"And so on, *ad nauseum*," said the farmer. "Let's get back to planet Earth, if you don't mind."

"Well, I was just trying to see if our lives could have a greater sense of purpose than just this idea that we are remembering something we've intentionally forgotten."

"But that's all our lives *can* be," the masseur said. "At the level of the Dao there can be nothing new. But for us many things can be new. I think our lives have an abundance of purpose by the very fact that we are searching for our purpose."

"I like it," intervened the young philosopher.

"You like what—my idea or hers?" asked the masseur.

"I like the fact that we are talking about things that may be beyond our ability to think! But perhaps we should get back to the planet Earth, as our esteemed colleague has suggested, if we hope to make sense of our purpose in this life."

"I can't believe it," said the farmer, "I think somebody just agreed with me."

"And I encourage you to continue," the young philosopher said to the farmer. "What do you make of our purpose in this life?"

"Our purpose? Well, I don't know about the rest of you. I believe my purpose in this life is to be happy. And be happy *now*, not in the future, not in some afterlife, but now. Becoming one with the Dao? Losing our individuality? What's the rush?"

"Well, maybe because being one with the Dao is happiness beyond measure, beyond anything we can hope to experience in this lifetime," said the masseur.

"And how long would that last?" asked the farmer. "If we actually were one with the Dao, as you say, then we wouldn't be able to experience anything. So we would probably want to get exploded back out into the universe." The farmer stopped for a minute. "I can't even believe I'm talking about this," he said, shaking his head.

The fire had become mostly embers with small flames flickering from the ends of a few twigs. Still, it generated some warmth for the four, who were now huddled more closely to the fire than ever.

"Why all this talk about purpose? All I want to know is how to be happy in my life," the farmer said.

"When are you most happy?" asked the young philosopher.

"When my work is done," the farmer replied.

"Why is that?" asked the young philosopher.

"Then I can do what I want. Eat. Sleep. Play around."

"Play around?"

"You know. Pick up a tool and fix it. Make it work. Or better yet, turn it into something new."

"Something that no one has ever thought of?" asked the young philosopher.

"Ha! I suppose that is the ideal," smiled the farmer. "Yes, I have many ideas, good ideas, that have come to me over the years while I was working. But they have remained just ideas. Time...responsibilities..." the farmer's voice trailed off.

"These ideas have come from your experiences?" the young philosopher interjected.

"Often, yes, through my struggles and toils. I could see how I could make my work more enjoyable, and make my life better. I could see how I could make other people's lives better."

"Something that would be your unique contribution to the world?"

"Yes. Yes!" said the farmer emphatically.

"How would that make you feel?" asked the young philosopher.

"Very...happy," said the farmer, with soft emotion in his voice.

The masseur was about to speak, but the young philosopher put his hand up gently to keep the silence. They waited as the farmer looked down thoughtfully.

"That's my purpose, isn't it?" asked the farmer quietly. "My purpose is what gives me the greatest joy. Everything else is a waste of time. My whole life..." the farmer stopped as his throat tightened.

"Your whole life has brought you to this moment, to this realization," said the young philosopher.

"So I guess the joke is on *me* then," the farmer lamented. "I mean, here I am talking about wanting happiness *now*, but I've been getting in my own way the whole time."

"We are all getting in our own way," said the schoolteacher. "The lessons we learn actually teach us how to get *out* of our own way."

"That is really what it is to heal, and what gets us moving forward along our path," added the masseur. For a few moments they were all quiet, allowing silence to speak.

"Well, my friends, the fire is nearly out," said the farmer as he wiped his eyes and gathered himself. As he extinguished the remaining embers, the others stood up and prepared to leave.

"Thank you for keeping it burning," said the schoolteacher.

"I didn't really need to near the end," said the farmer, taking a tall stretch. "It has not turned out to be such a bad evening after all."

"Amen to that," said the young philosopher.

The group rose and began their slow trek down the mountain, untroubled by the darkness as they made their way back to their homes.

Almost a year after graduating from university, without money or job prospects, I was quite fortunate to qualify from a long waitlist for a government-sponsored computer programmer's course. At that time the PC had just come into the spotlight, but while floppy disks were coming in and punch-cards were on their way out, it was still essential for a student of programming to thoroughly understand machine-level code and its *binary* system, a simple system made up of only two parts that continues to be the hidden driver of all computer operations.

The binary system governs the electrical flow of computer memory, where the basic memory cell, or 'bit', can be in one of only two states: it is either charged or not, on or off, lit up or dark. When the computer was first used only for complex numerical calculations, the orchestration of the binary system was fairly straightforward. But with the implementation of a keyboard and terminal, it became necessary to organize these on/off cells into units of eight, called a 'byte', so that a standard binary code set could be made with enough possible combinations of the 8 on/off cells (2^8 or 256) to represent all letters, numbers, and punctuation marks on the keyboard, as well as a few hidden characters. As an example, a capital 'A' is represented by the 8-bit pattern on/off/off/off/off/off/off/on, more commonly seen as '10000001' where 'on' is represented as '1' and 'off' is represented as '0'.

As the refinement of lower-level programs came to support more complex higher-level programs, the computer's character-based drone terminal gave way to an interactive window onto the world of colorful complexity and ever-growing possibilities for creativity and communication. Computer pioneers could never have imagined in their wildest dreams what would become of their room-sized calculators. And while we ourselves can scarcely imagine what new innovations will arise in future computers, there is one thing that is certain: they will all continue to be grounded in the simple shifting around of 1 and 0, on and off, light and darkness.

If this is staggering, and indeed I think it is, it pales in comparison to a proposition I would now humbly ask you to consider: that the entire range of human experience, emotion, thought, perception, and beyond that the *existence of the universe itself*, is founded on such a binary code.

In the binary code of the universe the '1' is the truth that we are all One, the '0' is the illusion that we are all separate. The truth is that the universe is One and is always 'on', but the only way to create separate and distinct things in the universe is to pretend part of itself is 'off'. Like the Dao folding itself in half, the light, which is the truth of the universe, first fabricated the darkness, which is the illusion of the universe.

And so from only two, light and darkness, it became possible for the universe to explode into an unlimited collection of different and unique things, forms that have become ever more complex over time, just like we have seen with the computer. Each one of us is therefore an ever-changing string of '1' and '0', an ever-shifting pattern of light and darkness, an ever-evolving hybrid of truth and illusion. As humans incarnate we all have a foot on each side of this duality and cannot escape it. That is the nature of our reality. It is impossible to be a distinct 'being' without always having some light and some darkness.

What makes us special as human beings is that we consciously experience this duality in how we see ourselves— as an Ego Self associated with darkness and illusion and as a Dao Self associated with light and truth. We perceive ourselves as individuals and yet, because we are self-aware, we know ourselves as 'perceiver' to be something more. That something more is our Dao Self, our connection to all-that-is. When we identify with our Dao Self we get closer to the truth of who we are and when we identify with our Ego Self we get closer to the illusion of who we are.

The complexity of the human experience is grounded in this primal duality, because, like an expertly cut gemstone, it gives rise to a multitude of facets than never cease to dazzle us. These facets of duality are ever-present in our lives and their poles are inextricable from each other, much as we might often want to identify with only one side. The following table is but a small sample of some of the dichotomies that give meaning to our lives and fodder for our ongoing conversation.

Ego Self	Dao Self
Illusion	Truth
Darkness	Light
Separateness	Unity
Individuality	Community
Doing	Being
Rationality	Intuition
Control	Flow
Matter	Spirit
Atomism	Holism
War	Peace
Reactivity	Creativity
Judgment	Acceptance
Resistance	Openness
Debate	Dialogue
Pessimism	Optimism
Competition	Cooperation

One special pair of opposites not mentioned above is worth exploring here, as I believe it can serve as a kind of umbrella under which many of these dualities are brought together. I think if we were to choose one word that most closely encompasses the spirit of the Dao Self the word would be *love*. Now while this word may mean many things to many people, let us call this Love with a capital 'L', and try to imagine it to be an absolute, pure, fully unconditional love. Our own understanding of what love is, no matter how imperfect, points us to experience a great force that binds us together, a state of being that unites, an energy that flows, and a 'rightness', a feeling that we have uncovering truth behind the illusion.

If the Dao is the essence of this Love, then in its full state of oneness it would lack the *objects* of its Love, and so the Love could not express itself. Our personal experiences of love are the experiences of oneness with the objects of our love. The universe may very well have been created to allow the Love that is the single truth of the One to express itself through separate beings such as ourselves. The only way this could happen would be through the creation of something that was *not* Love, and so it came to be that a darkness was created out of light, the opposite of Love, which I would like to call Fear. This Love/Fear duality is not an unfamiliar one in the language of the new conversation. While the word *fear* also has several connotations for us, let us define this pure Fear with a capital 'F' as beyond what we are capable of experiencing, and yet having a hand in everything we experience. This original division of light and darkness, of Love and Fear, is the prerequisite for existence itself. In Christian mythology, it is symbolized by the banishment of the Devil from the kingdom of Heaven.

Consider Love as the single fundamental truth of existence, the All, the One, the Dao. Love is rooted in the ground of being, permanent and everlasting, while Fear floats around, coming and going, rising and falling. Our own experience shows us that when we look towards and embrace love it reveals ever more of itself, and when we look towards and embrace fear it recoils and disappears. Fear disappears because it was never really there to begin with. It is illusion itself, and it only grows when we look away from it and do not face it.

Our Ego Self is driven by Fear. There are no exceptions to this. This Fear amplifies our feelings of separateness, making us attach ourselves to things. It fuels our insecurities, causing us to judge others in order to feel good about ourselves. It always leaves us wanting more, as though we literally need an ocean of abundance to drown our fears in. But when we are willing to actually face our fears we see that they don't drown, they simply float on the surface that is our ego. In those moments that we penetrate the surface and see ourselves as coming from the Love of the Dao Self, we are able to leave our fears behind.

Living from our Dao Self is like living from a spacious place of peace and abundance. Most of us only get glimpses of this paradise from time to time. Mostly we are living from our Ego Self, and our lives are all about limitation and being cut off by our self-built walls. Our task is to question if these dark walls, these limitations we have put on who we are, are real. The process of moving into the Dao Self is the process of shining a light from inside ourselves, pushing out and seeing that these walls are not really there. As we do this, the space around us expands, and with it is the expansion of our joy. Moving into our Dao Self is our desire of desires. It is what it means to gain self-realization, the message common to all spiritual traditions. It is the enlightenment, the *samadhi*, the Christ Consciousness.

But we should not be fooled into thinking this is a simple one-step process. It is a gradual unfolding that the entire universe participates in. Even when we do experience the light and spaciousness of our Dao Self, life makes it difficult for us to remain there. As soon as we activate our senses, or refer back to ourselves purely as individuals—by thinking that 'I' am having this experience—the gravity of the physical world starts to pull us back slowly into the darkness of the Ego Self we tried to leave behind.

We all face a choice day by day. There is not a single morning we wake up where it is guaranteed that we will live from the expansive space of our Dao Self, nor are we condemned to suffer from the limited and fearful vision of the Ego Self. When it comes down to it, that is the only real choice that we face in life: to go with the flow or to go against it; to see a unity in all things, or a separateness; to be a part of nature or apart from nature; to promote harmony or survival of the fittest. We have a choice in how we experience the world, as a celebration of unity or a battleground of duality, as communion or confrontation, as collaboration or competition.

But in this back-and-forth movement there is some growth. On occasion we will make a big leap, but our growth tends to be slow but sure. What is required to make a lasting step in the expansion of our consciousness is letting go or releasing some of our darkness—which can be difficult to do, since we may be quite attached to it. Seeking expansion, the Dao Self is constantly challenging us to let go and step into what is the unknown for the Ego Self. The process of shedding darkness is the process of becoming more whole, more who we really are. Some have described this as resolving our karma, learning our life lessons or going through our healing. But it is never easy, for the unique *quality* of our darkness is what makes each of us distinct individuals, and represents who we think we are. There is a natural resistance on the part of our Ego Self to let go of darkness because in doing so it must let go of *a part of itself*. The more we believe that our Ego Self is our true self, and the more powerful a role our Ego Self plays in guiding our lives, the more difficult it is to expand. This is the great quandary of the growth of our individual consciousness—in a way it is a constant threat to our cherished individuality itself.

Having said that, there should be no concerns that our individuality is going to evaporate away any time soon, during our time on Earth or even beyond. While we are all on a path that moves towards a union with the Dao, that does not mean our real purpose in this life is to see beyond the illusion and move away from it as quickly as possible. Our personal path back to the Dao is as unique as our inimitable configuration of light and darkness. Each one of us walks a path that has never been traveled before.

Herein lies our important contribution to our collective consciousness and to each other. Our lives are tales that have never been told, and when we share ourselves and our unique perspectives we help each other to refine our understanding of who we are. Nietzsche once said that "to have circled the whole periphery of the modern soul, to have sat in every one of its nooks, that is my torment and my delight." In a way he describes the agony and ecstasy of our interrelationship with each other, providing pieces of the larger puzzle of who we are to one another to help make us all whole. Our lives are intertwined so much more than we know, and as our consciousness expands we come to an ever finer appreciation of the supreme gift brought on by the original creation of duality—the capacity to express ourselves to each other, and to love one another.

19. The Path

After several tries, the astrologer finally managed to get the sculptor to accompany her on her weekly trek. She chose her favorite trail up the forested side of the mountain in the middle of the island of Allandon, which leads to a breathtaking view from the peak.

When they were about halfway up the mountain the trail split sharply in two, and there was a tree in the middle of the fork with a large arrow nailed to its trunk. The astrologer asked the sculptor to stop for a minute.

"You're supposed to spin the arrow," she said. "It will tell you which side of the fork you should take."

The sculptor spun the arrow, and it pointed to the right.

"So I'm supposed to take the path on the right?" he asked.

"That depends on you," she replied. "If you take the one on the right, it means you believe in destiny. If you decide to go left, it means you believe in free will."

"I suppose you think you know which path I'm going to take," said the sculptor.

"Well yes, I think I know you pretty well by now," the astrologer replied laughing.

The sculptor took a deep breath and marched forward right through the fork. He walked past the tree and continued directly between the two paths, trampling small saplings and crackling underbrush as he climbed.

"Hey, that's not fair," said the astrologer, struggling to follow behind him.

"Why not?" asked the sculptor.

"Well for one thing, this isn't even a path!"

"Neither were the other ones before the first person walked on them," he replied.

The metaphor for life as a *path* is an enduring image that is used in one form or another in virtually all spiritual traditions. Perhaps this is because the metaphor so simply encompasses the paradox of human life: that we are charting the course of our lives through our choices even as we seem to be following a predetermined route.

In a way it is hard to completely deny the deterministic quality of our life here on Earth. The study of genetics reminds us that the color of our eyes, our height, and the illnesses we are predisposed to are decided upon long before we leave our mother's womb. We seem to have no choice, further, as to which culture and parents we are born to, and which part of the world we grow up in. Are we also predestined to fall in love with a certain person, follow a particular vocation, and die at a time and place that has been etched in stone all along? If so, then where is the choice?

On the other end of the spectrum there are thinkers like existential philosopher Jean-Paul Sartre, who reject determinism out of hand. For Sartre, *choice* is the only precondition of being human. We are free to choose anything except to *deny our freedom of choice*. Life in and of itself is meaningless, and so we are called upon to create a path for ourselves out of nothing. This stance has some appeal, but it snubs the suggestion that we each have some transcendent purpose or mission in this life.

In the new conversation, a sense of both freedom and destiny are important components. There wouldn't be much use for a conversation to help each other get where we're going if we aren't actually going anywhere in particular. But without the presumption that we have the freedom to make choices, speaking about how we can navigate our lives would be pointless. Somehow we need to pull together both sides of the paradox in order to sustain a powerful vision that inspires us to live life *on purpose*, with vigor and enthusiasm. When we don't, we are left to live our lives lazily suspended between these two polarities, living like puppets on a string on one hand, and without the inspiration of a higher purpose on the other. If we never reflect on this matter, we might continue to default to the belief system we were born into, not realizing that we have long since outgrown it.

I think it is highly beneficial to try becoming more aware of the belief system, the *paradigm*, through which we make sense of our lives. When we identify the way we give our life meaning, we gain the capacity to ask ourselves if it still fits. Then as new experiences and information come in, we have greater flexibility to adjust and to try on a new way of looking at things, even if it's just for fun. The new conversation provides a space to explore our paradigms without judgment. All ways of looking at the world are respected and seen as valuable. It is not about trying to prove one *right*, or justify a certain point of view. It is simply putting our ideas out into the space, so that we can benefit from each other's wisdom and unique experiences as we choose. We share what works for each of us—by this I mean what makes us happy, what brings us fulfillment and the feeling of being truly alive. Inspiration follows naturally. I am fortunate to have been a part of many such conversations, which often facilitated important shifts in my own beliefs. If I may, I would like to share the paradigm that currently works for me.

In my view, freedom of choice and destiny don't have to play off against each other at all. We ourselves are dual beings, and we live at more than one level of existence at the same time. Destiny and free choice are reconciled when we assert that *destiny is a choice that has been made at a higher level of awareness.* In other words, if life could be seen as a predestined path that is ultimately of our own choosing, then everything falls into place. Never mind that we have forgotten that we have chosen this path, for that is the beauty of it all. A precisely measured dose of amnesia about the higher awareness of our Dao Self is exactly what sets the wonder of the human experience in motion. If we were fully ensconced at all times in the peace and serenity of our Dao Self, what would be the challenge? What would move us to heroic and courageous acts that make us feel truly alive?

Life is eternal. The fact that we associate life with a birth and a death is an important convention for our purposes here, but this is only part of the picture. Our current life on Earth is but one of a long line of incarnations we have experienced, and these incarnations are not necessarily all as human beings. Wayne Dyer reminds us that "we are not human beings having a spiritual experience, we are spiritual beings having a human experience." Our decision to have this human experience has happened of our own choosing, as part of our eternal life. And so it is likely that we have been party to the decisions of where we would be born, who our parents would be, and what the main purpose or goal or path for this particular cycle on the Earth would consist of.

Our path in each particular incarnation is a subset, a fraction of our larger path that leads us back to the Dao. We have designed the path for this current incarnation in a way that helps us learn something that we need to learn, or heal a part of ourselves that needs healing, or remember some aspect of who we are that we forgot when we separated from the Dao. In other words, we have moved by choice into the illusion, to follow a path out of the illusion to the truth.

If we can be less serious and have some fun walking our path that is a major step. We hear all the time that the purpose is not to arrive at the destination but to experience the journey. In this regard, while life keeps us busy with tasks we need to perform, agreements we need to keep, lessons we need to learn, or healing we need to undergo, none of these things really capture the ultimate purpose for being alive. Like Joseph Campbell, I believe the fundamental reason we are here is for the *experience of life itself*, which brings us bliss when we move into greater alignment with our higher self and rapture as we awaken to the greater wonder that we are.

For most of us, experiencing bliss and rapture is not easy. Nor is it supposed to be. The flow of life, which for each one of us is the path of our chosen destiny, is not the proverbial path of least resistance. We are not meant to live in perpetual comfort and avoid all obstacles, confrontations, and challenges. In essence, the flow of life really leads us *towards* resistance.

Imagine a running back in a football game. His path is a line to the opposing end zone, which, if reached, makes him the hero and brings about unbridled celebration. But to do it, he must get past eleven big men who will do everything to stop him. That is why the goal is of value: it is difficult and challenging. In a college game once a very funny thing happened. A running back carrying the ball got spun around after a couple of jarring tackles but stayed on his feet. Disoriented, he suddenly started running the wrong way without knowing it. As he rushed towards his *own* end zone, the players on the other team were actually clearing the way for him to make it. Only after he finally arrived in his own end zone and was tackled by the other team did he realize what he had done. Needless to say, he was not celebrating. Since football players understand the game they are playing, no player would ever want to be caught doing this. But in life we do this all the time. Instead of going where we really want to go, challenging the obstacles in our way to make a touchdown, we often run away from the obstacles, and then wonder why we're not the star of our own life.

In life we are not up against eleven big men in oversized padding: we are up against ourselves. The only resistance to our growth and personal transformation is our own resistance. We experience it as fear. It often stops us cold. So when we feel fear but still gather up the courage to move forward anyway, we feel at one with the current of the river and take in its power. Remember that the river represents *change*, and so when we are *in flow* we are travelling down the river without offering any resistance to what *is*, to the changes that life throws at us. The river of change through which our lives naturally flow can sometimes be turbulent rapids, and despite our fears we are asked to decide which way to turn. We suffer not when we feel fear but only when we resist what we are afraid of. This causes us to start paddling furiously back upstream, away from the turbulent rapids of change. Eventually we learn, at every stage of our evolution, that pushing through our fear is the only thing that can move us along our path, and so is the only truly worthwhile action in terms of human evolution.

When we are in the flow we could not be more happy to be alive. Life offers a thrill a minute, any time we are willing to follow its appeal. And while we are meant to experience peace, life never calls us to be complacent, or to conform, or to take the easy way out. It challenges us to take a risk, and face precisely what it offers us. Sometimes this means stepping into the darkness, the unknown brought on by change. In the process we evolve. Our consciousness expands and we move ever closer to self-realization. The path of familiarity, laziness, and suppression, what we commonly refer to as 'the path of least resistance', is paradoxically the path of *most* resistance, because we are resisting the most fundamental aspect of nature: change, growth, and evolution. Feeling truly alive will always demand taking chances. There's an old African proverb that says, "If you're not living on the edge, you're taking up too much room." This is not to say that we always have to be risking our lives, but rather we must be willing to risk who we *think* we are in order to make way for a bigger, grander vision of ourselves to emerge.

Of course this path is never forced upon us. We always have the choice as to whether we go with the flow or against it. Even if our life has a particular destiny, we can choose to resist it. And we all do resist sometimes, because we are afraid—of failure, of loss, of danger. Sometimes it does not seem safe when we don't know what is coming around the next corner.

But we are all perfectly safe. There is an invisible force that holds us with love and compassion at all times. Even though we sometimes feel alone we are never alone, because we are always connected to the source. Even though we sometimes feel confused and lost, we are never really lost because our every step is being watched and guided. The more I take the time to look back at my life so far the more I feel this. All the significant events of my life, especially the difficult, the scary, and the embarrassing, happened for reasons beyond my understanding at the time. Today I can see that they brought me to precisely where I am now—at the threshold of fulfilling a great desire.

The happier I become with where I am, the more grateful I become for all the events that led me here. It is impossible for me to regret any event that has expanded my consciousness. As time has gone on I have learned to trust more and more the quiet voice of my intuition, which I believe is the voice of this invisible force that kindles my deepest desires. When I align my actions with this voice, my whole life begins to make more sense.

But it is not only internally that this benevolent force guides us. It makes use of the external world as well, and not just in one or another particular way but in a multitude of ways, for it is connected to all that is. Particular animals may cross our path for a reason, or we may meet certain people at the right place at the right time. Doors literally open, signs come into our field of vision, books fall off shelves and songs come on the radio, aimed to give us clues as to which way we are headed.

There is not necessarily a fixed rhyme or reason as to how and when these 'meaningful coincidences' come into our lives. Our task is less about figuring them out and more about just noticing them and, if we so choose, following them with gratitude and curiosity. To do this is to acknowledge the invisible force that is pulling for each of us from afar to fulfill our destiny. From afar, because it cannot interfere with our free will, for this would negate the precious experience of life entirely.

Because we have freedom, it is quite possible that our destiny in this life could go unfulfilled. This is what it means to have ultimate responsibility for our lives. Whether we pay attention to the signposts that border the path of our destiny or ignore them is entirely a matter of choice. The more we pay attention to them, the more often these signposts crop up for us. A growing number of people today are coming to see that even the most tragic events in their lives were 'meant to be', and that everything happens for a reason.

It's no wonder we're so fascinated by conspiracy theories. We are all in the middle of the biggest conspiracy possible, as all the inner and outer forces of our world are conspiring to give each of us the chance to experience the bliss of fulfilling our chosen destiny, right here and now. Understanding this may be the quintessential way to be with *what is*, and from the many conversations I have had with people who live with this conviction, I am confident that it is a way to a happier, more peaceful, and more joyful existence.

20. The Character

Every summer the playwright provided a day of entertaining outdoor drama for the villagers of the island of Allandon. As he stood on this day under a bright blue sky on the stage in the village square, the large gathering of villagers were buzzing as to why no set had been put up on the stage and the players were nowhere to be seen.

"I have a surprise for you," said the playwright. "This year, instead of seeing a rehearsed play, this one will be improvisational. And the best part is, all of you will be the players!"

The villagers reacted with laughter and enthusiasm. As the playwright explained how it would work they appeared eager to participate. He told them that each person would be required to volunteer to play a role after he had described the character.

"The first character is a ruthless merchant," he said. "He does everything to kill off his competition, but is surprisingly gentle with children, even though he has none of his own. His main life lesson is to learn to cooperate and have compassion for others."

A few men and women raised their hands, and the playwright in fact chose one of the women.

"The next character is a single mother living in poverty who struggles to overcome her deep loneliness. She has a particular talent with music that she is not yet aware of. She is destined to enter into a relationship that will be difficult but will help to cultivate her courage."

Several of the villagers volunteered, and again he chose one. This continued until the playwright came to one character in particular. "This next role is of a man who has fully actualized himself. He is tall, handsome, intelligent and completely at peace with himself and his surroundings." When he looked out, he was surprised to see that no villager had raised a hand.

"Don't all be so humble!" he said laughing. He looked around but still saw no volunteers. When he pointed to people they simply shook their heads. Then he looked over to his friend the director, and implored him to take on the role.

"Pass," said the director with a smile and a brief wave of his hand.

The playwright looked around and asked, "Why will no one choose this character?"

"You of all people should not be surprised," said the director.

"Why? Doesn't this character represent who we all strive to be?"

"Exactly, he's already *arrived*," the director retorted. "Where's the fun in that?"

One image we find over and over again in our media is the image of the perfect woman or man. The message, while not always overt, comes through pretty clear: 'This is perfection. This is how you need to be to have a fun and exciting life.' It is motivation of a distorted kind, for it tells us we are not good enough the way we are. It leads us to believe that only once we have conquered all our imperfections and are beyond reproach can we relax and enjoy our lives. Problem is, we have largely gone along with this.

Without being fully aware of it, we push one another to feel shame for our personal limitations and weaknesses. If it isn't someone else quietly judging us for being too fat, too insecure, or too stupid, it is ourselves. So instead of just learning to feel good about who we are, we walk around with the belief that we desperately need to improve ourselves. And when we try, and find that our imperfections don't go away fast enough, we bury them deeper inside of us, so we can hide them from others and especially ourselves.

This is not growth. This is being reactive. Whenever we bury our imperfections we also suppress the passion of our true desires. In their place our attention is drawn to the prudent security goals that our society guides us towards. As we conform to this set of counterfeit desires, we get ever further from who we are and what we really want. And so when we succeed in fulfilling these counterfeit desires, it should come as no surprise to us when it does not bring the pure joy or sublime peace that we were really hoping for. "Is that it?" we may ask in a moment of self-awareness. "*Now* what?" If we are truly afraid to admit to ourselves that we are not really living *our* life, we may go back into our routine and think that the next prized possession on our list will bring us that rapture that justifies being alive.

The problem is that we've become too smart for that. We are awakening to the fact that we are not being honest with ourselves or being authentic in the world. We are becoming impatient with our own excuses that the pressure, the coercion, the demands of our lives have forced us away from the path of our deepest desires. We know that at the end of the day life always offers the choice to be authentic, albeit at a cost: being authentic could bring about disapproval, ridicule, or financial loss. Some even have to risk their lives for it. It is up to each one of us to decide what we are willing to pay for the blissful experience of *being who we are* in the world. As Emilia Earhart said, "Courage is the price that life exacts for granting peace."

When we are not being ourselves, it is hard to resist being judgmental of others. We become especially critical of those who are different, those who don't seem to feel the need to follow the party line when we do. They make us uncomfortable because they remind us that we, too, long for freedom of expression and action. And so in their presence we are presented with the challenge to be ourselves. Instead of continuing to bury our shadowy side, we are called to simply put all our imperfections out in the world for all to see, and deal with whatever consequences ensue. That is how we recapture our passion and our energy, and start to regain respect and confidence for who we really are. In showing the world that we think we are all right as we are, we help others believe they are all right as they are as well.

But how can we have pride and confidence in our fallible selves? We aren't all tall, dark and handsome. We don't all have the natural ability to play professional sports, or the talent to be a concert pianist, or the intellect to be a quantum physicist. We have our fears and insecurities, our moods and our tempers, our blind spots and our baggage.

So what. When we step back and look at the bigger picture, I believe we can truly see ourselves as perfect just the way we are. Being human in itself makes us brave pioneers worthy of the highest praise. We *chose* a set of circumstances to live in and a character to enact in this drama called human life, all in the interest of our own growth and evolution. So while we have to play the hand we're dealt, it is when we realize that each one of us has *stacked our own deck* that it becomes possible to see the perfection in our 'imperfect' selves and lives. This idea is a powerful beacon out of the dark confines of judgment and into a clearing of appreciation and wonder.

The new conversation does not dwell in the 'wrong' and 'imperfect'. It only sees learning opportunities and points of departure for great adventures. In fact these so-called 'imperfections' are what forge our uniqueness, and make it possible for us to play an important role in the drama that is human life. When we hear the oft-quoted words of Shakespeare that 'All the world's a stage, and all the men and women merely players,' it resonates deep inside us. At birth we enter the stage and at death we exit. Although to say that we are *merely* players—perhaps on this point I would take exception. Is there a more important or worthier task at hand for men and women than to *play*?

Our Ego Self would have us believe that life is not play at all but *work*, the serious work of survival. It could never endorse a life that was built for fun. Indeed, life for the Ego Self consists in hiding our fears from everyone and trying to meet with their approval. But if we could look behind the stage curtains and beyond the illusions created by the Ego Self, we would see that the entire production was created for our benefit, so that we could strut and fret upon the stage, and in so doing, slowly come to an ever-increasing awareness of who we are and what this play is really all about. An actor who steps on stage has a life much vaster than the character he breathes life into, and in a similar way, we are much vaster than the individual selves we typically identify with in our lives. Moving towards identifying with this vaster self, our Dao Self, enables us to see that the world is meant to be a stage that allows us to experience the joy of engaging, of participating, of *playing*.

Playing is the flow of life. It moves us forward along our path. And each individual's path, no matter how misguided or self-defeating it might seem by our standards, is ultimately on its way back to the Dao. It is interesting to note that the word 'Dao' in Chinese also means *the Way*. Even if we become powerfully transformed along our own path, that does not give us one iota of authority to judge the path of another. In fact, when we transform ourselves we are naturally brought into a greater appreciation of the unique ways of others.

At any given time our starting point is exactly where we are. There is no other place we should be. What difference does it make where we are on a path that stretches to infinity in both directions? To say we should be further along the path by now, that we shouldn't be making the same mistakes, we should be nicer, smarter, and more evolved is really just letting our Ego Self speak for us. If we are perfect the way we are, then 'evolving' is not something we *need* to do. We are free to stay in one place all our lives if that's what we want. However, I believe that making our way along our path is something that we naturally gravitate towards once we realize that *that's where all the fun is.*

Though we have all had moments when this resonates, we also have doubts. We will point to the suffering we experience and hold it as proof that life is not fun. And there is no question, from where we currently stand the suffering is real. There is loss, disappointment, and sorrow. How can life be fun with such suffering?

The point here is—how can life be fun without it? We all experience suffering because of the growing pains that tell us that we are stretching into a grander version of ourselves. Experiencing those pains need not invalidate our life or make us feel that we are going in the wrong direction. They are as much a part of our life as the joy that is our birthright. As William Blake reminds us in *Auguries of Innocence*,

> The World was made for joy and woe
> And when this we rightly know
> Through the world we safely go
> Joy and woe are woven fine
> A clothing for the soul divine.

Let us consider, in a brief sparkling moment of clarity, what life would be like if all pain, suffering, and fear were removed from the equation. Let us say a human body no longer needed food or drink to maintain itself. No consumption, digestion, or elimination functions necessary. Then, let us suppose that we did not need to breathe to sustain ourselves. And finally, that we could not possibly feel pain of any kind, that we could not become sore, tired, in fact would not even need to sleep. Our bodies would not age and would become impervious to any changes.

I imagine if that happened to me, I would at first feel a euphoria, being able to move around freely, without worry, without restriction. And then, slowly, I would start to wonder what there was to do. And, perhaps after thinking a long time and consulting with like-minded beings, we would try to invent a game in which there were actually some risks, some rewards, some pleasure, some pain, something at stake and something to care about. And this game we could play with passion and energy, taking pleasure equally in the joys and the sorrows. A game that sparks our interest at first, and then grows as we grow, changes as we change, and continues to challenge us at exactly the level we can handle in a given moment. Now *that* would be quite a game!

And if we heard about a game in progress that had a brilliant stage already set, a spherical stage spinning around a star, with mountains and oceans, plants and animals, risks and rewards, smells, sights, sounds and a panoply of emotions, and always providing new insights and discoveries, we would willingly stand in a long queue like crazy kids lining up to try the latest and greatest super roller-coaster at the amusement park. It would give a new meaning to the experience of *being alive*. Does this game sound familiar?

One of the reasons that life doesn't always present itself

to us as a game is that we get bored or jaded with experiences that once gave us some excitement. It seems that the luster wears off many of our experiences as time goes on, and we can't seem to recapture our youthful enthusiasm. But that is exactly the point: when we follow our Ego Self, we try to recapture some feeling that we had in the past by recreating the event, whereas when we are living from our Dao Self, we desire only to create new events, to give us a fresh sense of what is possible.

It is just like an actor going on stage, doing the same play every day for months. The great actors know that the only way they will stay at their best, and continue to be fresh and vibrant, is not to try to imitate what they did to be successful in past performances. They need to let go of what they did in the past and create something new. The temptation is very strong to just 'do what worked' in the past. But this is not the true craft of acting. Acting is not about faking, it is about playing a character to the depth of your being. This is what it means to be authentic and live life to the fullest. After a particularly brilliant performance of *Hamlet*, Sir Lawrence Olivier was told by friends and critics alike that it may have been the best performance of the Danish prince ever in history. He accepted the compliments graciously but not without a hint of rue, knowing that while they might expect to see that kind of performance for the rest of the run, he knew that it was unlikely that he would ever be able to recreate it.

Life presents itself to us not as an opportunity to redo what works, but to create anew. Each of us is unique, and we can always be looking to bring something new to the stage. We are actors, not *re*-actors! In life, no playwright will tell us what words to utter, for we write our own script. No director will tell us where to go, for we direct ourselves. Actor, director, playwright, we have all we need within. And we are called upon to create ourselves in every moment. Let us create ourselves in the highest vision we can imagine, for this is what it means to flow along our path towards the Dao.

21. The Two Tribes (Part 3)

While the running tribe kept running around the island of Allandon, exploiting it and fashioning it in the image of its own self-importance, the sitting tribe tried to sit quietly within whatever natural surroundings were left on the island. The sitting tribe had become small, as many of its members had switched over, feeling that the running tribe offered a better and more prosperous life. And yet life was not idyllic for the running tribe. For reasons they could not understand a collective restlessness had slowly come over them, a growing dissatisfaction with their lives. They no longer laughed at the sitting tribe, for every day they could see serenity on the faces of the sitting tribe members, a serenity that they longed for.

The sitting tribe could not help but be drawn to some of the obvious improvements that the running tribe had made to the conditions of life, but they approached the running life with caution, taking sporadic moments to try a bit of running. While this was happening more often, many running tribe members slowly took some time out of their busy day to sit, hoping to find the serenity they saw on the faces of the sitting tribe. The running tribe members each started to sit at different times to suit their own schedules. Eventually there was no longer an organized group that ran in unison, nor was there a group sitting in unison. In fact each individual developed their own unique pattern of the two practices. Amidst the daily confusion of sitting and running, the lines between the two tribes blurred more and more, until one tribe could not be distinguished from the other. It was around this time that a growing number of members of both tribes started to believe that one day the island of Allandon would again be home to a single tribe.

It is only because we are at a special time in the history of humanity that we have the capacity to talk to each other about creating ourselves and our lives in the image of our personal visions. Human consciousness has evolved to the point where individuals are starting to see a choice as to whether or not to follow the values and aspirations of the nation, race, culture, creed or even family that they were born into. In other words, individuals no longer need to identify with a particular group in order to manifest their personal visions and desires in the world. Certainly it has not always been like this. Nietzsche pointed to this when he wrote, 'Peoples were creators first. Only later were individuals creators. Indeed the individual is the latest creation.'

Although we tend to think that the entire history of humanity involved the choices, aspirations, and decisions of human individuals, in a very real sense the human individual as such only came into being through the development of the

Ego Self, which really sums up the history of Western Civilization as well as anything. There were of course a few remarkable individuals prior to the Classical Age of Greece, but those individuals were for all intents and purposes not humans but rather *gods,* who were deified as such by the vast majority of their culture. Only in modern times have 'everyday' individuals begun to identify themselves as creative, whole, self-fulfilling beings apart from any group.

While human groups such as cultures, nations, and religions have allowed us to fulfill a most basic human longing for unity, it is a limited form of this fulfillment. Within any group, a collective mind is created that excludes others, and actually limits individuals from fully experiencing or even actively aspiring to unity within the larger body of humanity itself. And so it makes sense that this larger unity, which Hegel called the 'full unfolding of the Spirit', is only possible when all individuals are free and capable of identifying themselves as entities unto themselves.

We have spoken at length about the pitfalls of our Western society founded on identification with the Ego Self, with its rampant materialism and disrespect for nature, its self-serving ideology and disregard for the communal fabric. Still, perhaps the growth of the Ego Self may not have been a catastrophic misstep of human development but rather an important, necessary stage in the evolution of consciousness. If we apply Hegel's dialectic to this evolution on a grand scale, Eastern thought would be the starting point, the *thesis.* Western thought, which emerged from the bosom of Eastern civilization, would be the *antithesis.* And the great synthesis of these two opposing forces is the leap of consciousness that we are living through today. If we can make it happen it will be the greatest synthesis the world has ever seen, a synthesis of traditional Eastern holistic spirituality that identifies with the Dao Self and modern Western atomistic materialism that identifies with the Ego Self. The promise of this synthesis is a life in which the best of both world views exist together.

We have seen in our recent history that an augmentation of individual freedom has brought forth a much steadier flow of creativity and innovation. Possibilities have opened up, not only for individuals to express themselves in the world and manifest their own destiny, but also for humanity as a whole to benefit from this creative expression. Individual development has moved to the forefront and has become more and more the leading edge for human progress. The development of the Ego Self has not only given individuals the opportunity to imagine a better way of life, it also provides the individual with the means to manifest this vision in the world.

Chief Seattle may have envisioned something like this even as Western man came over to America and obliterated his people's way of life. Remember he reflected that 'God brought you to this land and for some special purpose gave you dominion over this land and over the red man.' Although he could not see the purpose of Western man's dominance at the time, he still knew that it was all part of a common destiny of humanity that was much vaster than the particular aspirations of either culture.

As Westerners, I believe it is time to embrace that larger vision today, lest we continue to be swept away by egocentric self-delusion. It is very tempting for us in the West to be swayed by our sense of self-importance in the world, and to continue promoting our unconscious mantra that *the West is the best*. The very idea of 'better' and 'best' is a particularly Western convention.

With the Western model, mankind is on a linear path to evolution. With the Eastern model, mankind's evolution is seen within a cycle which returns back to the starting point. In the West we see ourselves going into uncharted territory, in the East we are simply returning home. With Western ideology the ability to progress *in itself* becomes the essential mark of a culture. It gives us a measuring stick as to the relative value and worth of a particular people. In other words, it appears to give us the license to *judge*. It should not come as a surprise that Hegel, author of this particular vision of human history, looked down with some disdain on traditional Eastern cultures. He once said that "the inferiority of [the Native Americans] in all respects, even in regard to size, is very manifest... [they are] still abiding in their natural condition of rudeness and barbarism." He likewise felt that the German society of his day was the height of human evolution to that point.

However when his indictment of Native Americans is measured up against Chief Seattle's assessment of the white man—a white man who had just ravaged his people and their land, I might add—one is left to wonder which culture was actually more evolved. Where Chief Seattle believes that his people and the white man are all as brothers equal under the same God, the Europeans who claimed America had no doubts that they were *better* than Native Americans, smarter, more evolved, more worthy of what life and the Earth have to offer. For them the material focus of Western civilization constituted *progress* over the spiritual focus of Eastern civilization, and this belief continues to this day. We are only now awakening to the uncomfortable proposition that this is simply an acute delusion of the egocentricity inherent in the Western mindset as a whole.

It is interesting that the extreme polarity of Eastern and Western civilizations can be traced to a single difference in their founding mythologies. Traditional Eastern cultures were founded on a mythology that saw the essential truth of life to be the unity of all things above and below the heavens. Everything is connected, and duality is the illusion of the world and can be transcended since the ultimate truth is unity with the One, the Dao. Western civilization has grown from the perception that this unity or oneness, such as existed in the garden of Eden before the 'fall of man', is the *illusion* that ultimately masks the fundamental truth of duality, revealed to man and woman by their eating fruit from the tree of the knowledge of good and evil, which had previously been known only to God.

Western religions that are derived from the mythology of duality are ethical in nature because of the belief that life is the battle between good and evil, God and Satan. The focus of Western religion is that man is apart from God, that he has sinned, he has fallen, and needs to redeem himself. In the Eastern tradition there are no sinners and no need for redemption. Their religions are not about ethics as much as alignment with nature, with one's true self and path in life.

Eastern traditions find their ultimate truth in the cyclical rhythms of day and night, the phases of the moon, and the seasons. By extension they see human life as cyclical. We are born, we live, we die, and we then are reborn.

Reincarnation occurs as we move around the cosmic wheel, to return to the source from which we came once we have resolved all of our accumulated karma. History itself is cyclical. In the Hindu model, for example, the universe comes into being when Brahma the Creator sleeps, and once a set of very orderly *ages* have come and gone, Brahma wakes up and the universe is whisked out of existence. Then Brahma goes to sleep once again and the whole process starts again from the beginning.

Western mythology, on the other hand, focuses on linear progress and does not deal with the nature of eternity in any deliberate way. Somehow we have one life to learn how to be good, and after this short experience ends we are to spend the rest of eternity either in a comfortable place of complete stagnation or, if we are judged by God to be bad, an *un*comfortable place of complete stagnation. The God of Western tradition seems to care about whether we are 'good' or 'bad', as though our being good would elevate this God in some way or make him expand, and our being bad would somehow bring him down or cause him to contract. In contrast, the Dao of Eastern tradition is completely unchanging and unaffected by our actions.

The ultimate question becomes: is the One/God/Dao evolving as we evolve, expanding as we expand? Or is it static and changeless, making our evolution simply an awakening to our eternal and unchanging nature? Is the universe evolving, really going somewhere, or is it just going around in a circle? The answer currently depends on which side of the fence we are on that divides Eastern and Western ideology. It is no wonder that the prevalent Western model of history, the Hegelian dialectic, implies linear progress, while its Eastern counterpart, the Chinese model of Yin and Yang, points to a history that is cyclical. Both models see one side of the duality emerging from directly within the other. Both models point to the interplay of these opposites as the driver of history. But while in the Western model this interplay represents a war of fierce opposition to reach higher ground, in the Eastern model it more closely resembles a dance of partners circling back to the same spot.

The new conversation lies on the razor's edge of these two polarities. It asks for us not to sit comfortably on one side or the other, but to learn to balance on the fence of paradox itself. We are moving past an age where we can choose one polarity over the other, thinking one is right and the other wrong. As we see beyond the limits of each polarity, there is no turning back. If we are to move forward, it will be with an understanding that Western thought is no better than Eastern thought, and vice versa. In a higher consciousness Eastern and Western thought complement each other, as the ultimate opposing forces whose tension bestows us with purpose, direction, and understanding in our world.

Our future can at once be a revival of the great and enchanting stories of the past and at the same time a tale that has not yet been told. Perhaps there is for the first time the possibility of conscious convergence, of a commitment to hold conflicting points of view at once, of identifying with both the Dao Self and the Ego Self at the same time. In this there is the opportunity to let go of judgment while still aspiring for a *better* life on the planet. This is the new possibility for consciousness, and the direction that the new conversation is taking us.

While I have so far represented the two great polarities as 'East' and 'West', I hope you have come to understand these more as a distinction of ideas than of geographical reality. While any culture's predominant founding mindset may sometimes be detectable, the joint presence of these opposing ideologies is at play in all of the cultures of the world, and to some extent always has been. Culture is not possible without some identification with both the Ego Self and the Dao Self, without some material and some spiritual awareness. Yet I believe it has been useful to make the distinction with regards to civilizations, in order to show how the play of these opposing forces has been the driving force of our human history.

Naturally these forces have continued to grow out of each other and further blurred the lines of division. Eastern society has faced a barrage of Western modernity for some time now. And yet Western society, for all its power and influence, has not been immune to the infusion of traditional Eastern thought and values into the life of its citizens. This has certainly not happened with all the hoopla of the dissemination of Western policies in the world, but its effects are certainly starting to be felt. If the spread of Western democracy, economics and popular culture has appeared like large, loud bombs dropping from the air, Eastern values have entered into our minds from the ground up, with the seeds of sublime ideas slowly germinating in our consciousness over time.

The result is a society that is on the brink of a quiet revolution never before seen, in which seemingly contradictory ideas and values will one day find a place to coexist in our minds. We are not there yet, certainly, but this is the work in progress of the new conversation. It has emerged as a way to foster an environment that encourages people of all different perspectives, with unique ideas and experiences, to share in the search for a common understanding of life and a common goal for mankind.

In our society the emphasis on the Ego Self has led to unbridled materialism. We can clearly go no further, and there are many signs that things have already started changing. The pendulum appears to have reached its height in one direction and is on its way back. If it is true that all change is directed by the pull of opposites, then this period of extreme materialism too shall pass, and we will be the better for it. We will not look to spirituality simply as an escape from the dense and dark material world but rather as a better way *into* it.

The heights of materialism that we have reached are actually serving to provide fertile soil for the growth of a new spirituality—one that does not dismiss materialism, but rather helps to give it a more profound and meaningful expression. As we become ever more aware of our excesses, our self-centeredness, and our alienation from each other, so we become more pointedly conscious as individuals of our responsibilities to our planet and our role as important contributors to our collective evolution, one that includes the unique dreams and aspirations of all people. We are both the created and the creator, on the threshold of fully becoming aware of our own divinity. The time has come for us to fully embrace the mission that we all share. We no longer need to deny the Earth to reach Heaven, nor deny Heaven to enjoy the Earth.

22. The Dragon

On the Western side of the island of Allandon the poet and his son journeyed deep into the forest until they came upon a hidden cave at the foot of the mountain.

"This is the lair of the dragon of a thousand and one heads," said the poet.

"Does it ever come out?" asked the son.

"Indeed. Each person on the island confronts it at some time. You will too."

"What if I just leave it alone?" the son asked.

"Eventually it will come after you, heads screaming and breathing fire. The question is, what will you do when it does?"

"I will run away," said the son.

"If you do, you will find that it will follow you until the end of your days, keeping you in fear and anxiety."

"I understand," the son said. "I must stand up to it and kill it."

"You can try. You could wield a mighty sword high and slice off one of its fearsome heads. But you would see that where one head falls off, two heads grow in its place."

"Then it is invincible!"

"In a way—but you should be happy about it. For killing the dragon would end your life also."

"So what am I to do?" the boy asked.

"Your life is designed to teach you that," said the poet.

The son looked into the blackness of the cave. "Has anyone ever tried to kill the dragon?" he asked.

The poet smiled. "How do you think it became the dragon of a thousand and one heads?"

They say that the first step to recovery is admitting that there's a problem, being willing to face the truth. After many years of denial, I declare myself ready for healing. My name is Richard, and I am an egocentric. I would like to say *reformed* egocentric, but I know I have not fully kicked the habit. And thankfully, I am no longer putting myself under the gun to do so.

It was only after graduating from university that I came to a full awareness of what *ego* meant, and first made a semi-conscious effort to begin to walk a spiritual path. My early reading of ancient spiritual texts seemed to indicate that the ego was something that eventually needed to be killed off. After all, the literature suggested that the ego alienates us from other people, is the source of the attachments that lead us to misery, and at every turn prevents us from experiencing peace, love, and a permanent sense of belonging. I felt that all spiritual masters had been able to perpetrate their own ego death. So for me, following the spiritual path meant learning to smother the life out of any expressions of anger, prejudice, jealousy, and other ego-related vices.

At that time I may have already had the appearance of some kind of master to a few people: I seemed quite composed, rarely judged others, and could speak eloquently on matters of spirit. I thought I was moving down a spiritual path in leaps and bounds. In truth I wasn't really going anywhere. I was still just a shy and serious kid with a tendency to think long and hard before speaking, a habit that was probably ingrained in me by my childhood fear of provoking my father's anger. It was easy for me to censor most expressions of judgment and self-centeredness because I had been doing it all my life. And I continued doing it, only now with added pride because I felt I was banishing my spiritually improper inclinations.

However, trying to relieve ourselves of the burdens of the Ego Self with a well-placed magic bullet misses one important point. The desire to kill off anything, including the Ego Self, is inevitably *sponsored* by the Ego Self. So in trying to commit this act we are actually keeping the Ego Self in control. The unwanted desires and emotions simply get stuffed down inside of us and continue to be a force in our lives. And so not only do we maintain our ego-motivated behavior, but our habit of controlling, censoring, and suppressing our expression also causes us to lose touch with the practice of living freely, authentically and spontaneously.

In more recent years, I have begun to understand that the path to mastery of the Ego Self requires exactly the opposite of control—it requires *surrender*. There is such a skill and an art to surrendering that it has taken me an eternity just to grasp it, and I'm not sure that I've really been able to fully apply it yet. It's like the lesson that keeps on teaching. The surrender of the Ego Self to the Dao Self is the quintessential act of courage, wisdom, and love. It is not a suicide but a succumbing. It is not a slaying of the dragon but a taming. It is not an excision of an unwanted part of ourselves but a healing.

While the Dao Self constantly bathes the Ego Self in love and acceptance, it is only when the Ego Self lets go of control that some of its hidden darkness can come into the light and, ultimately, be released. For the Dao Self all things are acceptable, even the desire of the Ego Self to lead and to control. The Dao Self will never impose itself since it has no 'will' as such, so what is required is for the Ego Self to *will* the Dao Self to be the leader and accept the designation of follower. Otherwise, we will by default be led by the Ego Self— which can only judge and condemn its own darkness and is incapable of healing it.

A spiritual master like Jesus was unwaveringly led by the Dao Self, which he called *the Father*. He was not without an Ego Self, for it was written that he could still feel the temptation of the Devil. But he never tried to destroy the source of this temptation, as he understood that the Ego Self—symbolized by the Devil—was an inextricable component of being human. Jesus had a choice, as we all do, and he consistently chose his Dao Self over his Ego Self. He had a clear vision that the larger plan for his life was more important than his pride, his safety, or any other ego-concern.

Like Jesus, we too have a larger plan for our lives. However, that does not mean we are all meant to live out the same plan as Jesus, nor can we be expected to follow our Dao Self as faithfully. There is no shame in seeing that Jesus was simply more conscious and more evolved than we are. That does not make him better. In fact he never thought he *was* better. He just was who he was. And very simply, that is all we need to do to follow our plan, and walk a spiritual path—*be who we are.*

This is not as easy as it sounds. This is because *who we are* as human beings is always in a state of *becoming* something greater. This means, paradoxically, that *who we are* is always in a state of moving away from aspects of who we are in any given moment. The way to see past this paradox is not to *judge* the parts of ourselves we are trying to move away from, for when we judge these parts of ourselves to be 'wrong' or 'unacceptable' they shrink back into the darkness and remain a part of us.

We all have darkness. But we are starting to find our way out of it. In the new conversation we have started to bridge the division of the spiritual and the material in our society. We no longer want to see spirituality as a separate domain of our lives, reserved for the hallowed halls of the church, the mosque, the synagogue, the monastery, the ashram. We also want it to encompass the office, the classroom, the sports arena, the restaurant, and any other place people get together in any human activity. Such a spirituality would not be about denial of ourselves and our selfish desires, and would not condemn the material focus of the Ego Self. Most importantly, it would not lead us into the seriousness of self-recrimination but out of it. It would help us all live according to a simple but fundamental idea: life is fun.

This is not possible if we continue to see ourselves as sinners needing redemption, compelled to pass the tests of an Almighty Judge in order to be worthy of Heaven, one who looks down upon us and is pleased when his rules are followed and offended when they are not. It is dawning on us that such a Judge cannot really be the One but is rather a projection of our own Ego Self.

We want to be allowed—nay, encouraged—to be our unique selves with all our flaws, to follow our inner voice of desire. The greatest times of our lives were not spent being obedient to the rules of others, but rather when we found a way to be who we are. In the new conversation we are encouraged to be who we love to be, not told to deny who we are afraid to be. As important as it is not to identify with the Ego Self, and not to let the Ego Self lead us in our lives, it is equally important to understand that the Ego Self is and will continue to be a part of who we are as individuals. Indeed it is the foundation of our uniqueness. One of the great triumphs of Western society has been the elevation of the individual and the blossoming of the expression of individual talents, gifts, and abilities.

Now we have to take the next step, and find a way to express our individuality while still moving together, hand in hand, towards unity. When we push for unity but ignore our individual needs, what some people would call a *nobler* path, we actually get farther from authenticity because we try to take a shortcut to unity. We suppress our dark side rather than honoring it and, perish forbid, let it be revealed to ourselves and the world. More often than not, this path of sacrifice and denial leads us to moral elitism and the sense that we are better than others who do not sacrifice as much or work as hard on being 'spiritual'.

What we really need today is for the spiritual path and the material path to come together, and pave the way for truly feeling alive in the world. The main requirement is for us to be authentic. For some of us that's exactly where the roadblock occurs. The proposition of being authentic itself is scary. We are tempted to act in a way that is more acceptable to others, that garners us some approval and status. But while choosing to act other than who we are may get us somewhere in the short term, it's never where we're actually going. It's like rushing to get on the first bus that arrives at our stop, even though it isn't the one that takes us home. No wonder we so often feel lost in our lives.

I always found it instructive to think very deeply about the following question: What is the worst thing that could happen by being authentic? Are we afraid of not fitting in, of being embarrassed, of being laughed at? So let's look at being laughed at. If, like me, you are on a mission to be less serious, there may be no better experience to go through than allowing yourself to be laughed at for being who you are. And if you have the courage you can laugh at yourself as well. As Milton Berle said, "If you can't laugh at yourself you're probably missing the joke of the century." Taking ourselves seriously keeps us in the domain of the Ego Self. If we are able to freely show to the world who we are and in the same spirit we are able to laugh at ourselves, then we give permission for others to live freely as well.

I believe the real spiritual masters understood this. They developed unlimited compassion for the egocentricities of others because they discovered how to have compassion for their own shortcomings. They are the ones whose facial wrinkles are forged by a peaceful smile, a sign of their constant amusement with their own fallibility and humanity.

When I started writing this book, I worked hard to make sure that people did not detect a hint of egocentricity when I spoke about it. After all, if I was going to present ideas about how to move away from one's Ego Self, the least I could do is show that I've mastered it successfully in my life. But as I got further into the writing, and more deeply into self-examination, I realized that this was not completely honest. I was just being cautious. If I was to be authentic I would have to admit that I have not evolved beyond all self-centered desires when it came to this book. In some moments I was captured by the prospects of gaining some fame and recognition. Sometimes I got caught up in how much money I might be able to make. I cannot in all fairness assert that my motivation to get this book written has come purely from selflessness and unconditional love.

At the same time, I *can* say that I have learned a lot since I started writing. I have seen that when I come from a place of self-interest it is much more difficult to write, to get good ideas, to be in a flow with the process. I am more prone to feel fearful of failure, to be worried about how people will react to what I am saying and to be doubtful that I actually have something of value to say. On the other hand, when I have been able to get more centered on this book being a contribution to others, suddenly the words and ideas come more easily, the process is less burdensome. So certainly I have tangible experience of the value of trying to move into my Dao Self.

But an even more profound lesson, one that brings me great peace and happiness, was learning to accept myself when I am *not* coming from my Dao Self. This is my highest experience of authenticity. I can be who I am and speak about what is true for me in a given moment without worrying that I might sometimes not be seen as such an 'evolved' person. Trying to be conscious does not mean having to be cautious. I recognize that I need to live at my current level of spiritual understanding, rather than pretending to be more 'holy', more 'spiritual' than I actually am.

And so I believe even our egocentric desires are not without purpose. Sometimes even if people who are rich and famous have told us that money and recognition don't bring happiness—and we believe them—we still feel the need to find out for ourselves. I recognize that I continue to be driven by the Ego Self from time to time, but then again so are most of us. To deny this is a subtle form of egocentricity itself. Let's all cut ourselves a little slack. In a way, we could say that if we were never driven by the Ego Self we wouldn't be driven at all. It's time we all got together to create a space in which we are free to make mistakes, do the wrong thing, play the fool. Even if our ego-desires lead to dead ends, we want the opportunity to play them out without being judged. Given the chance to find out we don't want what we thought we wanted, we get closer to knowing what our true desires are and living from our true selves.

In the West we have lived too long under the burning image of a spirituality that is divorced from the material. We walk away in sadness just like the rich man when Jesus told him to sell off all his possessions, saying to his disciples that "it is easier for a camel to go through the eye of a needle than for a rich man to enter the kingdom of heaven." We fear that spiritual mastery looks upon our materialistic strivings with disdain and disapproval. It seems that if we are to fully engage in spiritual practice, it requires forsaking our material desires. And if we are to follow our inner urges for material abundance, we must in those moments look away from our spiritual teachings. We try to make our lives work as best we can, but we tire of leaping back and forth across the chasm between our spiritual lives and our material lives. Our deep longing for a spiritual life is thwarted by a fear that we will have to give up too much. At the same time our enjoyment of our material life is tempered by a niggling guilt that we are not doing enough for those less fortunate. And so with all we have, and with all we can be, we are afraid to truly live either aspect of life with vigor and enthusiasm. We fear that trying to integrate our spiritual and material desires will make us hypocrites.

In truth Jesus never said that being rich was bad, nor that we have to abandon the material for the spiritual. He did imply that it would be a complex matter for someone rich to experience the treasures of a spiritual life. If we are to have a lot of money and not give material life any more of our focus than is needed, we are required to become complex characters ourselves, in order to avoid the traps the Ego Self lays in our fields of material abundance.

I believe we are ready for it. I believe this is the true challenge of our time, to bring forth a spirituality in harmony with our growing capacity for material wealth. We have started to ask ourselves: Why would our souls have been delivered into this wondrous world of the material if not to enjoy its fruits? All we need is some guidance, not away from the material, but onto that fine line that balances our material needs with our spiritual needs.

Of course this is not an easy path. This is why we need to be in conversation with one another, ready to accept each other's help. Since our consciousness has evolved, we have started to become able to guide one another through the pitfalls of an integrated life. In the new conversation we can condone our Ego-Self desires without being driven by them. We are able to witness our own egocentricity in the space that is provided, when we are most ready to see it. The new conversation is in service of allowing us to stand in a place where the spiritual is not a denial of the material and our human desires, but rather the material and spiritual are balanced in a whole and vital life. If we guide each other carefully, I believe it will indeed become possible for us to put a camel through the eye of a needle—while riding shotgun.

23. The Competition

One morning a young boy and his older sister were fishing on a small stream that ran through the forest on the Western side of the island of Allandon when the branchless trunk of a fallen tree floated slowly by.

"Look, a tree!" said the boy.

"So what?" replied the girl.

"So we can play 'tip-over'!" he said.

"Ha! You've never beaten me at that. Why do you keep asking me?"

"Ladies and gentlemen," started the boy in a tone mimicking the village crier, "we are now ready for the finals of the main event, the tip-over! Will the contestants please take their positions on the tree!"

"All right," she said, "get ready to lose again."

They waded into the shallow stream and got onto the tree trunk. As they slowly and stutteringly rose to a standing position, he continued his announcement: "Ladies and gentlemen, the contestants are set. When one contestant falls in the water, the other will be declared the winner. Ready, steady, and go!"

The girl stood nonchalantly, trying to make it look as effortless as possible. But minutes started to go by, and he was also staying steady. She knew if she could get the tree spinning he would fall. He had always fallen. After a bit of effort she got it started, but this time he was spinning it right with her.

"Why aren't you falling?" she asked.

"I've been practicing!" he replied.

She tried to reverse course and stop the tree trunk from spinning in the hopes it would put him off balance. Instead, she slipped and fell backwards into the stream while he remained on the tree trunk. "It's over!" he said, and jumped into the water with an exuberant splash. He followed his sister out of the stream with arms raised, exclaiming, "He's done it! He's done it! Ladies and gentlemen, we have a new world champion!"

"All right, enough," she said, looking back at him with annoyance.

"What?" he said. "It's the first time I've ever won!"

"Relax," she said, "it's just a game."

"*Just* a game?" asked the bemused young boy. "Do you mean there's something *else*?"

My search for a more spiritual life after university, inspired by a growing interest in Eastern philosophy and practices, brought with it an unexpected byproduct: it compelled me to become more acutely aware of my highly competitive nature. Competitive soccer, for example, was a major part of my life. Doing activities that did not lead to 'winning' were still somewhat foreign to me. I remember the difficulty I had during my first ever yoga classes around that time. I'm not simply talking about the fact that I was preoccupied with holding my postures longer and stretching further than the middle-aged women around me; I'm referring to the internal clash of emotions I was feeling just as the postures and the rhythms of the yoga began to relax me. My mind kept conjuring up vivid images of battling on the soccer field and passionately celebrating victory with my teammates. Although I was convinced that yoga could bring me some much-needed peace of mind, I left those first few sessions feeling restless and even somewhat ill. I had a vague sense that doing yoga was a threat to my competitive instinct and lifestyle. And since I didn't feel ready to give that up, I did not practice yoga again for over a decade.

In the back of my mind I imagined that being competitive was a phase that I would eventually grow out of as I matured. Some of my own experiences and the literature I had been reading seemed to support that. And yet today, even as I have returned to yoga, meditation and other holistic practices, I still have not been able to pull myself away from the lure of competing. Not only that, but I continue to follow some professional sports competitions with pointed interest. I realize there are more than enough things going on that should have turned me off of that whole scene, with the outrageous salaries and image-related endorsement contracts, performance-enhancing drug use, gambling, match-fixing, and other distractions. Yet I still sometimes find myself in front of the TV, captivated by the unfolding drama of my home team's game or an important golf tournament. Sometimes when I am watching an event and my wife comes in, I will enjoy making a big production about the importance of the moment. "There's only a minute left," I will say, "he *has* to make this free throw," or "this putt is *so* important." She will often sit with me through the moment of truth to humor me, even though the drama usually has little impact on her. Of course I understand her perfectly. I would agree that in the grand scheme of things it really makes no difference for my life whether my team wins or not. In quiet moments after the final buzzer has sounded and the teams have left the floor, the thought will occasionally occur to me: Do I just need to grow up and get over all this?

For me this question has been more complicated than it might seem. At first blush, the desire to pit individuals against one another to see who is stronger, faster, and better appears to be the epitome of Ego-Self-motivated fulfillment. Indeed, it was during the emergence of the Ego Self at the dawn of Western Civilization that formalized competition first came into prominence with the inaugural Olympic Games in Ancient Greece in 774 B. C. However the Greeks had some noble reasons for initiating their Games, not the least of which was to facilitate the pursuit of *areté,* which was perhaps the most esteemed value of ancient Greek culture. *Areté* can be translated as 'virtue,' but actually means something closer to 'being the best you can be,' or 'reaching your highest human potential.'

Looked at from this point of view, competition may in some cases hold value for our lives. Being the best we can be, striving to reach our potential, is *who we actually are.* And so the pursuit of *areté* is an exercise in being our true selves. Our true self is not the self that we outwardly identify with, the self of a name and job and habits and addictions. Our true self is the high water mark of self-actualization that we have achieved to date, and it is only when we consistently attempt to reach and surpass our high water mark do we gain the real sensation of being fully alive.

I think that beyond the commercialism and corruption, our competitive sports heroes can still inspire us towards this. They demonstrate that peak mental and physical performances result from commitment and dedication, courage and focus. If our heroes are to be of benefit to our lives, it is through the way they model grace under pressure, and a willingness to face and challenge their own fears to rise above and perform. Athletes can still exude a simple, almost childlike love for the game, and demonstrate unabashed joy when they individually or collectively overcome the greatest challenges of their sport.

There is a danger for us, however, if we always remain spectators, living vicariously through the achievements of professional athletes. We must recognize that the victory of our home team or sports idol is not really our own. Our joy is short-lived, a pale imitation of the feeling the victorious athlete says "cannot be put into words." Our own euphoria is reserved for the times when we face the challenges that have *our* name on them, and lead ourselves to victory by our efforts. The more we focus our emotions on the exploits of others, the more we will shrink in fear when we get the opportunity to step onto the playing field ourselves. We will not be prepared and we will look for the comfort of the sidelines. The only thing is that, in life, there are no sidelines. We are always on the field of play, even when we're just curled up in a ball trying to avoid all the action.

It is important for each one of us to determine whether or not competition is serving us in our lives. If winning has become everything, and we are willing to cheat to earn victory, then competition is no longer a context for reaching our highest potential. It only echoes the dog-eat-dog mentality rampant in our society where one person's gain is always another's loss. However, while the design of competition puts one of us *against* the other, I believe it can still give us the feeling that we are in this together. When we do it with an awareness that winning is not the *only* thing, competition can bind us to an unspoken understanding that we really play together in order to celebrate life. The famous saying that 'It's not whether you win or lose, it's how you play the game' rings true—because in life it's possible to play the game in a way that everybody wins.

While we may be in danger of taking the game of life too seriously, there is also a danger of not taking the game seriously enough, of playing it too safe and not really engaging in life. Remember Helen Keller's words that 'life is either a daring adventure or nothing.' There is a fine line that we need to observe, because it is in the balance that *life is fun*. A common misconception is that a spiritual life demands we withdraw from the game. I believe a spiritual life urges us to walk that fine line, and play the game as though everything was at stake while being wholly detached from the outcome of our efforts.

We all cross both sides of that fine line throughout our lives, but in some magical moments we can get it just right. In one of his lectures, Wayne Dyer recounts a true story told by the father of a young boy with motor and learning disabilities when his son wanted to join a baseball game in progress.

The boy's father thought it was unlikely that the players, who were his son's age, would let his son play. So he was pleasantly surprised when one of the players he asked actually consented, albeit hesitantly and a bit out of embarrassment, to let his son onto his team. The young player rationalized that that it was already the 8th inning and his team was losing badly, so the boy was given a glove to play outfield and was promised an at-bat in the 9th inning.

His son's team made a courageous comeback, however, and by the 9th inning they actually gave themselves a chance to win. They were only down by three runs and had the bases loaded. The only problem was that there were two outs and it was his son's turn to bat. The father, who could appreciate the drama of the moment, highly doubted that the team would let his son go up to bat at this critical moment. After all, his son could not even hold the bat properly, let alone swing it. But to his surprise, he saw his son making his way timidly to the batter's box.

The players could see right away that his son would not be able to get a hit, especially after he missed the first pitch clumsily. So one of his teammates came up behind him to help him hold the bat while the pitcher moved closer in order to lob the ball in softly. On the next pitch the two boys swung together and hit a weak ground ball to the pitcher. The father thought that the pitcher would easily throw his son out, and that would be the game.

That is when something remarkable started to happen. The pitcher instead hesitated for a moment, and then threw the ball high over the first baseman's head and down the right field line. The young boy's teammates started yelling to him, "Run to first! Run to first!" Never in his life had he run to first. He scampered down the baseline wide eyed and startled. By the time he rounded first base, the right fielder had the ball. The father knew that the outfielder could have thrown the ball to an infielder who would tag his son out, as he was running along the base path aimlessly. But the outfielder suddenly understood what the pitcher's intentions were, so instead he threw the ball high and far over the third baseman's head, as everyone yelled, "Run to second! Run to second!"

The father saw his son run towards second base as the runners ahead of him deliriously circled the bases towards home. When his son reached second base, the opposing shortstop actually ran to him, gently turned him in the direction of third base and shouted, "Run to third!" As his son rounded third, the players from *both* teams gathered behind him screaming, "Run home! Run home!" Together they guided him home, and as soon as he stepped on home plate all 18 boys lifted him on their shoulders and made him the hero, as he had just hit a *grand slam* and won the game for his team.

There is perhaps no greater feeling than when, focused as we get on a game that pits one against the other, we transcend our Ego Self to touch the world of unity beyond. But to have this experience, we need to chalk the foul lines, fasten the bases in place, and have a sturdy umpire behind the plate telling us to "Play ball!" The rules of the game provide the context for some of the most magical experiences in life.

In those moments when we feel the rules of the game are brutal and unfair, whether it be from having a loved one die, or losing our fortune, or being born with a disability, it is a good time to stop and reflect for a moment. When the totality of life is taken as a game, all of its difficulties can be seen as the challenges that make the game worth playing, where the emphasis falls on the experience of life rather than its outcome. The struggle towards self-actualization, the pursuit of *areté*, is no easy ride for any of us. But if we were really looking for an easy ride, we likely would not have come onto this field of play in the first place.

24. The Map

One day the arborist and the scientist were rappelling down the steep southern face of the mountain in the middle of the island of Allandon. They came upon the mouth of a cave and stopped on a ledge that protruded from it.

"I have always wanted to explore this cave," said the arborist, still catching her breath. "I'm curious about the mysteries that it holds."

"So why haven't you?"

"Well, it's so dark and so vast," said the arborist looking inside. "I suppose I'm worried about getting lost."

"Well this must be your lucky day," said the scientist. "It just so happens that I have extensively explored this very cave."

"You have?" she asked with excitement.

"Yes, and I have even made a complete map of all its nooks and passageways."

"Really! You are my hero!" exclaimed the arborist. "If you don't mind, I'm going to go in to look around."

The scientist started searching through his backpack for the map, but on finding it he looked over and saw that the arborist had already unhooked her lines and ventured deep into the cave.

"Wait!" shouted the scientist into the cave. "Don't you need the map?"

"Certainly not," the arborist hollered back, "you've already given me what I need!"

We are all on a path of growth. We are never compelled to walk this path, but if we want to experience the rapture of living authentically, we need to be open to where it leads. In a way this puts us between a rock and a hard place. If we resist growth, we suffer from the weight of unexpressed passion and unfulfilled desire. When we embrace growth, we face the growing pains that come with it. There is no way to avoid them. And if there were, life wouldn't make sense. The *context* for striving towards anything would be gone, and moving forward would actually feel like sitting in the same place, stagnant, until the end of time. Buddhism puts this right up front in the first of its sacred truths: *Life is suffering.* When we recognize this truth as more of a cause for celebration than commiseration, we go a long way towards understanding the Buddhist ethos.

In order to grow, we must expand beyond the borders of what we know. We have all had some experience of the deep satisfaction that results from moving into new realms and expanding our field of play. The world is infinitely more captivating when we penetrate into the unknown than if we simply remain in the known. Yet to some extent we continue to be afraid of the unknown. We are literally scared of the dark. And so we are afraid to truly *live*, because it is in the darkness that our light really shines. At every moment of the day, wherever we are, something novel, amusing, unusual or fantastic might occur to us, if we were open to it. If we could find the courage to remove the self-imposed blinders and be truly present to the world as it *is*, not just as we *know* it to be, that's when life becomes fun—an adventure worthy of story books.

Still, a life of fun is not without a certain amount of anxiety. If we reflect back on our greatest moments, we would remember that anxiety has always been present. What monumental achievement was not preceded by butterflies in the stomach? What euphoria did not rise out of doubt and uncertainty? And in the grand scheme of things, what gives being alive the potential for such unmitigated joy but the fear of death? We have anxiety precisely because as humans we have self-consciousness, which gives us the power to act, to choose. The anxiety fuels our sense of responsibility to make choices that help us continue to grow and evolve. If we ignore it or avoid it, not only do we miss out on all the fun, we are actually choosing to be other than who we really are, to walk a path that is not our own. This leads to depression and despair, which unlike anxiety actually makes it more difficult for us to act. Anxiety calls us to make our move. It ignites the transition from reflection to action. As philosopher Peter Koestenbaum notes,

> In any endeavor, how do you feel when you go from one stage to the next? The answer: You feel anxious. Anxiety that is denied makes us ill; anxiety that is fully confronted and fully lived through converts itself into joy, security, strength, centeredness, and character. The practical formula: Go where the pain is.

Many of us have become so used to avoiding our own darkness that we actually conspire with each other to live life on the surface, and pretend together that our darkness doesn't exist. When we are struck by those impulses of anxiety that lead us into our darkness, we may try to soothe one another until they go away. But somewhere inside us we may suspect that these impulses are the calling of a vital life. If we wait until the stillness of our deathbed to confirm our suspicion like Ivan Ilych, we are likely to look upon the missed opportunities of our life with similar deep regret.

The good news is, the opportunity to truly live is always here now, whenever we are ready to explore darkness rather than avoid it. When we reframe our life as a journey of personal evolution rather than simply a struggle for survival and comfort, all the difficulties we are beset with are much more meaningful, and can in fact be celebrated.

In the introduction to the Star Trek T.V. series, the climactic line before the starship races towards us is "...to boldly go where no one has gone before...". This idea excites us, even if many of us would not join the crew of a real Starship Enterprise if one were launching off tomorrow. But we wouldn't really even need to. Each one of us is going where no woman or man has ever gone before, because of our unique nature and perspective. We each bring a different pair of eyes on the visible, a different mind to every action, and so the experience itself is always unique, and adds an important entry into the ledger of our collective consciousness.

In the end, it is our struggles in the darkness that will be the foundation of what we have to offer the world. When we are able to move through our darkest places, that is when our experience can inspire others. Is it any surprise that people who speak powerfully to alcoholics in an AA meeting were alcoholics themselves? Is it strange that cancer survivors are the ones that have the ear of others battling the disease? Why is Nelson Mandela the voice of peace and forgiveness, but for his ability to transcend resentment and the desire for revenge, and forgive the captors who had imprisoned him for countless years?

When we are faced with darkness in our lives, troubles, difficulties, scary but necessary choices, it can be helpful to draw inspiration from stories of others' heroism. After all, we really are all in this together, and becoming inspired may be the best way to honor the great models of bravery and heroism. As Joseph Campbell notes in *The Hero with a Thousand Faces*:

> We have not even to risk the adventure alone, for the heroes of all time have gone before us—the labyrinth is thoroughly known. We have only to follow the thread of the hero path, and where we had thought to find an abomination, we shall find a god; where we had thought to slay another, we shall slay ourselves; where we had thought to travel outward, we shall come to the center of our own existence; and where we had thought to be alone, we shall be with all the world.

Heroism is not the absence of fear and anxiety. It is the willingness to get on with our journey and act in the face of fear. Stories of heroic redemption and glory help us believe that we too can be brave. They help us believe that when we honor our yearning to leave a relationship we are not doomed to be lonely for the rest of our lives. They help us believe that if we act on the desire to speak up to our boss we will survive the repercussions. They help us believe that it is worthwhile to reach for the stars, and risk everything for our greatest dreams. And when we choose to be inspired by these stories and act on our inner impulses, we are taken on a journey that may eventually go on to inspire others in ways we could never imagine.

I am reminded of a story I heard a few years ago that continues to evoke awe and amazement inside me. Bethany Hamilton was an aspiring young surfer who was competing by age 11. In 2003, at age 13, while surfing off Kauai's North Shore, she was attacked by a 14-foot tiger shark, which tore off her entire left arm at the shoulder. She lost 70% of her blood trying to make it back to shore and needed several surgeries to survive.

In a circumstance where most people would feel justified in turning to a life of fear, shame, and self-pity, Bethany chose to do what I consider the quintessential heroic act: She decided to *get over herself*. In other words, she put aside her Ego Self and chose to live from her Dao Self. And she seemed to do so almost immediately. What astounded me was to hear her talk about losing her arm with such aplomb, while maintaining a cheerfulness and equanimity rarely seen in anyone, let alone someone of her age and circumstances.

Bethany even said that she was glad this happened to her, because it enabled her to share with others the profound experience of feeling part of something bigger than herself. Her identification with the part of herself connected to the divine—which I call the Dao Self—made it possible for her to deal with this tragedy with such grace and apparent effortlessness. When I first saw her, a slender left arm conspicuously absent from her side, I could not help but be immediately struck by the utter conviction she had of her own wholeness. It inspires us to believe that, in the face of our limiting beliefs of ourselves, we too can be and feel whole.

Bethany's confidence that she would be surfing again was unwavering. Her attitude and love for her sport could not help but give rise to heroic action in the world. She returned to the water less than a month after the incident, and unbelievably, only eight months after losing her arm, she placed fifth in the U. S. National Surfing Championships.

Traditionally we have looked at heroic acts as the victory of good over evil, like the slaying of the dragon that leads to a life lived happily ever after. But actually life holds a more subtle challenge than that. If our heroic struggle in life were captured as a holographic video game, it would be more than our 'good' guy trying to kill the 'bad' guy. The 'bad' guy would be a part of us. We could never kill him, but we had to find a way of dealing with him to reach paradise. We would want to push forward, but the 'bad' guy would always try to hold us back. And he could attach himself to all our skill and even our thinking, until we had trouble discerning who we really were. This is our challenge.

In our world of duality, of yin and yang, darkness comes from light and vice-versa. Even the most heroic actions in the world displace both light and darkness, and yield results that are both good and evil, positive and negative. It is only when we change our state of *being*, when good *embraces* evil, when the Dao Self *loves* the Ego Self, does our act move into the realm of the truly heroic and does our consciousness rise up to the next level. If we look at all things dark as simply crying out for light, then there is no longer a need to annihilate the darkness. Besides, there is no way to annihilate the darkness. It shows up again and again, in different forms, until finally light is shed on it. That is when it disappears.

The heroic act brings inner transformation and moves us ever closer to a clear perception of the outside world as only a game, a context for an internal change. For every heroic deed moves us up the evolutionary steps of consciousness, where we drop some of our arrogant, self-centered illusions, and realize ever more profoundly that the joke is on us.

The same can be said for the path of humanity as a whole. The elevation of the Ego Self to prominence in Western Civilization need not be condemned as a horrible mistake or a wrong turn. Maybe we are not on this planet, as the Eastern mindset might suggest, only to move as quickly as possible to a unity with the Dao. Physicists tell us that the physical universe is in the process of expanding, while biologists note that the nature of living things is to become more complex and diverse. Perhaps in the larger plan our current mission is to continue to sophisticate our uniqueness rather than simply contracting back into the source.

From where I stand, it does not seem for now that we are ready to shed our individuality just yet. Indeed, in the new conversation, we are just coming into a greater appreciation of it. Despite the devastation and alienation that Ego-Self domination has brought to the world, perhaps it was a necessary step in the evolution of consciousness. In fact, it has even been said in some circles that we are on the leading edge of consciousness in the universe, expanding into new territory, where the growing complexity of our individual minds is helping us find a way to move towards greater diversity and greater unity *at the same time.*

The more complex our mind gets, the more conscious we become as individuals, and the more exquisite the experience of life becomes. We as individuals become clearer, more refined channels for the light of the Dao. The darkness of the Ego Self becomes more translucent and, at the same time, goes further into the background as the *context* for the experience of life rather than the experience itself. From this powerful place our senses come alive, and our appreciation grows for everything around us, the sights, the sounds, the shapes and textures, the tastes and fragrances of life. Such, I believe, is what the next level of consciousness promises to bring.

25. The Flower

In the village flower shop on the island of Allandon the mason was looking through the selection of flowers and, finding nothing to his satisfaction, waded out back where the florist was tending to her extensive garden.

"I have a special request," the mason said. "Cut me a fresh flower that has just reached perfection."

"No problem," said the florist. She smartly clipped one of the nearby flowers and handed it to the mason with a smile.

"No, I don't think so," the mason said. "This flower is still too green; the buds haven't opened enough."

The florist moved quietly to another flower bush, again cut one off and gave it to the mason.

The mason looked at the flower in dismay. "Can't you see this flower has already started to decline? The petals are wrinkled and it's falling apart," he said, shaking the flower and spilling some of the seeds from its mouth.

The florist calmly picked up one of the seeds from the ground and held it out in her open palm. "Perhaps this is what you're looking for."

The mason shook his head. "What's wrong with you? Can't you tell when a flower is perfect?"

"Of course I can tell when a flower is perfect," the florist said. "I just can't tell when it's not."

I have been in the habit of trying to figure out how life works for most of my adult existence. This probably started from my acute inability to flow with life when I was younger. I was confused and fearful, and my only defense at the time was to try to understand it in order to control it. This was a fairly solitary pursuit, for often when I attempted to have conversations with my friends about it they would tease and rebuke me for being overly 'intellectual'.

I find it happily ironic that my persistent reflection, reading, and practices—driven by insecurity though they may have been—helped me come full circle to a place where I no longer feel the need to try to control life. In fact I now hold an unwavering conviction inside me that life is perfect just the way it is. It is a belief that is ever strengthened by my ongoing experiences, like a potter's urn fired in a kiln. Today, if I ever notice myself feeling down or discontent with my life, I know that it is because of who I am choosing to be in that moment and not about life itself. Life is like the sun, which continues to shine even when it is hidden by clouds and we see only rain. It always is and always will be an opportunity to experience new heights of joy, exuberance, and passion. Life stands ready to offer us its bounty in all situations.

That does not mean to say that things always go in my life the way I want them to. My Ego Self takes me on rides to far away places—far away from my true self, that is—and as a result it can be quite a struggle to return to a place of peace and centeredness, a place where I really do feel at my best. If I am struggling with anger, sadness, jealousy, fear, guilt or despair, sometimes all I need is to remember to ask myself the question: *Have you forgotten that life is perfect?* No matter how badly things have gotten for me, I will never deny this. This conviction helps me to accept that whatever is happening to me in the present moment is exactly what needs to happen, and becoming more conscious in the moment will eventually be enough to pull myself out of the manhole I have slowly and inconspicuously slid into.

The Ego Self fights the idea that 'life is perfect' tooth and nail. For the Ego Self life is dangerous, because we are alone. We need to learn strategies to cope, compete well, and make tactical alliances while being careful who we trust. When something happens that we don't like we must call it *bad*, *wrong*, or *unjust*—presumably to prevent it from happening again. Our Ego Self might cleverly argue that if life were perfect then we wouldn't need to do anything. We wouldn't try to make our lives or the lives of others any better. We would become complacent, apathetic, bored. We wouldn't need to *change*.

This is just the kind of reactive thinking that we need to save ourselves from, a thinking that says we have to wait for the pain of a relationship or the boredom of a job to be intolerable before we are willing to take on the discomfort of making a change. When we step back out of the clutches of the Ego Self and into our Dao Self, that is to say when we become more conscious, we see that it is our resistance to change, sponsored by the Ego Self, that is causing the suffering and preventing us from seeing that life is perfect the way it is. When we become more conscious, we can shift from beings who change because we *have to* into beings who change because we *want to*. Instead of being driven by a fear of the suffering of life we are driven by a love of the rapture of life.

Change is actually embraced when we are in the flow of life, because as we have said, life *is* change. The desire to change something does not first require our condemnation of it as something wrong or bad. In my experience, condemning something and making it wrong has never changed it or made it better. If anything, it brings hopelessness and causes the painful situation to persist.

I was once coaching a client around her desire to change a situation and move forward in her life. We went through a visualization process that helps to free the client up to see the source of the problem. In her visualization she saw herself stuck, trying to climb out of a heavy pool of mud. In the distance, she envisioned a clean, vibrant oasis, which represented where she wanted to get to. She was very unhappy and frustrated with being stuck. Her eyes were looking forward towards the oasis but she seemed to be unable to dislodge herself. When I asked her about the experience of being in the muck she just kept saying how difficult it was for her to get out. She described how awful the feeling of being stuck was, how much effort it was taking to try to move out of it with no avail.

After a few moments something came to me. I suggested that before trying to get out of the muck, she might try to be OK about being *in* the muck for a while, and describe what it felt like. In other words, I wanted her to pretend that things were perfect *in the moment*. She was a bit surprised by her own resistance to this at first, but she visualized being still, and stopped struggling with what was *bad*, what *should not be*, long enough to speak about what it actually felt like to be in the muck. To her surprise, the muck was no longer so uncomfortable once she had settled into it.

After we had done that, I asked her what happens next. With great excitement, she saw herself suddenly flying out of the muck with a full burst of energy, and getting easily to the paradise on the horizon. This was the trigger she needed. When we ended the visualization with her moving happily towards the oasis, she felt that she was no longer stuck in her real life. She saw the possibility for enthusiastic action, and the next time I spoke to her she told me that she had already made important progress. The powerful lesson we both took from that session is that in order to have any power to make changes, we must first acknowledge and accept where we are in the moment, in the *now*, the wellspring of the perfection of life.

When we look upon the cycles of nature, we can see the stage of each moment cannot be 'wrong'. We can appreciate that no season is better or worse than the next, no phase of the moon or time of day is the 'right' one. They are all essential parts of their respective rhythms. But when we try to apply this principle to our lives, it is easy to miss the perfection. We don't see the times we have become depressed, or the times we have fallen ill, or the times other people let us down as part of the perfection. We believe that there are a great many things wrong in the world, direly and desperately evil and unjust, and feel the need to fight against and destroy these things if we are to get where we are going.

In actual fact, this only blocks us from where we are going. When we are so serious about the game of life that we forget it is a game, we also lose our appreciation for the fact that life has been set up for the benefit of all of us. If we keep a clear mind and an open heart, we can see that we always have within ourselves the faculties to meet and overcome any of the ongoing challenges that life provides. When we learn any sort of game, which stage of it is really the most satisfying, the most joyful? Is it the beginning, when we are just getting familiar to the rules and are open to the new challenges that lie ahead? Is it soon after, when we first show signs of proficiency and have evidence of our improvement? Or is it when we come close to mastery of the game?

I would suggest that the stage of life that is the most satisfying and joyous is always the one you are at in the moment. That's where the perfection in the universe lies. The stage you are at in this moment is exactly where you need to be; it is the source of your greatest possible experience in life. It is only when we look away from the moment, to the aspirations of the future, to the way things ought to be, or to the passing of a time gone by, the way things should continue to be, that we are taken out of the potential wonder of the present moment.

When we lose sight of the perfection of life it is even possible to take the miracle of the flowering of human consciousness and turn it into nothing more than a dire race to save ourselves and our planet from extinction. Now true, I do believe that we are being called upon today to save our planet, what I'm saying is that we don't need the guilt or shame or despair of having been inactive up to now. As big and as urgent as saving our planet might seem, it is still just a part of the game, set up for the benefit of the individuals within it. From a higher perspective, we see that we are participating in the biggest, fullest cycle in the universe: our separation from and return to the Dao. And it looks like we are well on our way. We are sitting somewhere on a timeline of eternity. Does it really matter where we are on this line, at some point between the beginning and the end? From this perspective, there is nothing 'wrong' in the world now. The world is perfect just the way it is. There is nothing we should do. There is nothing we have to do. We can do as we desire. We are free to choose. This is the way it has always been. This is only just now dawning on us, as we enter a new level of consciousness.

Life is what we make it. Literally. We give meaning to it, we are capable of shaping it with our own vision. At the same time, our lives have a common thread. We have all come here to explore our darkness and bring our light to it. That is the process of expanding consciousness. Our darkness is our *karma*, the mechanism by which our path in life is drawn up. We take on our darkness one small piece at a time, as we become ready for it. Each time we shine our light intensely on that piece of darkness it crumbles and evaporates. We are reminded over and over again that this darkness is not real. Each time we do this we get an ever-clearer glimpse of who we really are.

But how we get there is up to us. There are an infinite number of ways to play. If we see life as a race, our darkness is the obstacle we have to move around and through. If life is a play, the darkness of our character is the basis for the drama. If life is a classroom, our darkness is our ignorance of what we need to learn. It's why we play all these games in life, because we know deep down inside of ourselves that life literally is such a game, the grandest game, and all these other things that we invent and play help us to engage fully in our lives.

Do you get a thrill from climbing to the top of a large mountain? Then let your life be that climb. Do you get the highest satisfaction in honing a great talent, like becoming a revered painter or talented musician? Then let life be this path of mastery. Is your fulfillment found in nurturing and teaching the young, so that they may enjoy the greatest fruits the world has to offer? Then let your life be the unfolding of your love. *We have chosen this life.* We come here for entertainment, adventure, the unique experience of being alive in human form. Let your life be a celebration of that!

26. The Banker

In the banker's office at the village bank on the island of Allandon, the glassblower was just completing a loan application for renovations to his glass shop. He was about to sign when he noticed something peculiar about the final sentence.

"What's this?" he asked as he read the final line: "Warning: late payments will *not* lead to prosecution."

"Yes, what about it?"

"Well, it must be a typo. Surely you meant '...*will* lead to prosecution.'"

The banker smiled to himself for a moment. Then he said, "Do you want me to let you in on a little secret?"

"Sure," said the glassblower.

"A while back many people were not making their monthly payments on time. They had every excuse in the book. So I had that line added to the bottom of the contract to prevent them from taking advantage of me. And so you're right, it *is* a typo. The printer put in the 'not' by mistake."

"Well, don't you think you should change it right away?" asked the glassblower.

"Well, I was going to when it first came to my attention," said the banker. "The first customer that saw the new contract pointed it out. But he thought it was my way of showing my trust in him. He promised that he wouldn't let me down. I was too embarrassed to tell him it was a typo."

"But then you *didn't* change it."

"I was planning to, but before I could get in touch with the printer, another customer also noticed it. She was amazed at the way I was willing to do business. She made quite a big fuss about it."

"Sounds like a recipe for disaster to me. What if the word got out that you were doing this?"

"Well, long story short—it did. She told a lot of people and suddenly they were coming to me, calling me 'the trusting banker,' and 'the caring banker'. And certainly they would all be looking for that line in their contracts when they came to me for loans."

"And so you were stuck."

"You could say that—but I promised myself that I would fix it the next time someone was late with a payment." After a slight pause the banker added, "That was twenty years ago."

Whenever we want to ensure *right* action, whether it be in a business deal, teaching our kids, or holding a vision for humanity, we tend to automatically resort to discouraging *wrong* action. This is the persistent temptation we face living in a world of duality.

Proclaiming 'Thou shalt not...' followed by a threat of retribution has long purported to be what is required to maintain an orderly and harmonious community and world. The underlying assumption here is that there are universal 'right' and 'wrong' actions, an absolute code of what is good and what is evil. In many religious traditions, there exists a supreme Being who is the author and enforcer of an absolute code of moral conduct, the rules and commandments that we must follow in order to be saved. This supreme Being presides on our 'day of judgment' after our death, to determine if our cumulative actions in the world merit either eternal salvation or eternal damnation.

Ahem.

I'm not saying this state of affairs is *impossible*, but it has long puzzled me how an all-powerful and omniscient Being could ever find the motivation or desire to judge good acts from evil acts, since this Being is ultimately the source of *all* acts. The idea that this Being would somehow have a need for our obedience, or have any needs whatsoever in fact, doesn't make any sense to me. It smacks of anthropomorphism—our tendency to give human attributes to something that is not human.

This 'supreme Judger' appears to me as a projection of our Ego Self onto the Being that I have called the Dao. When we come from the perspective of the Ego Self, then we tend to be deeply involved in matters of right and wrong, judgment and retribution. We are likely to believe that some among us are basically evil, not to be trusted, and if given the freedom to act from an inner compass will undoubtedly seek to harm others. This becomes a self-fulfilling prophecy, because in coming from an environment of mistrust and fear we continue to create mistrust and fear.

This perspective is only reinforced by the media, which sells copy and maintains ratings by clearly distinguishing the heroes from the villains in our society. It is easy to buy into it, as it can be comforting to know who the good people are and who the bad people are—especially since we consider ourselves to be on the side of good. And so naturally it appears more than obvious that we need to have some common form of morality to contain the potential damage coming from the bad guys.

The idea that we will be considered *good* if and only if we follow some universal code of moral responsibility towards others is very tempting, as it saves us the work of figuring out from the inside how we should act. But therein lies my firm objection, and why I take the opposite tack: I believe we have *absolutely no moral responsibility to others*. We do not 'owe' people respect, compassion, or charity. Of higher importance is that we actually feel that we have a choice.

Our true moral obligation, our path, our destiny, and also not coincidentally our greatest bliss, is to endeavor to find and be our true self. But this is not even a real obligation, it's a choice we made that we have forgotten about, the choice to come into this world. If we owe other people anything it is to get to know *ourselves* better so that we can act from our connectedness while sharing the gift of our unique perspective. The closer we move to the center of our being, the more we become aligned with our freedom of choice, of *real* choice, not of choice based on compulsion or command. My experience of life has shown me that when I am free to act in accordance with my true self, my Dao Self, I act out of love. The love flows easily, and is genuine and empowering. When I am 'loving' as a result of some outwardly proscribed moral directive, the expression is always dry, stunted, and unenthusiastic.

What is morality but one person's idea thrust upon another? No system of morality ever sponsored great love, compassion or true acceptance. All commands, orders, rules and imperatives come from the fear of the Ego Self. Even the greatest commandment of all, 'love thy neighbor as thyself,' loses its essential power if it is taken as a commandment rather than as a proposal freely offered to consider. Enlightened masters who spoke powerfully about love such as Jesus understood that real love is a natural expression of our true self. Throughout our history the tendency of humans has been to misinterpret this call to love as a 'you must do this' rather than a 'try this on'. I don't believe it has ever been the intention of the truly enlightened masters to have their offerings hardened into mandatory moral codes.

When we stand behind a moral code we can become righteous about our own moral superiority. From on high, it is easy to condemn and judge others for what we have determined are 'evil' acts. But this judgment and condemnation is actually the lynchpin of the entire problem. Someone might say, "I believe that everyone should respect each other," but in saying so they might feel justified in closing the door to respecting people who do not respect *them.* And so the person who most desperately needs respect and love—the one who cannot in a given moment respect and love others—does not receive it, and we all get stuck. It is only when we are able to move closer to our Dao Self that we get in touch with our authentic desire to respect others, out of the pure joy of expansion and expression of love. This respect is afforded even when—especially when—the other has no respect for us, because this is where the respect is most pressingly needed.

Consider the possibility that right and wrong are never absolute, and in fact we are all continually making it up as we go along, to create dramatic effect in the unfolding of the play called human life. In the old *Spaghetti Westerns*, we could tell the good guys and the bad guys apart, since the good guys wore the white hats and the bad guys wore the black hats. The difference in real life is that everybody thinks that they are the good guy. They really do. And do you know why they think so? Because they are. We are all good. Wars and fighting only occur between some good guys who have one idea of what is good and other good guys who have a different idea about what is good.

The sooner we see that good and evil is really a fabrication of the Ego Self, the sooner we will be able to take the next leap in consciousness, and come more fully from our Dao Self. When we do, we will gain an understanding that we are all fundamentally good, and when we are able to act authentically we can be trusted to exercise our free will in ways that will benefit others. It stands to reason: from the perspective of the Dao Self, we and others are the same. Coming from our Dao Self we would never harm the world because our Dao Self *is* the world.

No matter how 'moral' we consider ourselves to be, if we are still judging others for being less 'moral', then we are instantly pulled by our judgment out of the realm of our Dao Self and back into our Ego Self. For the time being, I think the best we can do to move things along is to realize that those who do 'wrong'—that is to say, detrimental to others—are simply acting out of fear, and are unaware of their true nature. Rather than being condemned and castigated they need to be understood and accepted. The condemnation of evil should not be confused with the celebration of good. The emotional need to exact revenge by condemning people who have perpetrated crimes is the same as the emotional need behind the crime itself. We actually circulate divisive energy by overtly demonstrating our opposition to ignorance of self. And so to me, whenever I see on the news the hordes of people standing outside a prison, vilifying a man or woman who is to be executed for a heinous crime, I can only think that those people are projecting the very darkness that they are condemning.

The attempt to legitimize the separation of people as good and evil, worthy and unworthy is itself a denial of our unity and connectedness as human beings. As Khalil Gibran says,

> Oftentimes have I heard you speak of one who commits a wrong as though he were not one of you, but a stranger unto you and an intruder upon your world.
> But I say that even as the holy and the righteous cannot rise beyond the highest which is in each one of you, so the wicked and the weak cannot fall lower than the lowest which is in you also.
> And as a single leaf does not turn yellow but with the silent knowledge of the whole tree, so the wrong-doer cannot do wrong without the hidden knowledge of you all.

When we come from a place of oneness, judgment is pointless. We are captured by the joyful feeling that we are all in this together. Eventually it is possible to see that *all* acts, those we call good and those we call evil, are really on a continuum of actions all motivated by the same basic human desire—the desire for unity. The low point of this continuum is total ignorance of who we are and the high point is fully embodied knowledge of our true nature—as One. The acts that emerge from a knowledge of self try to arrive at unity by embracing diversity. Acts of charity, humility, and compassion are obvious attempts to unite with others. The acts that emerge from an ignorance of self tend to try to arrive at unity by suppressing or destroying diversity. The need to conform is a good example. So is jealousy, which stems from the desire to be united with another. Even the act of genocide is founded on an attempt to unify one's race or culture—by killing people who are different.

Easy now. Let's not misunderstand what is being said here. The assertion that there is no absolute good and evil does not mean that we need to consider all acts as the same. When we let go of judgment we are still left with the power of *discernment*. We know an act of kindness has a significantly different effect from an act of violence. We know from experience that the kind of unity that the Ego Self seeks inevitably tears us farther apart. But if we as witnesses of such acts can frame them not as evil but rather as simply ignorant, then it helps us to maintain a vision of ourselves and the other as One. From there we can see that if people knew more about who they were and what they were doing that they would be seeking to unify not out of a fear of being alone but out of a love of being One.

Of course as individuals we are not there yet. We are all at various stages or levels of awareness of our true self. And that is all well and good. Being at one place on the continuum of awareness is no better than being at another. Being self-aware is not 'better' than being ignorant. It simply is what is. For each of us I believe a time will come in our evolution when we will realize that our diversity is our greatest gift. It is actually what makes any worthwhile experience possible. And the easiest way to achieve unity without rejecting diversity is to act with the belief that there is already a unity underneath our differences. This, in all its shades and nuances, is what it means to act out of love.

I am not saying we *ought* to act this way. There is no 'should' in love. Love flows naturally. So rather than enforcing moral standards, informing each other what is right and wrong, we are better off trying to be gentle and accepting, creating a space that is big enough to allow each person to think, speak, and act in accordance with what they believe is good. The new conversation honors your personal morality based on your unique set of values and experiences. It does not support a fixed and universal morality since this can actually serve to hide you from your true nature. After all, if you follow rules that oppose your desires, how will you ever learn about your true nature? How will you ever come to face your own ignorance? It is only in a space where we feel we are allowed to show our ignorance, our darkness, that we become capable of dissolving our ignorance and seeing who we truly are. And as we go forward we become more able to help others discover the same thing about themselves—not out of some moral imperative, but out of the joy of expressing and expanding ourselves into the world.

The new conversation is a call to heal our darkness together. There is no one we need to look to but ourselves. There is no guru, no expert, no savior, because all of us have darkness. All of us need healing. As imperfect beings we will create the space as best we can, a space without right and wrong. We only need to be authentic, and speak the truth of our desires. In an environment where we no longer feel the need to suppress our true desires in favor of the 'right' way to think, speak and act, we are likely to enjoy a far more empowering sense of ourselves as beings of pure love.

27. The Testament

By noon on Remembrance Day most of the villagers had found their way into a large circle in the village square. Remembrance Day on the island of Allandon was a celebration of the present through an embracing and owning of injustices and atrocities of the past. Any one would have the opportunity to give testament, in their own words, to events from their collective history that they felt needed to be remembered.

After several minutes of silent contemplation together, the orchard owner was the first to rise. He put his hands in the air and bowed his head.

"Let us remember a time when we gathered up the harvest for the few, so that we could grow fat while others starved."

"We remember," the villagers said in unison.

The renovator stood up next. "Let us remember a time when we burned homes and villages, so that we could strike fear in the lives of others."

"We remember," the villagers said.

The old woman who cleaned the village square banged her pail on the ground signaling that she wanted to speak: "Let us remember a time when we tortured those who thought differently, massacred those who looked differently, a time when we raped the defenseless for pleasure and dismembered the innocent without remorse."

"We remember," the villagers said.

After a short silence, the orchard owner encouraged the young man who planted seeds in his orchard to say something. As the seed planter stood up and looked around shyly, the villagers clapped to encourage him to speak. And so with a deep breath he began.

"Let us remember that when the news of these acts of cruelty came into our ears and eyes—often as these events were still going on—we felt deep sadness in our hearts and anguish in our minds. But at the time we did not consider them *our* acts. We only judged them as wrong and mostly did nothing."

There were audible gasps among the villagers. Some bowed their heads while others looked about perplexed. The seed planter bent down to the orchard owner and whispered, "Did I say something wrong? Aren't people supposed to say 'We remember'?"

The orchard owner smiled wistfully and said, "Give us some time. We will."

If we step into the future just a little bit, it is not hard to imagine that we will look back to the present day and marvel at our relative inaction in the face of the human suffering and need on our planet. This is not at all to discount the incredible work that is being done by people to directly address the sickness, the starvation, the disease and the injustice; but it is still the work of the few, the exceptional, and the money that we provide for this work remains a drop in the bucket of global wealth, especially when compared to the amount being used to manufacture the tools of war and destruction.

More than ever in our history, we are front and center to the misery that is occurring around the world. We are hearing more about the aftermath of natural disasters, becoming more acutely aware of the spread of deadly diseases, and witnessing in graphic detail the catastrophic consequences of wars and conflicts as they happen. It makes us wonder if this is occurring because of the advances of modern telecommunications, or if the world really is headed towards fragmentation and eventual self-destruction. Either way it has become nearly impossible to turn a blind eye to it.

And perhaps that is a good thing. Not because we are more likely to be *guilted* into giving a donation, or to drop everything to become a relief worker abroad, or even to be forced to appreciate all that we have. The reason I say it is a good thing is because I feel that the broadcasting of human atrocities of the past and present sharpens our collective self-awareness and propels the evolution of our consciousness, which is the only avenue that will lead us to that long sought-after dream of world peace. Before Adolf Hitler orchestrated the holocaust, few people would have considered such massive crimes against humanity possible in the twentieth century. However they occurred, not because of the twisted vision of a single man, but because of the complicity of so many whose darkness had gone unexamined.

In a way, few people made a greater contribution to the eradication of discrimination than Adolf Hitler, because through his actions the darkness that was in humanity as a whole rose to the surface, like a disease that moves from deep inside us and erupts on our skin for all to see. The holocaust is rightly kept in memory not as a reminder that an evil man perpetrated unthinkable deeds, but that something in the darkness of our collective soul made such an event possible.

In the new conversation humanity is a true community, in which we share ownership of the darkness and fear that explodes into the world. As the development of the individual reaches new heights, so too is there a greater opportunity to see ourselves as One. So long ago Jesus implored that 'he who is without sin should cast the first stone,' to show us that the blame placed by one person or group on another is not really where the solution is but actually where the problem lies.

Blaming others for all the suffering in the world is a rather limited way to empathize with that suffering. We are better off being straight and simply saying that it causes us suffering as well. We may deny that we are affected, but denial is an acute form of that suffering. For a long time we have used coping mechanisms to escape from the guilt, the shame, the sadness that the current state of the world brings to us.

But can we be faulted? Can we really be expected to fathom what it is like to be an innocent bystander in a war zone and be captured, terrorized, and finally have our head sawed off? Can we grasp the anguish of a woman who is dying a painful death from AIDS as a result of having been raped repeatedly by soldiers of her own country? We might be excused for avoiding much more than a cursory, detached glance at these events, for fear of being overwhelmed and not being able to get on with our lives.

But this fear is only reasonable at our old level of consciousness, the one we are growing out of. It is coming from a place where we feel absolutely helpless and powerless, disconnected from our world and what goes on in it. From the point of view of our old consciousness, being at peace with what is going on in the world can only be seen as complete ignorance or unmitigated apathy. And so we proclaim righteously that these horrible events in the world are *wrong*, that they should not be happening!

Ah, but this is where we need to be the most careful, because—I'll say it again—herein lies the lynchpin of the whole problem. What is most pressingly needed, in this matter as with all human matters, is not our judgment, but rather our acceptance.

But that seems absurd! How can I suggest that we lend acceptance to these horrible events? If we don't judge these events as wrong, then why would we ever act to make things right? In accepting the occurrence of these events, are we not automatically condoning these human actions and sending a message to the perpetrators to keep right on doing them? These are the questions we ask ourselves. What we ask less often is: how effective has our judgment been in bringing peace and harmony to our world? If we look at the evidence honestly, we will realize it has been wholly ineffective.

In order to bring about lasting change we are required to bring our consciousness to a level above the one in which these problems were made and continue to perpetuate. Let's face it once and for all: judgment does not lead to action, it only leads to *reaction*. Look at what has been happening in the Middle East since the end of the second World War. It is a chronicle of reaction. But history does not have to be about reaction. It can be about *creation*. The only thing we need to do is stop being informed on how to act based on what we know from our past, the favorite stomping ground of our Ego Self, and act instead from our deepest voice inside, from our self that is connected to the All, our Dao Self.

Let us begin with the most obvious of propositions: what is, is. In other words, if an event has occurred or is occurring, then judging it to be bad or wrong or horrible does not change or affect or negate the event one iota. It only changes *us*. It separates us from the event. It makes us feel powerless, because it makes us feel as though we are not part of the event, that we are not connected to it in any way. If we are not connected to it then we have no power to affect change.

Now true, our governments show us that if you have enough might, you can effect some changes in the world using the old paradigm of good over evil. But these are not the deep lasting changes that get to the source of any problem. These are more like the superficial shifting of lines on a map and titles of governments, while the real energy behind these events are pushed down into the depths of men and women, to re-emerge at the first opportunity. Ever wonder when the wars will end? The War on Terror? The War on Drugs? The War on Cancer? They will end the moment we stop believing in the need to wage war, the moment that our consciousness evolves enough to see that war is self-perpetuating.

It is tempting to pronounce ourselves on the side of good, but believe it or not, being on the side of good is actually the problem. Being on the side of good is really equivalent to being on the side of evil, for we will always be 'evil' in the minds of the group that we are opposed to, the side that we have called evil. This old consciousness is driven by our fear, and makes us proclaim to others that "you are with us or you are against us." Even those who want to remain neutral become the enemy. It is only with an elevated consciousness that we can arrive at the truth about all the fighting we do— that 'we have met the enemy, and he is us'.

In war, everybody believes that they are on the side of good. Everybody believes that the One, the Dao, God, Allah—is on their side, and their fight is in their Name. But this is the most absurd of contradictions. When you are on a 'side', it means you are in *opposition to*. It means you are *fighting against*. If we are truly with the One, the Dao, then we are not against—anything! There is only the One! Duality is transcended, duality which is fueled by judgment, by right and wrong, good and evil. Mother Theresa may have encapsulated this best when asked to join an anti-war march. She declined, and then added, "but if you have a march *for peace*, I will be there." Perhaps, finally, we are ready to step into a consciousness that sees beyond the very human obsession with good and evil.

We have always had visionaries throughout our history who have known about this, and in their own way have tried to inspire people to a consciousness of unity. They realized that this consciousness cannot be forced, cannot be pushed, but can only be offered softly and humbly as a choice. We may have heard the words of this wisdom thousands of times in hundreds of different settings, but seldom have gotten to its core. No matter. The words will continue to be there for when we are ready. And when we are able to let our minds become still, it may be possible to hear those words again inside us as if for the first time, words of a stirring speech, a sacred text, or even a song like this visionary *oeuvre* by John Lennon:

Imagine there's no heaven, it's easy if you try
No hell below us, above us only sky
Imagine all the people, living for today...

Imagine there's no countries, it isn't hard to do
Nothing to kill or die for, and no religion too
Imagine all the people, living life in peace...

You may say I'm a dreamer,
But I'm not the only one
I hope someday you'll join us
And the world will be as one

Imagine no possessions, I wonder if you can
No need for greed or hunger, a brotherhood of man
Imagine all the people, sharing all the world...

You may say I'm a dreamer,
But I'm not the only one
I hope someday you'll join us
And the world will live as one [10]

We are ready to be moved by great visions like this, and we are preparing to share similar visions of our own. The move to a new approach has started to change the way we are all thinking about healing the divisions on our planet. When we approach life from our Dao Self, we think globally rather than locally. We take ownership of the ills of the world rather than opposition to them. A recent campaign for AIDS awareness read 'We All Have AIDS', which shows the growing awareness that each one of us is complicit in any condition that befalls humanity, and we are an essential part of the healing of that condition as well.

Many organizations are now being created which, although certainly supportive of action in the world, are focused on the proliferation of a consciousness of unity. Initiatives like *Humanity's team*, *Alliance for a New Humanity*, and *the One campaign* believe that when a critical mass of

---

[10] *Imagine* Words and Music by John Lennon©1971 (Renewed 1999) LENONO.MUSIC All rights Controlled and Administered by EMI BLACKWOOD MUSIC INC., All Rights Reserved, International Copyright Secured, Used by Permission

people have elevated their consciousness to the point that it is abundantly clear and self-evident that we are all One, something will become immediately obvious: there is nothing more pressing to do than to put all our energies into helping the most desperate among us in any way possible. This means no longer marginalizing people and nations when their ways are different from ours. This means making a priority of sharing our food, water, medicine and other resources.

This happens in the most spontaneous way. When we gain greater self-awareness our hearts are opened. If enough people move into this higher awareness, it is not impossible that one day the world will be freely willing to offer up all its resources—yes, ALL its resources—until each human being on the planet is free from worry and suffering.

Imagine if your young child was sick and needed immediate medical attention to survive. Would you decide that since you have budgeted 3.5% of your total wealth to this matter, that you would stop after it runs out? You would let your child die? I don't think so. When we think about humanity the way most of us currently think about our immediate family, when we realize we are connected in just the same way, our behavior in the world will naturally change.

In the new conversation caring about others on our planet is not a command or even a request. The new conversation is simply an exploration of the experiences in life that we truly want, in a space provided for the expression of our truest, clearest, most grounded selves. In itself life isn't bothered with the prospects of people starving and the planet disintegrating through war. Life will go on regardless. Our world is the backdrop to our experience, providing us with the possibility to make choices. When the situation in our world is dire it just makes those choices more meaningful, more *felt*. If we really could free ourselves from our old consciousness, we might have no greater desire than to care for the less fortunate among us and help to heal our planet of the Ego-devastation it has experienced throughout its history.

This does not all have to be overwhelming. In the consciousness of unity we realize that as goes the microcosm, so goes the macrocosm. Each shift in our individual consciousness affects human consciousness as a whole. Each gesture, each interaction with others in our lives has global consequences. And so if we want to exercise our choice to help make the world better for all people on the planet, we need to look no further than healing our everyday relationships.

28. The Hairdresser

One day the choreographer walked into the village hair salon on the island of Allandon and went straight to the hairdresser, who was her best friend as well as her boyfriend's sister.

"Can we talk?" said the choreographer.

"Well, I'm a little tied up right now," said the hairdresser, who was busy cutting the hair of the renovator's apprentice.

"It's about your brother," said the choreographer.

"What a coincidence," the hairdresser said without lifting her eyes.

"Why's that?"

"My brother was just here getting a haircut. He said if I saw you he wanted me to tell you..."

"Oh, he has something to tell me, does he? And now he's getting his sister to do it?" The choreographer shook her head. "Have I ever told you that your brother is impossible to be with?"

"Yes, you have actually," teased the hairdresser. "You said he knows nothing about relationships." The apprentice shot the hairdresser a grin.

"Exactly. Why I'm still going out with him I'll never know," said the choreographer.

"Are the two of you not talking again?"

"Of course not. He's making no effort to have a real conversation with me."

"Perhaps he finds you difficult to talk to."

"*I'm* difficult to talk to? He's the one that just wants to hear himself talk," the choreographer said. "It's always about what *he* needs."

"What does he need?"

"What does he need?" the choreographer mocked, arms up in dismay as she walked back towards the door. She turned and said, "Do you know what he really needs? He needs someone to tell him to just listen for once."

The hairdresser stopped cutting for a moment and said, "You know, that's funny, because..."

"In fact, the next time you see him tell him that, would you? Tell him next time to be ready to listen for what *I* need!" The choreographer left the salon, slamming the door shut behind her.

The hairdresser looked at the apprentice. "That's just what my brother asked me to tell *her*," she said with a wink.

When I look back to my earlier relationships, I see that I had the whole thing backwards. I was very controlling, felt that I knew better, and tended to be quite judgmental of behavior that did not lead to where I thought the relationship should be going. Often I encountered opposition from my significant other, and when there wasn't opposition there was resignation. In my mind I was just trying to help my girlfriends communicate better, be emotionally stronger, and basically *grow up* so that we could both enjoy a better relationship. I thought I was helping to heal problems but I was probably causing more damage than anything. While my end goal may have been to develop a relationship of trust, openness and acceptance, I couldn't see that my means of achieving it were anything but open, trusting, and accepting. And therein lies all the difference, a lesson I would learn in small steps over the course of a long climb.

One step I remember very well involved a girlfriend who had a tendency to be critical of how I talked, how I dressed, and how I acted with people. No matter how hard I tried to get her to stop it, whether through pleading, building a strong argument against it, getting angry or not talking at all, nothing worked. Fed up with the situation, I approached a friend and coach for help on the sidelines of a workshop she was facilitating. I remember the conversation almost verbatim because it was such a long-standing problem that I thought that only prolonged hours of analysis would scratch the surface of the issue. Instead:

Me: I'm having a big problem with my girlfriend.
Coach: What is it?
Me: She's not allowing me to be myself.
Coach: Does she really have the power to prevent you from being yourself?
Me: Do you mean that she doesn't?
Coach: (knowing smile)
Me: All these things she says and does, they aren't actually preventing me from being myself?
Coach: What do you think?

That was it. Now admittedly, I must have been ready for this revelation. Or more precisely, I was ready to apply it to my life, because the idea was already familiar to me. Her final question triggered a shift in my perception, and suddenly I was no longer a prisoner to my girlfriend's opinions. I realized that I didn't have to change her behavior at all. Nor did I have to change my own. I just needed to accept *what is*. This short conversation changed nothing in the world, and yet it made me feel free.

For me, relationships used to be about changing what was *out there*: convincing, arguing, threatening, cajoling, or appeasing the other in order to get them to change in some way and do what I wanted them to do. Even that old standard, *compromising*, rests within this old paradigm. When we compromise, we make changes *out there*, changes as to how we behave in the world, so that the other person makes changes as to how *they* behave in the world.

The new conversation is about changing the world *in here*: the only change that really affects us has to do with ourselves, while our partner can remain free to keep doing exactly what they are doing. We are not changing our *behavior*, we are simply changing our perspective, the way we look out upon life. From this inner change, our outer appearance and behavior is transformed naturally. We become an ever fuller *authentic* self. Just seeing things from a different place—shifting from the Ego Self to the Dao Self—makes it possible to be at peace in our relationships. As a result of deciding to foster change *in here* rather than *out there* we gain control of all the changes we seek in our lives, and conflict begins to vanish. We become agents of healing in our relationships, almost as a byproduct of our personal consciousness work within ourselves.

My conflict with my girlfriend stemmed from my desire to get her to change her behavior. In my mind it had to be done somehow. I could see no other options. The irony of the situation is not lost on me. I was angry with my girlfriend for not accepting me for who I was. But I was doing exactly the same thing: *I was not accepting her for who she was.*

This just reinforces the notion prevalent in the new conversation that our relationships are like mirrors. Eventually the behavior we are putting out is the behavior we will get back. When I stopped trying to change her, lo and behold—the landscape of our relationship was magically transformed. It's not just that her behavior didn't bother me any more, which would have been enough. It's that over a short period of time her behavior actually *stopped happening.* When she no longer needed to react to my desire to change her, she must have started to lose her own desire to change me.

When we create a space in our relationships founded in acceptance, the experience of unity which we call love inevitably shows up, not as something coming from the other as much as something whose expression we allow within ourselves. Rumi said, 'Your task is not to seek for love, but merely to seek and find all the barriers within yourself that you have built against it.' If we approach our intimate relationships not as a way to *get* love but as an opportunity to unblock the love that flows through us, then our relationships become an eminently satisfying way of helping one another move into our Dao Self where our already-connected state of being, our love, is revealed to us.

If we want a relationship in which openness, acceptance, and freedom exist, then obviously we have to begin by providing that for the other. This is what love in a relationship really represents for me: an acceptance of exactly who the other person is, or even more—a reverence for their uniqueness. But what if *they* are not doing it? Well, somebody has to make the first move. We cannot simply wait to be inspired by the other to act. We need to be the change we want to see in our relationship.

In order to play a role in the evolution of human consciousness we don't have to start a big movement or speak to thousands of people at a time. Creating space in our relationships, one by one, is the fundamental way we participate in making the planet a better place to live for everyone. In fact, it is only through relationships that a change in consciousness can happen in the world at all.

We are all in this together. Our common journey is to help one another on our individual paths. If we can somehow find the patience to just listen, and the strength to withhold our judgment, at least for a moment, we will help in the growth of an environment of trust and healing in the world. Perhaps we don't realize the impact of creating a space for others—sometimes we still act as though only our advice and our opinions are helpful. But then, we need only reflect on the conversations in our past that really had an impact on *us*, where someone listened and really gave us the space to hear ourselves think. The more we become interested in listening without judgment, the more likely we will get our turn to express ourselves when we really need to.

We have the opportunity to make a difference not just with our significant other but in *all* our relationships. Whether it be letting go of expectations we put on our children, accepting our parents and relatives as they are, or forgiving our friends for past mistakes, we can make a difference in the awakening of their consciousness but more importantly we can awaken our own. Creating a space for others to *be* is actually one of the greatest acts of self-love we can perform. Accepting others always brings us peace. Forgiving others always makes us more free. As we get more ambitious, we can even work on creating a space of love and acceptance for the people who we least get along with, the ones that really push our buttons, knowing that this will truly lead us further down the path of self-realization.

Always keep in mind, though, that none of this is achieved through compulsion, obligation, or duty. It is essential to come from *choice*. When being accepting, forgiving, and non-judgmental is a duty, our power is lost. When we identify ourselves as people who *should not* judge others, then what happens when we falter and stumble? We judge *ourselves*. We fall into thinking that our jealousy, our anger, our judgment is *wrong*. And so we call ourselves wrong. We feel shame. We censor what we say and suppress our feelings. And this is where the devastation really happens. Now suddenly we've taken away all the space for *ourselves* to be. Without giving this space to ourselves, we can hardly provide it for others. We hide our darkness from the world not only because others disapprove of it, but because we disapprove of it ourselves.

To avoid the spiral of self-recrimination, it is important to establish a starting point. I have had success in healing my relationships with others only to the extent that I healed my relationship with my self. I needed to get to the point where I could look in the mirror and say "I love you". To be with *what is* in the world was anchored in being with *what is* in myself.

When I was younger I searched desperately for love and approval from others because I had not given it to myself. The great relationship I had been searching for, the one that would finally make me feel right with the world, was within me the whole time.

In a way our relationships with others serve us best when they strengthen our relationship with ourselves. When others create room for us to safely express *everything* inside of ourselves, not just what is easy to say and hear, they can help us move forward in our evolution. Our judgments are important clues for us, direct pointers to the part of our own fear and darkness that is crying out for our attention. Whether it manifests as jealousy, anger, blame, or pessimism, all judgment will be uncovered at its root as *self*-judgment. It is ironic that many of us who aspire in earnest to expand our consciousness by letting go of judgment get stuck when we judge ourselves for not being able to fully let go. In these instances it becomes invaluable to have a trusted other to remind us that not only our judgments but also our inability to let go of our judgments is perfectly OK.

There is perhaps no single choice we can make in the world more powerful than the choice to work together to embrace and transform our darkness. This is the choice to enter the new conversation. Rather than politely side-stepping our fears, we can allow them to be one of the topics of discussion. When the conversation is founded in trust and authenticity, we are able to provide each other with some valuable perspective. As we help each other to become more conscious of our own fears, and we get to realize how much they are driving us in our lives, we move into greater choice. As a consequence we become ever more powerful in helping each other face these fears—so goes this upward spiral. Fostering simple awareness begins the transformation of our darkness into something noble and beautiful.

While the cloud of darkness that hangs over the world today is undeniably vast, there is no reason to be overwhelmed by it. We are best to focus on one relationship at a time, and even then, we have to accept that all our relationships are works-in-progress. Still, the prospects are exciting. As we become able to provide the space in our relationships to heal through awareness, we become part of the evolution of our collective human consciousness, which will one day amass the power to heal the world.

29. The Astrologer

On a clear night on the island of Allandon, the astrologer was peering through the telescope in the village observatory when the scientist walked in.

"How's the view now?" asked the scientist.

The astrologer stepped away from the telescope and turned to the scientist. "Brilliant! The changes you made to the lens are perfect. Everything is so much clearer."

"I'm glad to hear it's working well," said the scientist.

"Yes, I don't know how I can repay you," said the astrologer.

The scientist moved up to the telescope. "Oh, I don't know," he said casually as he peered quickly into the eyepiece. "Perhaps you could, you know, do one of those chart things you do."

The astrologer was surprised. "You would like me to do your birth chart?"

"Oh, just for fun, you know," he said. "I don't really believe in those things."

"Uh-*huh*," she replied with a smile.

"Now don't get me wrong. I mean no disrespect. But isn't it completely irrational to think that the position of the stars could really have anything to do with our lives?" he asked.

"Perhaps it is," she said.

The scientist frowned. "That's not what I wanted to hear."

"No?"

"Well, I was hoping that you could give me some proof that this stuff is real."

The astrologer looked into his eyes. "Do you have a feeling inside you that wants it to be real?"

"Yes, I suppose I do," he conceded.

"Look there for your proof," said the astrologer gently.

In life there is no getting away from duality. As I have said, it is a requirement of existence itself. However this does not mean that it is ever necessary for us to identify firmly with one side of a duality and be in opposition to the other. We don't need the battles of the sexes, the pitting of Democrats against Republicans, the wars of opposing ideologies. We have started to become so overtly aware of the damage caused by polarization that we are getting very clear in both our hearts and our minds what will be required of us to heal our divides.

As we bridge the rift between the West and the East, the material and the spiritual, reason and faith, innovation and tradition, both sides benefit. I am reminded of a movie I saw a few years ago entitled *The Painted Veil*, in which Ed Norton plays a bacteriologist and physician who has volunteered to go to a remote village in China to help stem a major cholera epidemic that has broken out. Through a series of deductions he realizes that the village's water supply is continually being contaminated as a result of a local spiritual tradition to bury the bodies of the dead within the banks of the river. His orders to remove the dead bodies from the river banks are met with fervent opposition by the locals, who can't comprehend that this is actually contributing to the outbreak. It is only when his reason-centered approach is allowed to influence their faith-based tradition and that the outbreak is brought under control.

On the flip side, our society is seeing a growing number of people of reason looking to people of faith, openly searching for something they realize is missing in their lives, something they cannot find through rationality alone. I personally have benefited from learning that I was sometimes best to follow my intuition even when the prudence of reason spoke otherwise. Living life not only through the intellect but also through the heart has made me much happier, more self-aware, confident, and perhaps even a little more humble. I have seen much of my fear fall by the wayside. I no longer feel the need, as I did up through university, to express my cynicism and outrage at all the darkness that I felt around me. My optimism about life today is unlimited. My life is no longer just about strategies to cope with fear and isolation, but also about connecting to a unity that has been there all along, just waiting to be discovered.

We begin to fulfill our potential as human beings when our reason and intuition both have a voice, when we develop both the left and the right sides of our brain, and perhaps more importantly when they are working together. We can move from our heart saying one thing and our head saying another thing to a more integrated experience. This is what it means to feel whole. I truly believe these two forces were made to complement each other, and when our rational and intuitive sides are both active and in harmony, we are positioned to have the most sublime experiences life has to offer.

On a larger scale, I believe the healing of the planet is also the bringing-into-balance of two sides, a profound merger in all facets of life of East and West. This is the last great synthesis, which promises to bring together the two fundamental ways that we look at life. This synthesis does not always unfold as smoothly as the harmonious interplay of yin and yang in the East. Neither, however, is it the fully confrontational battle of thesis and antithesis in the West's Hegelian dialectic tradition. The tone of this final resolution of materialism and spirituality, of atomism and holism, of reason and intuition, of individuality and communality, appears to be borrowing from both systems of thought. Perhaps this is a good indication that the healing of these two polarities is well underway.

In our society, what is occurring in the healing arts and sciences *themselves* is a prime example of how this synthesis is taking place. The ways we seek to cure what ails us, physically, mentally, emotionally and spiritually, have started to converge. This is notwithstanding the fact that many proponents of the Western medical model have been fighting the rise of Eastern medicine in our society at every turn. Our health coverage is still designed to advantage practitioners and patients of Western medicine over the so-called 'alternative' modalities offered by Eastern practitioners. But over the last few decades, Eastern modalities are no longer considered 'alternative' as such, and are ever gaining on Western medicine as the preferred choice for treatment and prevention. Note that the term 'alternative' was first popularized when people who had been given no hope by Western doctors for chronic and often life-threatening illnesses searched for an alternative approach.

Western medicine is atomistic, based on the principle of dividing an organism into its component parts and dealing directly with the part that is diseased, so that this inherently *bad* part can be eradicated. Cancer, for example, has generally been treated in one way: if a tumor is found, the doctor will look for ways to excise it, shrink it, or render it inert and stop its growth. There has been little consideration given to the complex organism—the human being—that the cancer emerges out of. Now truth be told, the undistracted attention on the *part* rather than the *whole* has led to significant expertise in some areas. Surgical techniques that have saved the lives of many and improved the quality of life of countless others are the product of a Western mindset. So is the development of prosthetics, hearing aids and artificial organs, to name just a few important innovations. The focus of Western thought on the individual and the separateness of all things has honed the skill of the Western doctor in dealing with the minutest detail of an individual event or symptom—at the expense of gaining expertise on how to deal with the person as a whole.

Eastern medicine, by contrast, is holistic. That means that any organism is considered to be more than the sum of its parts. The interrelationships of the parts with one another and with the organism as a whole are the focal points. For this reason, the Eastern practitioner may treat identical cancer tumors located in exactly the same spot in two patients quite differently. The tumor itself is not the focus of treatment, since the tumor is considered a symptom of a deeper illness. The focus is the state of the organism and the conditions that gave rise to the tumor in the first place. The tumor itself is not considered *bad*; it is simply the manifestation of *dis*-ease, a message from the consciousness of the organism that its system is out of balance. And so the Eastern practitioner strives to help bring the organism back into balance, such that once the balance is restored, the organism is empowered to deal with the symptom of imbalance, in this case the cancerous tumor.

Up until very recently in the West, we only saw the doctor as a kind of 'fixer', a dispassionate expert whose words and prescriptions were not to be questioned. He was somehow *above* us rather than in some kind of relationship with us. It is not a surprise that Western doctors were typically known to have very poor bedside manner, and would speak to us about our disease conditions impassively or at best with misguided sympathy. There was no relation, for the Western doctor, between our condition and the emotional impact of the doctor's behavior towards us or the actual manner in which the treatment was conducted. If there is cancer, it was thought that it will either grow or be killed off solely based on the efficacy of the radiation, chemotherapy, or surgery.

In contrast, the Eastern doctor is the 'healer' who forms a partnership with us to restore balance. It is more common for the Eastern practitioner to get to know us in areas other than those directly related to our medical condition. Their concern tends to be not only our physical but also our mental, emotional, and spiritual balance. The manner in which treatment is administered is often an essential aspect of the treatment itself.

The proposition that Eastern and Western modalities could work together, hand in hand, has only started to come about recently. On the one hand, many Eastern practices have been modernized and enhanced by Western technology and diagnostics methods. On the other hand, there have been a growing number of pioneers in the West who, while still grounded in the practice of Western medicine, believe that Eastern practices and techniques can be used in conjunction as complementary modalities. As an example, Western-based Cancer Centers are popping up that understand that illness must be addressed on the multi-dimensional levels that make up a complete human being—not just because it is what patients want, but because treating a patient as a whole person and not just a collection of body parts is becoming recognized as an effective component of healing. This is backed up, by the way, in clinical studies.

Individually we are becoming aware that *healing* is not just taking a pill or applying a cream to mask symptoms or give temporary relief. It is not painting a happy face over a legacy of pain and sorrow. And so too in the world, healing does not take place when one force tries to annihilate another, or when a society's external order masks the internal suffering that rises from discrimination and intolerance. Healing is really getting to the source of our pain, bringing our darkness out into the open so that we can look at it and allow it to *be*. It is in acknowledging that we have fear and giving ourselves the opportunity to shine our love on it that healing occurs, for in submitting our fear to the light of love, it suddenly is transformed.

The transformation of our fear is complex, and occurs at many levels. If we follow the Eastern vision, the universe is a single living organism that we as human beings are a part of. We are also ourselves an organism made up of smaller organisms—heart cells and liver cells and blood cells, all with a life of their own but which contribute to the functioning of the larger organism. These organisms are therefore all interrelated by purpose. That is why our own personal path is inextricably linked with the journey of humanity, and the destiny of the universe. We are all on a common path—a healing path—back to the full unity of the Dao. We each have a unique pattern of light and darkness, of Love and Fear, and are on a path to let go of our darkness. When we have let go of all of our darkness then we will have let go of our individuality too, for our individuality is the ultimate illusion. As a being of pure light we would become self-identical with the Dao. This is the melting of the island into the ocean from whence it came.

But the Western vision sees the transformation of our fear differently. From the mechanistic standpoint we are separate and distinct. Our evolution is certainly not driving to dissolve our individuality but rather is seen as strengthening it. We wear the overcoming of our fear like a badge of courage, emblematic of our personal growth. We are not going back but rather we are going forward, evolving on the leading edge of consciousness.

In the final synthesis of East and West there must be a sacred merger of both of these visions into one. Perhaps our path is not simply a return of the island back to the ocean, but also the flowering of the island into increasing complexity. When a part of us heals, we could say at one level that we let go of darkness, but at another level we could say the darkness is transformed. We can see it as a maturing of the character of our Ego Self, making the veil of the illusion of our individuality finer, more transparent, and yet at the same time stronger and more sophisticated. In this way it is possible to move towards greater individuality while moving closer to a unity with the Dao at the same time.

It is as though we are each a sacred abode for the Dao, and our maturation moves us from simple to complex. At one time in our history we could be compared to simple caves and now are each becoming magnificent cathedrals. As caves, it would have been very difficult for the light of the Dao to penetrate into our limited consciousness. In fact we would practically have to go outside ourselves to become aware of the light of the Dao. But imagine us now becoming grand cathedrals, vast, spacious, with colorful stained glass windows on all the walls, letting in the light of the Dao. Our expansion from the cave to the cathedral is our move towards enlightenment. It is the march of consciousness. As our abodes become more complex, more intricate, more sophisticated, the more they allow in the light of the Dao. And so the more they become cherished houses for the Dao to experience itself from a particular perspective—our individuality.

As the flow of life moves us into ever-greater complexity, we will experience our grandeur as never before. If the purpose of life is to provide each one of us with the most exquisite experience possible, one could equally say the purpose of life is to provide the Dao with the most exquisite experience of itself *through* us. We are at a time in history where our cathedrals are undergoing major transformations, to give us more space and bring in more light for our experiences.

For now, it is enough to be aware that we stand on one side knowing that part of the truth is held on the other side. And if we can begin to see the possibility of having a foot in both camps, of thinking two ways in parallel, then we are indeed participating in bringing humanity through a watershed in the evolution of our consciousness. To get there we must become beings who can stand comfortably in discomfort, loving our own fear and accepting our own judgment. This move to greater complexity is our true coming-into-balance, the healing of the dichotomy that makes up who we are. And the more we are healed, the better we are placed to allow the source of all Creation to shine through us and fulfill the highest expression of ourselves, as beings of boundless creativity.

30. The Waiter

After a successful performance of one of his plays at the village theatre, the playwright went with the cast to the village restaurant to celebrate. Once they had placed their orders, the playwright noticed that their waiter kept looking at him from a distance.

When the waiter brought their drinks, the playwright asked him: "Is there something you want to say to me?"

The waiter was a bit startled. "Uh, no," he said with eyes down as he put the drinks on the table. He began to walk away, then he hesitated, turned to the playwright and uttered, "I saw your play tonight."

"Did you enjoy it?" the playwright asked.

The waiter stood and looked around, his tight lips ready to burst.

"Oh, how I envy you!" the waiter finally blurted out. "You have such a way with words."

The playwright laughed. "What do you mean?"

"Well, you know what I mean. Your talent with...images, with metaphor."

"Hmm," the playwright mused, "Can you elaborate?"

The waiter stepped back. "Well surely you know what I mean! Tonight, your words, they, they welled up inside your characters, until the clash of their tongues became dark clouds crashing together, piercing lightning bolts through our hearts and leaving a downpour of sorrow in our wake."

"Really? Well...thank you."

"And your hero's final soliloquy, well, his words of anguish and regret thundered through our bodies, fracturing any fossils of hope his courageous journey had imbedded in our bones."

"But that's wonderful," said the playwright.

"Yes, of course it is," the waiter said woefully. "If only *I* had that kind of talent."

Many of us discount our creative abilities, or deny that we have them altogether. This belief may very well have resulted from getting our creativity trampled on at an early age, when our efforts were subjected to judgment and ridicule. Being creative entails being different. It means leaving ourselves open and vulnerable without a safety net of established order to fall back on. And so instead of continuing to follow our magical inner voice, we were forced to *grow up*, to follow the rules that would allow us to gain acceptance by fitting in and acting like everyone else. In other words, we were under a lot of pressure to be *normal*.

As a result we will sometimes state flatly that we are not creative when we are asked to be artistic or make use of our imagination. But the assertion that we are not creative is far more that false modesty: it is actually impossible. True, some people may display more talent in rendering oils, expressing themselves musically or consistently being able to find the *bon mot*, but this does not mean that we do not all have the ability to create. If you have ever cooked a meal you have created something. Whenever you speak you are creating meaning from words. If you are alive—and I suspect that everyone reading this book is—then you are creating a stamp on the collective human consciousness with every thought you think and every move you make.

To be human is to be creative. Demonstrating it is a matter of tuning into and trusting our intrinsic abilities. And getting in tune with our true nature is greatly facilitated by getting in tune with nature itself. When we walk into a forest everything around us is alive and growing. If we stop taking for granted that the trees and the birds are just *there* and look more closely at their activity, we get reconnected to the world as creation. We see the harmonious growth, where everything has its place and purpose. We can be swept up by the feeling that we are a part of this world, and that creativity is within us as well. We may even get a glimpse of our life as a process of ongoing creation, creation that admittedly we are not always conscious of.

However our modern lifestyles generally make it difficult to be connected this way. Working in lifeless high-rise buildings, moving from place to place on pavement in motorized vehicles, we lose touch with growth, change, creation. Instead we live amongst cold, permanent concrete, steel and glass. Our lives get modeled around this permanence, and we get into the routine of the daily grind. We stay with what we know, continuing to do the mundane activities that we're used to and have become familiar with. When even our leisure time is spent more and more in safe and predictable confines, our imagination is neglected. Our thinking itself tends to stay within the known, rehashing the same ideas over and over again in our minds. In the process, our creativity atrophies like an underused muscle.

Still, it remains within us, ready to be activated. Our creativity can never die. It is who we are. And even if we are not conscious of it, we continue to create as our life goes on. When we are not conscious of our abilities, when we are not actively seeking to create something new, then we are fully influenced by what is around us, and simply re-create what comes into our field of perception. This is perhaps why we do not consider ourselves creative, because habitually all our thoughts, ideas, and even dreams are based on what we see before us and not our imagination. But this does not prove that we are not creative—it just means that we are not fully conscious. Consciousness really demands looking inside. Without consciousness we are like sleepwalkers, on track to continue replicating only what we see and know so that the conditions of our life generally remain the same.

But life sees to it that we have our moments, and will ultimately push us in the direction of becoming more conscious of who we actually are at some point in our lives. For example, when a couple gives birth to a child there is not only a sense of amazement but also a deeper clarity and a sharper focus. It is as if there was something they knew all along but only truly awoke to it in the moment that they first saw their newborn. So even if they had been oblivious to it all their lives, this moment cannot help but produce an epiphany for the couple: *we are creative.*

Typically we have looked at our creative moments as extraordinary in the context of our normal lives. But there is a budding suspicion nowadays that these moments actually put us in touch with the highest truth of who we are. When we are thrust by some powerful event into a recognition of our creativity, we are at one with the world. This is what it feels like to have the power of our Dao Self flowing freely through us. For a moment the ecstasy and excitement are difficult to contain. Soon enough, however, this state of being becomes just as difficult to retain. The feeling gradually fades away like a dream, as the gravity of an environment dominated by reason returns us to the familiarity of our Ego Self. We start to question whether those feelings were real and authentic, or if we were just on some momentary anomalous 'high'. Purely speaking it is not *reasonable* to be creative, so it should come as no surprise that being creative has precious little support in our society. And without support, these moments of clarity and heightened awareness soon give way to a dwindling-back into relative unconsciousness.

In his day William Blake fought tirelessly against the numbing effects on an overly rational world, saying, "I will not reason and compare; my business is to create!" His was a call to live in accordance with our passion, which leads to the desire to create, not just in artists but indeed in all humans. Creation is the true *business* of human life, even if it has not been our business *as usual*. It requires us to let go of control, to loosen the grip reason has on our thinking, and work more from the passion of our intuitive side. It is no wonder that this is uncomfortable for us, since it leads us away from the secure grounding of the tried and true. But then, how can we ever expect originality if we are simply following what has come before? The sublime and the beautiful rarely reveal themselves through the controlled application of established guidelines. Fostering our ability to create requires the courage to go beyond formulas and dig for the source in the unmarked terrain of our own minds.

I have had many challenges with the creative process on my writing path, going through periods of doubt and uncertainty about how to proceed. On the one hand, I have come to understand why writers keep talking about the *muse*, the mythic woman who shows up on her own schedule to inspires writers to find the words and ideas they long to use. There is no question of the feeling sometimes of some outside 'presence' that brings me calm, focus, and inspiration. In this state my writing is clear, strong, and sometimes even beyond what I thought I had in me. Five minutes with the muse can often bring me better results than a full day of forced effort.

On the other hand, I have a deep respect for the many successful writers who treat writing like a nine-to-five business and keep a set schedule in which they fasten themselves in front of their typewriter or computer. Certainly the adage that 'writing is one percent inspiration and ninety-nine percent perspiration' resonates with my experience. Persistence has probably been the most essential ingredient to the whole process. And yet I no longer see persistence as forcing myself to write when I'm not in the mood—because the results are almost never any good. Persistence can easily become control, and I believe the work of creativity is a letting-go of control.

Learning to walk the fine line between the two poles of allowing and persistence is, to me, learning about writing and about creativity. We don't 'do' creativity as much as we open ourselves to it. In order to create we must somehow be in touch with—and have a strong measure of trust in—

something bigger than the self we usually identify with. This doesn't mean that all we should do is sit around and wait for this bigger self—our Dao Self—to come by and enter into our lives. In actual fact our Dao Self is always there, but we often need to get out of our own way to be present to it. Our persistence serves to move us more deliberately into the *now*, where we can tap into our creative source.

Historically, artists have endowed us with reminders to move away from the mundane and live in the realm of the imagination. Great works of art provide us with models beyond the checks and balances of our rational world. When we go to a museum and see the glory of a great work of art, we are reminded that its beauty originated as a thought in the artist's mind. Every brushstroke is guided by this inspiration, this thought. The grander the thought, the grander becomes the creation.

If creating brings into being what originates in thought, then it is not reserved for what we formally call art. Creating art can be seen as a microcosm of creating life, the ultimate work of art. While it seems obvious enough that a painting or skyscraper or even a rocket was once a thought, it is a bit of a challenge for us to grasp that the very shape and fabric of our lives emerges from our thoughts. And yet this is the premise of the new conversation. It maintains that we are all creative, and we have the power to create the kind of life that we most deeply desire for ourselves.

This is an idea that has been expounded upon by many of the great thinkers and sages in history. Only now, however, is it starting to take hold in the hearts and minds of a significant number of people in our society. We are still in the early stages of fully practicing the deliberate and conscious creation of our lives. And it is not easy. The disproportionate influence of the mechanistic world view is still prevalent. It tells us that we can only believe what can be proved rationally. It tells us that our future is dictated by our past. It tells us that we are small and separate beings, at the mercy of the external circumstances of our lives, driven to behavior rather than driving it, as though we were billiard balls being knocked around a table in a deterministic manner. The mechanistic world view has left a deep mark on us, making us fear that we are merely unfeeling machines, and consciousness simply the result of random material processes. This has reinforced an ingrained habit of living unconsciously, without directed thought, without focus, without *intention*. In other words, it has reinforced the habit of *acting out of habit itself.*

But we are at the dawn of a new era. The time has come for us to talk each other out of this habit of habits, and open the way for our thoughts and beliefs to drive the circumstances of our lives forward instead of the other way around. We are ready to move beyond a life where external circumstances knock us around like billiard balls. Our growing complexity is tuning us in more to the plea of our inner voice that there is a choice, and that choice is to be creative. It allows us to soar beyond the strict boundaries of behavioral cause and effect and respond to the conditions of our lives in unique and unpredictable ways. To deny that we are creative is to resign to a life without purpose or direction. To accept it is to acknowledge that we are responsible for everything that happens to us, and have the potential to experience ourselves consciously as the creators of our lives.

31. The Fisherman

Around noon on the East beach on the island of Allandon, the fisherman sat at a makeshift table gutting and cleaning his morning catch. He was so focused on his task that he took a while to notice his dog standing beside him patiently, wagging his tail with a large stick in his mouth.

"I don't suppose you came here to help me prepare the fish for market," he said playfully. The dog continued looking up at the fisherman, eyes full of anticipation.

"No you just came to play," he said as he scruffed the dog's head briskly. "Play, eat and sleep, that's your life, isn't it?"

He put down his boning knife and wiped his hands off with a nearby cloth. "Well, I suppose I could take a break," he said to his dog. He took the stick from his dog's mouth and ran along the beach, leading the eager dog with the stick. Then he threw the stick far down the shoreline, and his dog ran after it at full speed and retrieved it for him.

After a while they returned, and the fisherman put out some of his dog's favorite food, which the dog dove right into.

"Sometimes I wish I had your life," said the fisherman as he picked up the next fish to work on. "I mean, you seem to have it all."

The fisherman looked over to the dog, as if he was expecting a response. Of course the dog paid no attention to the fisherman, and kept on eating.

"Well there is one thing I have that you don't, even though it probably causes more trouble than it's worth," said the fisherman, raising his boning knife with mock pride. "At least I can wish for a different life!"

What differentiates us from the animals that grace our planet is our self-awareness. We recognize ourselves as separate and distinct from our environment. More than any other we are the species that has traveled furthest from the Dao and have forged deep into the darkness of the universe. This is what puts us on the leading edge of consciousness, and what actually makes the discovery of who we really are all the more exciting and magical. If we identified solely with the source, the act of creation might be felt as something happening outside of us, rather than through the prism of our individuality.

Since animals are closer to the Dao than we are, they are more or less in flow with life all the time. They don't have much of an Ego Self holding them back, and so they cannot help but live in the moment, grounds for occasional envy amongst us humans. And yet, even if it were possible to do, few of us would honestly want to trade places with them. Down deep we sense that the greatest experiences life has to offer are predicated on awareness, and the more conscious we become, the more sublime our experience of being *inspired* becomes. This inspiration has grown with the growth of our consciousness, and today is moving us towards the penultimate revelation: that we create our reality by the way we think.

Kernels of the idea that our mental state actually has some creative impact on our world and what happens in it have been circulating in our society for quite some time. In recent years, the conversation has intensified around the power of positive thinking, the value of visualization, the influence of intention. The full extent of the effect of our thoughts and the role they play in our endeavor to fulfill our deepest desires is something that I believe we are just coming to grips with today.

It is not a matter of much debate that we will be able to more easily 'win friends and influence people' if we think and act confidently and positively in their company. And with the power to draw strength from our relationships it is no big stretch to see how we can directly improve upon our esteem, our career and monetary success, and our overall enjoyment of life. The idea of visualization is a bit more amorphous, but it has certainly penetrated many aspects of our lives in relation to the outcome of our performance. My own experience in sports like golf, for example, has made me a solid believer in the assertion that we have to visualize a good result in order to ensure a good result. The clearer our vision is of what is to come, the more likely the intended outcome will occur. *Be the ball*, a conscientious golfer may remind himself.

In general, the idea that we will be successful if we *believe* we will be successful is not so hard to accept when we can make a direct link between our attitude and our own behavior, and then see that our behavior has a direct effect on our environment in terms of the way in which people and circumstances react to us. However it is entirely another thing to suggest that the way we think can affect the world around us *at a distance* as it were, with no visible ties to what we are affecting. Can we really believe that positive thinking can attract the right person into our lives at the right time? That visualization can bring us abundance from an unexpected source? That intention can actually affect the weather?

Actually, in some sense, it is only modern Western societies that have been skeptical about these possibilities. In earlier times these ideas were not only accepted, they were the foundations of tribal rituals and religious practices of all kinds. These practices ranged from carrying out personal vendettas to bringing much-needed rain to the communal crops. Perhaps the only difference is that rather than believing the power to be within the minds of each individual in their culture, they vested it in the particular deity that they were devoted to. There was no doubt in their minds, however, about the invisible connection between discreet things in their environment, and the ability to tap into this ever-present web of influence through prayer and other acts of devotion.

The advent of science, which ushered in the mechanistic world view, has made it difficult for us to give credence to these invisible connections between our thoughts and what actually happens in the world. More than ever in human history, our attention has been focused on the material connections between things, because it has been seen as the only way to gain the power to get what we want in our world. This in part explains the all-consuming supremacy of money in our modern world which, for all intents and purposes, we have made into a material 'thing' that is the main source of acquiring the other 'things' that are supposed to fulfill our desires.

When a claim is made that someone has brought something material into being and fulfilled a desire by their thoughts alone, the inclination of our materialist mindset is to write it off as superstition, voodoo, or the opiate of religious fervor, maintaining that we have evolved beyond such mysticism. When uncanny events occur that seem to present us with exactly what we want, need, or have been asking for, and no clear cause-and-effect relationship can be found in the visible world, our habit of thought has been to simply attribute it to coincidence and haphazard randomness.

Like many habits, this habit of thought has been hard to break. But we have begun to do just that. The evidence to the contrary has started to become too overwhelming. And more and more this evidence has been coming from an unlikely source—science itself. Contemporary research in physics and other scientific fields demonstrates that the mechanistic world view itself may be one of the greatest superstitions in human history. Mechanism has no choice but to maintain that our thoughts are simply random offshoots of physical processes in the brain, without transcendent design or purpose. The notion that we have any intelligence outside of the domain of our physical bodies, and that this intelligence can actually have an effect on matter, is untenable in a mechanistic world. However the discoveries of modern physics beg to differ. They are actually demonstrating that it has become more *reasonable* to assert that mind creates matter rather than matter creating mind.

It is no surprise that Albert Einstein, whose driving ambition in his scientific pursuits was to 'understand the mind of God', was a key player in the modern revolution of scientific thought, and of thought in general. In his seminal 1906 paper *On the Electrodynamics of Moving Bodies*, Einstein essentially put our idea of objective reality on the shelf forever. He showed that both time and space—the underpinnings of objective measurements—were themselves subject to the conditions by which they were being observed and experienced. In other words, the *actual* passage of time and measurement of space are relative to the perspective of the observer. With relativity, the *nature* of things breaks away from the cold calculations of pure objectivity and suddenly becomes subjective. *Relative* is how things REALLY ARE, meaning that there is no absolute or objective reality as such.

While it has taken quite some time for us to catch on to this fundamental idea—over a century, to be precise—our way of thinking and living is starting to come around. We are beginning to discern that what we used to consider to be objective truths are simply unconscious agreements, collective habits of perception that are so ingrained that we consider them unchangeable objective facts. Now certainly we need many of these agreements in order to live and relate to each other, but that is not the same as saying they exist independent of us. In other words, they need an observing consciousness to become 'real'. The proverbial tree that falls in the forest with nobody around, then, actually *does not* make a sound—although it is debatable as to whether there could ever be 'nobody around'.

The discoveries of quantum physics, which studies the behavior of sub-atomic particles, have only further refined Einstein's notion, showing that the objective world is not so 'objective' after all. Let us take for example any experiment conducted by a scientist, purportedly an unattached and objective observer who desires to report on exactly what he sees and draw conclusions from it. This seems all well and good for 'traditional' observation in which a scientist can stay unobtrusively a safe distance away.

The only problem is that with sub-atomic physics, the physicist cannot stay a safe distance away because he cannot escape an intimate relationship to that which he is observing, *influencing its behavior just by observing it.* In fact, it has been shown now that some kind of exchange goes on between the observer and the observed in *every* act of observation. Its effects are simply more noticeable at a sub-atomic level. Heisenberg's famous uncertainty principle confirms this very fact. Electrons exist around a nucleus not as 'things' as such but rather as 'probability clouds' that *necessarily* wait for the attention of an observer to bring the electron to an actual position in space. Without that attention, the electron is actually and truly *nowhere in particular.*

Now in the broader phenomenal world that we live in every day, the effects of observation are not so instantaneous. There is much more to do than to position a single electron. However, while the processes might be more complex, science is starting to prove that consciousness is a participant at all levels of activity. As Lynn McTaggert says in *The Intention Experiment,*

> The implication of these early experimental findings [of quantum physics] were profound: living consciousness somehow was the influence that turned the *possibility* of something into something real...living consciousness is somehow central to the process of transforming the unconstructed quantum world into something resembling everyday reality.

The study of sub-atomic particles, the building blocks of life as we know it, has brought scientists to the unavoidable conclusion that consciousness affects matter by way of a unified energy matrix that orders the universe and weaves an intelligent design throughout the largest and smallest of entities, and all those in between. The long search of science for a unified field is now being conceived as an energy storehouse of all possible events in space and time. All things material originate in an energy state, as potential, waiting for consciousness to put sufficient attention on one possibility to bring it into material existence. In other words, material events don't just *happen*, they all originate from the focused attention of an observing intelligence on a given possibility.

The next big step science is in the process of taking is determining whether we are restricted to the role of observer, of passive consciousness, or if we can actually affect the world of our everyday lives with our consciousness in ways that we actually want. What spiritual traditions have been claiming all along—that we can shape our world and our lives with our *intentions*—has become the subject of rigorous scientific inquiry. Ground-breaking work done by people like biologist Rupert Sheldrake is opening up a vast new field of possibilities. His explorations demonstrate that not only *can* intention intervene in the bringing-into-being of matter, it is actually the foundation of such processes.

> There's a kind of intention, a kind of goal-directedness inherent in the very nature of life in the most fundamental processes that enable embryos to grow and even protein molecules to form. And I think that the kind of conscious intention we experience as part of our mental life has its background in this goal-directedness which is inherent in all living creatures, and is an essential part of the nature of life and an essential part of the nature of the organizing fields that organize living organisms.

At the height of scientific materialism in the West, large numbers of people were skeptical of all things immaterial and came to doubt that there was any purpose to our being created at all. But purpose, goal-directedness, and intention are being seen more and more as the foundations of material life. As science gets turned on its ear, it shifts from being the strongest proponent of a universe devoid of meaning and conscious design to validating the role of consciousness and the existence of an invisible world of spirit out of which the visible world emerges.

It was not long ago that science took pride in its orderly mechanistic vision, one which had us living in an unspeakably beautiful, highly sophisticated and fully functioning natural world and yet seriously doubting that there was an intelligent design behind it and a purpose to our own existence. Today, no longer is science strictly the domain of the visible and religion the domain of the invisible. The line in the sand has been crossed, and the tacit agreement between the two camps has begun to dissolve. The result is that we are starting to feel whole again.

This did not all happen by accident. For me, this is the master stroke of Creation itself. It was *intended* that the illusion of materialism become so powerful that we could doubt there was an intelligence behind it—because this doubt *itself* had a highly transcendent purpose. With this doubt, born of the emergence of the Western paradigm, of the aggrandizement of rationality over intuition, of the separation of science and spirituality, we have been brought to greater heights of individual self-consciousness. We have been propelled into a complexity that distinguishes us even more from our source and yet holds the possibility that we can feel ever more of its power.

In the universe consciousness cannot contract, it can only expand. Expanding consciousness is the flow of life and the inherent mandate of all living things. Our capacity as human beings to be conscious of ourselves brings us to the brink of a great epiphany about our purpose here: we were created to experience *being creators ourselves*. We have begun our ascent into a higher level of complexity, one that empowers us to create our world anew out of our conscious intentions, grounded in our deepest personal and collective desires.

32. The Poet

For days the poet had been diligent in getting the word out about his poetry reading. Yet when the time came, he stood on the stage in the village square looking at row upon row of empty seats. Only his friend the mason was in attendance, sitting patiently in the front row at the designated time.

"Whenever you're ready," said the mason.

"Are you kidding? I'm not reading for just one person."

"Why not?"

"And anyway, you don't really appreciate my work. You're just here as my friend."

"Not at all, I think your poetry is great."

"It's *brilliant*, which is why people should be here to hear it!"

The poet looked out to the empty seats and then up to the sky. "Why have you made things happen this way? What did I do to deserve this?"

"Who are you talking to?" asked the mason.

"Whoever made nobody show up, the powers that be, the universe, whatever," the poet said. "You're the one who keeps talking about how the universe responds to our desires, how whatever happens is exactly what we ask for."

"Yes."

"So what about this?" the poet asked as he sat down brusquely on the front edge of the stage. "I create some great poetry and the universe responds by creating an empty audience."

The mason approached him and said calmly, "Perhaps it's the *universe* that created some great poetry and *you* responded by creating an empty audience."

"Shut up!" said the annoyed poet. He banged his fist continuously on the hollow floorboards of the stage, reverberating out the sound of his frustration. The mason was unmoved, and maintained his calm demeanor.

The poet sat pensive for a few minutes, and slowly a change came over him. His face softened and his eyes welled up slightly. He leaned over and put his hand on the mason's shoulder. "Could you go back to your seat?"

"Sure. Why?"

The poet took a deep breath and rose to his feet. "I'd like to read you some beautiful poetry."

I first heard about the idea that 'we create our own reality' from Jane Roberts' book *Seth Speaks*, which my father had passed on to me when I was still a teenager. While the concept of conscious creation aroused my curiosity, there were very few people in my social circles interested in talking with me about it at the time. Fortunately, this has changed in recent years. These days, this fabled *secret* of life seems to be coming up more and more in my conversations with friends as well as with strangers. Most people I talk to now have either read about it, seen a film about it, or at least have heard the buzz around it. It has been exciting to see the subject of conscious creation begin to get widespread attention.

At first blush the concept of conscious creation seems simple enough. We take a desire (i.e. 'I want more money in my life'), put it in the form of an intention ('I *will* have more money in my life'), and if we focus on this intention with every fiber of our being then it cannot help but come true. When I first caught on to the idea I became excited by the possibility of having money come flooding into my life from the comfort of my living room sofa. I sat by myself at a certain time in the morning on several consecutive days and followed a particular set of guidelines that were supposed to announce my intention to the universe that I was ready to receive abundance.

I believed what I had read to that point about the power of intention, and I thought my will-power and discipline would see me the rest of the way. I was quite enthusiastic the first day or two, but soon I could feel it waning. Try as I might to think positively while going through the exercise, some inner uncertainty slowly crept in. By the end of the week I was sitting there, arms crossed, waiting for the universe to prove itself. This was suddenly no fun at all. Amidst my growing doubts the task became more loathsome until thankfully I gave up.

But that was not the worst part. The worst part was that I was turned off of the whole process, and blamed myself for my lack of success. I must not have tried hard enough, I thought, or didn't focus enough, or wasn't patient enough. Whatever the case, the experience left me feeling more disempowered than when I started, and for a long time I was reluctant to revisit the process of conscious creation simply because I didn't want to go through the self-recrimination again.

Although this experience was difficult, it was important for me to see it as a necessary part of the learning curve. As we collectively get swept up in the buzz of excitement around conscious creation, my concern is that many of us will get stuck in this type of disillusionment and self-blame and will give up. It's a symptom of our *modus operandi*, to seek instant gratification, to want to be given a set of action steps that we can follow mechanically to our destination.

Certainly there are those out there willing to accommodate this habit, busy at work packaging the idea of conscious creation for mass consumption, tempting us with the promise of riches and fulfillment if we follow a particular recipe for success. However when the process of conscious creation is getting sold as an off-the-shelf, stand-alone product without being part of the larger human pursuit of self-awareness, I have only two words: buyer beware.

The ability to consistently manifest what we desire is inextricably linked to our personal growth. If we are to make any real progress bringing things that we truly want into our lives, it actually requires us to take an honest look inside and begin to heal and transform our darkness.

I have come to experience that an essential ingredient to conscious creation is being aware of where we are coming from. In my early attempt to manifest money I was coming from fear, from scarcity and lack, from the type of thinking about money that my parents had. If we are coming from fear rather than love, from our Ego Self rather than our Dao Self, then our desire is imprinted with a skepticism about the connectedness of all things, and housed in doubt about the possibility of conscious creation itself because Ego Self desires do not have roots in the source of creation.

Remember the Ego Self is all about *control*, and if we try to control the process of conscious creation we will become even more disconnected from it. Control may work to a certain extent in the physical domain, where tactics such as intimidation and force have a certain amount of power over people and the environment. However in the realm of conscious creation the desire to control is useless. And so there is no real way to consider conscious creation until we are first able to move into, and *come from*, our Dao Self.

The process of moving into our Dao Self for the purposes of conscious creation is described in a powerful way in an important work on the teachings of Abraham, *Ask and it is Given*.[11] Abraham introduces the quantum-physical perspective that we are vibrational beings,[12] and we live along a scale or continuum between low and high vibrations. The higher our vibration, the more we are *allowing* our connection to source energy, or, in my language, the more we are coming from our Dao Self. The lower our vibration, the more we are inhibiting source energy, or the more we are coming from our Ego Self.

Abraham makes the distinction that our emotions are no more than *indicators* that reveal our current level of vibration. At the highest levels of vibration we find pure Love, and at the lowest levels of vibration we find pure Fear. Every other emotion in-between reflects its own relative level of vibration. The revelation is that when we want to feel better we can focus on raising our vibration rather than changing our emotion, for as we raise our level of vibration, our emotion—the way we feel—will naturally be raised. And as our feelings

---

[11] The material in this book actually comes from a non-physical entity named Abraham channeled through Esther Hicks and complied by her husband Jerry Hicks. In the time remaining in our conversation I will only be able to give the most cursory of references to this book, and would highly recommend it to those interested in a profound elaboration on conscious creation.

[12] As vibrational beings we are governed by the *Law of Attraction*, which states 'that which is *like* unto itself is drawn.' The idea is that we are always attracting into our lives, manifesting, those objects and events to which we have a vibrational match.

are raised, so then do we become more capable of conscious creation. Here is an example of this continuum of emotions relating to levels of vibration.[13]

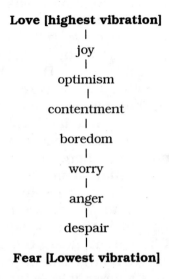

Love [highest vibration]
|
joy
|
optimism
|
contentment
|
boredom
|
worry
|
anger
|
despair
|
Fear [Lowest vibration]

Abraham notes that we can change our level of vibration by changing our thoughts. Our thoughts are *creative*, whether we are aware of it or not. When we are not aware of our thinking, then whenever we are coming from a lower vibration, our Ego Self, we are creating things we don't want—like when we're afraid of something, it is often more likely to happen to us. The thing about *conscious* creation is that we can create the things that we want, that we would love to have in our lives, if we learn how to move up the vibrational scale. And we can use our feelings as indicators, successively choosing the thoughts that feel better than the ones we have been thinking, so that we can slowly but surely move up the scale.

So the key to this all is to think better thoughts. But this may not be as easy as it seems, for underneath the thoughts we are aware of there are deep unconscious core beliefs, the kind of long-standing, solid thoughts that seem imbedded into our very essence. My intention to bring money

---

13 There is no definitive list, as different words describing emotions mean different things to different people. Still, this small sample reflects the idea of being able to step up a continuum from negative to positive emotions.

into my life was squelched by limiting core beliefs. While I had learned some important lessons from my parents around money, there were still remnants in me of their *scarcity thinking*, their belief that abundance was limited, that there wasn't enough for everyone, and that we have to scrimp and save to have enough money to live well.

In a way, this is part of the reason that the rich get richer and the poor get poorer. Being brought up in an environment of abundance tends to reinforce the idea that there is abundance in the universe, while being brought up in an environment of poverty and lack will have the opposite effect. Even though I believed, intellectually, in the power to manifest through intention, there was a much deeper core belief at work, telling me that when it comes to abundance, I could not bring it into my life effortlessly.

For any intention to work, we need to be able to transcend the limiting beliefs that contradict it. These limiting beliefs are grounded in fear. They are the brick and mortar of our personal darkness. To a large extent, what shows up every day in our lives manifests directly from these beliefs.

I experienced something a few years ago that began to show me the power I had. I was mentioning to my life coach that I hadn't been feeling at my best lately, which for me meant I wasn't feeling inspired, alive, and motivated. She suggested that I wake up the next morning and *act as if* I felt inspired, alive, and motivated, so that eventually I will start to believe it's actually true. It sounded like a novel idea—I am very much enamored with the craft of acting—so I took it on as a challenge. I started the next day, and made all attempts to have the external appearance to my wife and others that I felt inspired, alive, and motivated. It seemed very awkward at first, but by midday, I was starting to feel the way I had been *pretending* to feel. The next day was the same. The third day, it was even easier. The shift from acting to really feeling it was occurring faster. I was truly inspiring and motivating *myself*.

Now I must make a very sharp distinction between this kind of acting and actually being fake and inauthentic. Here is the key: If you are acting for the purpose of altering your limiting beliefs so that you can make the internal shift to become who you want to be, then it is an authentic act of creation. It is an act of courage and it will strengthen you inside. It is the stuff of heroes, sponsored by love. If you are acting for the purpose of fooling and convincing others that you really feel that way, with no conscious intention to shift your internal belief, then it is being inauthentic. It is the stuff of charlatans, sponsored by fear.

A life well lived is one in which we are consciously acting—as the person we want to become, as that highest vision of ourselves that we know we can be. If we let how we feel dictate how we will act, then we will always be at the whim of circumstances, we will be reactive. The greatest gift bestowed upon us as human beings is that we can always choose to be creative.

For me, I realized that bringing money into my life meant having fun with *acting* rich. This entailed being more generous, not worrying about what's on sale where but just buying what I need and not putting off what I want to do on the basis of cost alone. Now remember that to be authentic, this all has to be done with the intention of changing my limiting beliefs around money. And it feels great. These days my wife and I have absolutely no worries about money. We are growing in confidence that when we need it, it will come into our lives. Now as I write this we are in debt, and by no means am I ignoring that fact. But from my practice of acting rich over the past few years the truth of the abundance of the universe is sinking in and evidencing itself. I now have what money cannot buy—an empowering belief about money.

Over the past number of years, I have slowly cultivated a core belief in the overall beneficence of the universe, not just around money but all things. As a result, my life has seen more and more moments of freedom, joy and peace. Today I am not even trying to manifest money—I have the confidence that it will come as I need it for the fulfillment of my deeper dreams. There is a certain flow to my life, founded in an ever-growing trust in the source of creation and my ability to tap into it.

In a provocative movie that explores the basis for conscious creation in quantum physics entitled *What the Bleep Do We Know*, I was moved by a profound description of this process by Dr. Joseph Dispenza:

> I wake up in the morning, and I consciously create my day the way I want it to happen. Now sometimes, because my mind is examining all the things that I need

to get done, it takes me a little bit to settle down, and get to the point of where I'm actually intentionally creating my day. But here's the thing. When I create my day, and out of nowhere little things happen that are so unexplainable, I know that they are the process or the result of my creation. And the more I do that, the more I build a neural net in my brain, that I accept that that's possible. Gives me the power and the incentive to do it the next day.

So, if we're consciously designing our destiny, if we're consciously, from a spiritual standpoint, throwing in the idea that our thoughts can affect our reality or affect our life—because reality equals life—then I have this little pact that I have when I create my day. I say, "I'm taking this time to create my day, and I'm infecting the Quantum Field." Now, if it is in fact the *observer* watching me the whole time that I'm doing this, and there is a spiritual aspect to myself, then "show me a sign today that you paid attention to any one of these things that I created, and bring them in a way that I won't expect, so I'm as surprised as the [dickens] at my ability to be able to experience these things, and make it so that I have no doubt that it's come from you."

There is a very fine line that we need to walk if we want to be conscious creators. We need to have utter confidence that we can create experiences that seem to manifest from outside of us, where the causal link tends to be hidden. We need to feel that we are somehow in control of what happens in our life and yet we have surrendered control to our higher self. This is only possible in a complex consciousness, where the Ego Self and the Dao Self are aligned, where the Ego Self serves as the vehicle of the experience and the Dao Self is the source of the experience. As dual beings, we experience a balance of active participation and patient observation of the process. We need to have a deep sense of trust and connectedness to what Dispenza calls the *observer*, the Dao, the One from which all of creation springs. Another way of saying this is that we have to be *coming from* our Dao Self, from Love, from an authentic sense of unity and connectedness.

And this is what is often missed: if we need to be coming from our Dao Self in order to manifest our desires, then those desires themselves will be coming from Love. The desires that come from our Ego Self are counterfeit desires, founded in ignorance and Fear, leading us to greater alienation and opposition to others.

This is not a moral imperative concerning which desires we should try to manifest. It is just the way the whole thing works. The only thing we are likely to manifest coming from Fear is more of what we fear: scarcity, lack, isolation. But this doesn't mean we need to abandon our individual goals and focus only on communal goals. Not at all. As we increase our self-awareness we will recognize that our *authentic* individual goals are aligned with our universal goals because they are the *same goals*. Our individual purpose is aligned with our universal purpose because they are part of the same purpose. What gives us the greatest joy and bliss and rapture in our lives is *ipso facto* what the universe 'wants' us to pursue as well.

If our darkness is the sum of our limiting beliefs, then healing moves us towards experiencing ourselves as unlimited. This is the flow into our most worthwhile experiences, our move from ignorance to enlightenment, the evolution of our consciousness. It is the careful and constant refining and refitting of the mask that is our Ego Self, so that we can see ever more clearly through the eyeholes that we are the creator of everything we see.

Conscious creation, while not yet a major part of my life, is no longer the source of self-judgment it was the first time I tried it. Rather than focusing on the heaviness of control and predictability, I am noticing my desires being fulfilled in ways that restore my sense of surprise, wonder and enchantment with life. It has been a slow trial-and-error process of gaining the confidence that we can relate to the source of creation in a deliberate but still mysterious way. I have done much reading, experimenting, reflecting, and, perhaps most beneficially, I have gotten together with like-minded people to discuss successes and failures, insights and questions around conscious creation. In recent years, I have witnessed the spontaneous emergence of intention work groups and energy discussion groups all around me. I have felt the enthusiasm grow as the possibilities for our lives become better articulated. Enhancing our ability to create our lives and our world in the image of our highest visions is our reason for coming here, and one of the most important frontiers of the new conversation going forward.

33. The Ocean

On this morning like most every morning since the beginning, the ocean rolled its waves rhythmically onto the beach on the island of Allandon. Over time the waves had milled the sand into tiny granules, making the beach a pleasant conversation-space for the ocean and the island.

"Today I am at peace with the rush of your waves upon my shore," the island said, his tone on this day alive with curiosity and bereft of bitterness. "But other days it brings me unease. Why is that so?"

"I commend you for your growing awareness," the ocean replied. "You are starting to see that ours is necessarily a relationship of love and of fear, of joy and sorrow, of acceptance and denial."

"I don't fully understand," said the island.

"Of course not," she laughed. "What would be left to do if you fully understood?"

And as had happened many times before, the island fell into silent frustration.

"My dear island, if only you could see that understanding is no greater than confusion, then you could just revel in your search for understanding."

Still, the island was silent. And the ocean tried to soothe him with the gentle sound of her waves.

"Behold the life that has been created upon you, the trees, the flowers, the creatures that walk and buzz about."

"Do you wish me to thank you for it?" the island asked.

"That would hardly be necessary—if you could see that *you* have created it."

"And how can I see that? When I fully accept that I am a part of you?"

"It is no longer a question of accepting that you are a part of me," the ocean said tenderly, "but rather of fathoming that I am a part of you."

Nobody ever said the game that is the evolution of consciousness was an easy one to play. However, in a very real sense, it's the only game in town. And we have all chosen to participate in it, just by being here. We are at a fascinating stage of the process, on the cusp of our *definitive awakening*, which will bring us to a collective awareness of ourselves as the fountainhead of consciousness itself, playing out as separate beings in a material world.

The great difficulty of this part of the process has been facing the intense loneliness and isolation, more profound than at any time in our history. It's like moving out of childhood, when we get weaned off those things that give us a sense of security and belonging, and have to stand on our own two feet and become responsible for our lives. As conscious beings we have been driven ever further from the womb of creation, plunged into the darkness in order to forge a complex 'I' capable of self-awareness.

To make way for this move to a heightened self-awareness many of the traditional structures we have relied on at other times in our history have broken down. Blood-line ties are no longer the bond they once were. Religious structures have lost much of their power and have become splintered and fragmented. All manner of social conventions have been challenged. And those things that we once relied on to bring us together, our nationhood, our culture, our values and beliefs, are also being brought into question. So many of us feel the discomfort, either from clinging to beliefs that we have outgrown or from sensing there is no belief that we can count on at all. It is no wonder that ours is a society driven to distraction, rushing and competing, fighting and acquiring, using each other simply as a means of validation, all the time getting less satisfaction from it all.

Perfect.

For it is amid the disappointment, the despair, the dissatisfaction and the desperate seeking for something real to believe in that the definitive awakening occurs. When we grow tired of the tried and untrue avenues and feel like we have nowhere else to turn, we may finally choose to look into the teeth of our loneliness with a sincere mind and an open heart, and truly be humbled by something beyond ourselves. It is at this moment that, in spite of our disdain for religious dogmatism, we awaken to the fact that we are never really alone, that there is a loving presence that has been waiting patiently for us to open our heart in order to guide us. Once this is grasped, or more properly when it is *deeply felt*, a new doorway into possibility opens for us. We suddenly understand what it means to pray to be an instrument of a greater purpose.

This guiding presence answers our most sincere and probing questions, in the quietest and softest of our internal thoughts. The tone is much more subtle than our interaction with the physical world—and that is as it was meant to be. It is only when we perceive our interaction with this guiding force in freedom and choice can the experience truly impact the evolution of our consciousness. To follow the dictates of a higher force out of obligation or duty is often a helpful experience, but to do so fully out of choice is pure and utter bliss.

We have personified this guiding force in many ways: as a god such as Krishna of Hinduism or Zeus of Greek mythology; as a transcendent master such as Jesus, Buddha, or Mohammed, or the founder of a spiritual tradition that has spawned a long line of gurus; as spirit guides or angels, or even a departed loved one; as animals that cross our path or indeed nature itself, the wind and the sun, the moon and the stars; as signs that emanate from our physical bodies, or our dreams; even as the synchronicities that occur in our everyday lives.

All can be valuable in putting a face to the faceless One, the Brahman, Allah, God, Dao. Which is the right one? Simple. The one that personally resonates with us the most. For they all provide clues that guide us in the direction we really want to go. All we need to do is decide whether to pay attention to them or not. This is our ultimate choice, the foundation of our free will. Do I go with the flow, or against it? Do I choose Love, or Fear? Do I live consciously, or unconsciously?

I have called this guiding force our *Dao Self*, and I do so to particularly emphasize that our guiding force is actually *who we really are*. But because we have forgotten who we are, we don't fully recognize the Dao Self as *Our* Self, we see it as an *Other* Self. This allows our Dao Self to guide who we *think* we are—our Ego Self—into the experience of being alive. In fact it is the only way experience itself is possible. Our Ego Self is really our *ticket* into the material world, but in order to have the experiences that we most deeply desire, it becomes essential to let the Dao Self lead and the Ego Self follow. As the Ego Self gets more complex, it becomes more capable of choosing whether or not to follow—which then makes following the Dao Self an increasingly profound and exhilarating experience.

Our Dao Self bathes us in guidance with the regularity of waves on the beach. But this is done ever so quietly, patiently and without judgment, providing a space for us to step into when we are ready. In this way, our conversation with the Dao Self is like the new conversation. In fact it is the *original* new conversation, a model that has been with us since the birth of consciousness, since the first day the island awoke and noticed that it was separate from the ocean.

From that moment we have had a deep longing to return to oneness, but life itself has a longing of its own—for ever greater diversity. In the evolution of all species there is a pull towards greater variety, greater complexity. Our lives are animated by the dance between the longing for unity and the longing for diversity. Today, this dance is moving us towards a more integrated and functional relationship between our rationality and our intuition, our darkness and our light, our Ego Self and our Dao Self. These polarities are getting closer together as our evolution proceeds, but like an exponential curve on a graph, the curve approaches the axis but is never able to touch it.

While the guidance of our Dao Self can come through gods and prophets, spirit guides and angels, more and more today it is coming through *each other*, for we too can serve as personifications of this guiding force. Despite all our flaws and foibles, faults and failings, we are becoming better placed to be a face and voice of each other's Dao Self—after all, we share the *same* Dao Self. There is only One.

For this to work, we are called to establish a sacred trust in our conversations, one that grows the more we create a space of non-judgment, and live from a paradigm that is inclusive of all others—just like our Dao Self does. The better we get at doing this, the more we are able to provide one another with the leverage and traction to evolve, to move into a self that is much bigger, more powerful, more loving than we know ourselves to be.

Certainly we are free to try to go it alone, to insist that our path is uniquely ours and we cannot be following someone else. This may get us a little ways down the path, but eventually it will leave us stranded. If we are to fulfill our deepest desire to unite, part of our mission will always involve accepting help from others. And when we become lost or stranded, the best way to find our way again is by helping another to find *their* way. Our purposes become ever more entwined as we get closer to the top of the mountain and sense our profound connectedness.

> Brave climber, fret not
> When the slope is steep and,
> Anxious to ascend,
> You reach up for that helping hand
> And find none.
>
> For this moment too is precious.
>
> It invites you not
> To reach up but down,
> To another who may be searching
> For *your* helping hand.
>
> For we chase the heights together,
> Tethered by purpose,
> And moderated by a rhythm
> That delivers the most and least likely among us
> As one to the view from on high.

Herein lies the perfection of our universe. If we look at the miracle that is the human body, we see billions upon billions of individual cells working together, each with a very specific function and purpose. And these cells are in constant communication with each other, governed by a single mind, checking and testing that their own functioning is perfectly aligned with the purpose of the organism as a whole. Every one of these cells are organisms themselves, which are graced in the same way by the synchrony of each atom and molecule that constitutes them.

From on high we can see that the entire universe is a living organism, where the individual destinies of its component parts are bound by a unified purpose. From the microscopic to the macroscopic, there are organisms nested within organisms, atoms and molecules, our individual bodies, our communities and nations, our planet and our solar system and in the universe beyond. *Uni-verse* literally means 'one song', and represents a stage where we are all part of one great and harmonious choir. Chief Seattle was right when he said 'Everything is connected'.

What is special about human beings is that we can be fully conscious of our role, and actually have been given a choice as to how we will participate in this grand process. Here we can finally understand why the all-powerful, omniscient Creator doesn't step in to set things right when the planet goes out of balance and we are not working together. It is because we are meant to have the opportunity to realize that *we* are the all-powerful creators of this world.

Like the cells of our body, we are all connected by a single mind. We are forging new pathways of communication with each other in order to unite around our common purpose. The mandate of the new conversation is to bring a critical mass of people to a certain threshold, one that will rouse the whole of humanity to its definitive awakening. While we certainly don't need to talk to every person on the planet to reach this critical mass, every human being is invited to step in whenever they choose. One conversation at a time, we are waking each other up from the slumber of unconsciousness, so that we can be present together to the wonder of our creation.

34. The Busser

On a bright summer morning on the island of Allandon, the jeweler was sitting alone out on the patio of the village restaurant enjoying a cup of steaming coffee. The busser came out to clear a nearby table, noticed the salt shaker, and then took the nozzle off and began working meticulously to clean it. When he had been at it for over a minute, the jeweler couldn't help but make a remark.

"Do you have to clean out *every* grain of salt?" he asked playfully.

The busser turned and thought for a moment, and then answered: "I guess that depends on whether I think I'm cleaning a salt shaker or changing the world."

The jeweler was intrigued by the busser's comment. "What do you mean by that?"

"Well, imagine I knowingly put this salt shaker down with one nozzle hole plugged. Maybe a woman sitting at this table one day would be having a conversation, and a wisp of a thought enters her head just as she is sprinkling salt in her soup. The woman might faintly sense the stuck nozzle, and put in an extra dash. With her attention going to the slightly too-salty soup on her first spoonful, that wisp of thought might float off. This may have been an important thought, a building block to helping her friend heal her marriage. But if it went unexpressed, the marriage might not get healed and could continue to manifest in other areas. Perhaps it would contribute to her son growing up angry and choosing to act out violently when confronted with difficulties in his own relationships. The son might end up in jail, and the ripple effects..."

"Now wait. All this from unblocking a single salt shaker nozzle hole?"

"Not necessarily. It could be the way the cutlery is arranged or how fresh the coffee is. It could be how I interact with the customers or the way I listen to what the waiters or the cooks need. It's all about providing a space for people to be at their best."

"Is this part of the job description of being a busser?"

"I like to think it's part of the job description of being human."

The jeweler took a sip of his coffee. "I'm impressed," he said. "You know, I could really use someone like you in my business. How would you like to work in my shop?"

"I already am," replied the busser.

It is always fun for me to meet someone who feels they have found their mission, their calling, their *purpose* in life— whatever it may be. From my experience these people are happy, motivated, and able to deal with anything life throws their way. Best of all, they can bring everyone around them to life. They remind me that my life works best when I am aligned with a purpose that not only fulfills me but also serves others in some important way. I know it's not always easy to come to know what our purpose in life is. But working to discover it can really be half the fun.

One good way to move closer to our purpose in life is to help someone else. We can help others discover their purpose by pointing out their skills and talents, by noticing what brings out their passion, what makes them feel alive. Sometimes people are so busy doing what they think they are supposed to do, they need us to notice where their energy really wants to take them.

If we think about our own lives, we are sure to remember moments when we needed others to tell us that our lives meant something, that we mattered. Sometimes we need to be acknowledged for exactly who we are. We need someone to point out our beauty and value when we don't see it in ourselves, when we don't think we measure up or have anything worthwhile to offer. And when someone ennobles what we perceive to be our greatest faults, it can change everything. Note this charming parable that I received in an email a few years ago:

> An elderly Chinese woman had two large pots, each hung on the ends of a pole which she carried across her neck. One of the pots had a crack in it while the other pot was perfect and always delivered a full portion of water. At the end of the long walks from the stream to the house, the cracked pot arrived only half full. For a whole two years this went on daily, with the woman bringing home only one and a half pots of water. Of course, the perfect pot was proud of its accomplishments. But the poor cracked pot was ashamed of its own imperfection, and miserable that it could only do half of what it had been made to do. After two years of what it perceived to be bitter failure, it spoke to the woman one day by the stream.
> "I am ashamed of myself, because this crack in my side causes water to leak out all the way back to your house."
> The old woman smiled, "Did you notice that there are flowers on your side of the path, but not on the other pot's side? That's because I have always known about your flaw, so I planted flower seeds on your side of the path, and every day while we walk back, you water them. For two years I have been able to pick these beautiful flowers to decorate the table. Without you being just the way you are, there would not be this beauty to grace the house."

Acknowledging people for who they are and recognizing the beauty and greatness of their unique selves is the currency of the new conversation, and a skill worth developing. I'm still working on it. I learned a great lesson on this from a girlfriend several years ago. Early in our relationship she asked me to meet her at a center for mentally challenged people where she worked. I pretended that I had no problems with it, but in fact was very uncomfortable about entering into that environment, especially if I had to interact with some of *those people*. I suppose the only reason I actually agreed to go in was because I wanted to impress her with my, ahem, open-mindedness. Instead, I was the one who got impressed, by the way she spoke with her clients as human beings, without a hint of condescension. She exuded confidence that she could communicate with them, and I could see that she was able to. Her authentic expression slowly drew me into the conversation, and as I started speaking with a few of her clients I felt an invisible wall that I had built up between me and *those people* coming down for the first time in my life. It was a wall founded in my own judgment and fear. And when the wall came down, I started to get an inkling of the connectedness we shared. All my life I had shunned *those people*, dehumanized them, and unconsciously believed that their life was an unfortunate mistake and had no purpose.

Like most humbling experiences, this one came with a gift. It got me closer to a deep awareness that everybody has a reason for being here, and each person's life has purpose, no lesser or greater than anyone else's. There are no 'those people' except within a judgmental mind. We are really all connected by our individual and collective purpose. When we see that, then we see every interaction as an opportunity to wake each other up to our destiny. That is why everyone is invited in to the new conversation. We are all in this together. As John Donne said, we are all 'the same author of the same volume.' And as we boldly seek to fulfill the true desires we hold individually, we contribute to the ongoing story of humanity.

We are at the precipice of a collective leap of consciousness. Our entire history has brought us to this point. And when we look at our own lives, we can see how our own history, our own experiences have brought us to this point, to reading this chapter in this book, to thinking about our own transformation. It is time for each of us to stop believing that we can't make a difference, that we're not part of this. Since we are all distinct individuals we each bring a unique spin on the universe that nobody else could provide. We have a role and we play a part. The world is waiting for us to use that unique spin to consciously *create*, a sport previously reserved for the gods of myth and lore. In the new conversation we are moving quickly towards a critical mass of people who are becoming aware of how we are creating our circumstances, our lives, our world. And as we continue to encourage each other to experiment, to remember who we are, and to live in possibility rather than dwell in inevitability, our lives become ever more intertwined.

Some time after I had begun writing this book I was looking through some old papers and came across a folder of my father's writing which I had kept. There were only a few pages of scant notes and the beginnings of a few stories. Under the title *The Game Called Life* was written the following introductory statement:

> I guess what this book is about is to make the following statement, and have it heard, miraculously, by myself and others: "I am god and you are god!" The ravings of a madman? I don't think so!

Up to that point I had always resisted seeing a connection between my father's life and my own. I considered my life a moving-away from my father and his influence and behavior. But in that moment, with my book now well underway, the evidence really became impossible to ignore. I was clearly following something that he had started. Our purposes seemed to be aligned, as though I was meant to continue what he had embarked upon. Indeed, it would not be inaccurate to say that in *The Game Called Life* my father wanted to expand on the idea that we take ourselves too seriously. It was through the trials of a difficult life filled with fear and uncertainty that he had moments where a clear and breathtaking vision of a life of peace and exhilaration were possible. He never finished the book, nor did he really fulfill this vision in the way he lived his life. But just seeing those hand-written pages again, I could not help but feel a greater connectedness to a larger whole, and see my life itself as part of a plan far vaster and more complex than I could imagine.

Much like my father, my own path has been fraught with fear, sadness and loneliness. As a child I was painfully shy, and growing up I was rather uncomfortable in social situations. As I became older I had a great desire to understand the mysteries of these social situations, so I made it a point to put myself in those situations, despite the discomfort, so that I could experience them and learn more about them. At least this way, if I got to know what other people were thinking and feeling, I wouldn't feel so uncomfortable or stupid. Perhaps this was the original motive for my strong desire to 'figure things out' in life.

Today, my past no longer causes me shame or regret. I have come to see why I had to experience those things to fulfill a greater plan. If I have experienced the dark side of human life during this lifetime, then all the more precise will be my language in talking about the possibility of emerging out of it. Who better than the most serious of people to speak about the possibility of creating a life that is fun? As Shakespeare's young Prince Henry the Fourth remarked,

> Like bright metal on a sullen ground,
> My reformation, glitt'ring o'er my fault,
> Shall show more goodly and attract more eyes
> Than that which hath no foil to set it off.

If we could help each other see the difficult experiences that we have had in our life so far in this way, as a foil against which our true nature can shine, as the darkness that brings out our light in greater relief, then perhaps it would become easier for us to believe that we have a very important contribution to make to the evolution of consciousness in the world, not in spite of our so-called 'imperfections', but *because* of them. Our active participation in life is what will help us heal, when we bring our darkness into our lives rather than shut it out of our lives. Our darkness, after all, *defines* our uniqueness. As Nietzsche reminds us, 'Be careful when you cast out your demons that you don't throw away the best of yourself.'

It is not important for us to push ourselves to be *perfect*, we need to simply encourage each other to be who we are. *Who we are* will naturally move us in the right direction, because at root who we are is love. My conversation with you has helped me to see that my purpose is fulfilled when I get out of my own way, that my mission to take life less seriously does not itself have to be so serious. In a way, just this thought makes me feel a bit lighter.

35. The Parable

The mayor of the island of Allandon loved to spend time with his daughter. They would explore the island, play games together, and also have some unusually serious discussions. He loved to recount to her all the great stories of myth and lore. Although she was still very young the mayor's daughter was quite intelligent and infinitely curious.

One calm and cloudy day, as they were finishing their lunch in a clearing in the south meadows, she suddenly posed, "Why are we alive?"

"Uh, why do you ask?" he asked, slightly taken aback.

"I've been wondering about it for a long time. I mean, shouldn't we know why we're alive before we try to do anything?"

"That makes sense," the mayor said as he stroked the top of her hair gently.

"So why are we alive?"

The mayor stood up and took a deep breath. "OK, let me tell you a parable. One day, in a—"

"Dad," the little girl interrupted.

"Yes?"

"I think I'm getting too old for parables."

"Oh, too old for them, are you?" said the mayor with a smile.

"Yes. I'm ready to hear about exactly the way things are. I don't want just a story. I want the truth."

"I see," said the mayor. He settled back down beside his daughter and sat thoughtfully for a few moments. "Well I'll try. But you have to promise not to interrupt."

"I won't," she said with anticipation.

"Are you sitting comfortably? Listen carefully."

His daughter awaited with rapt attention. She had been looking forward to this day when she would finally learn the truth about life. She waited, but her father said nothing. She thought he must be thinking about how he would explain things. But time went on and on and still he said nothing. Whenever she would look over as if to speak, he would simply put his finger to his lips. Finally, after thirty minutes, she could stand it no longer.

"What am I listening for?" she asked. The mayor, sitting calmly, simply put his finger to his lips once again.

"I don't understand!" she screamed. She was so distressed that the mayor felt he had better break his silence.

"It's OK," said the mayor, trying to comfort her. He said, "The reason we are alive is—" and then abruptly stopped. He took a breath to gather himself, and then gave her a warm embrace. "The truth is, I don't really understand it myself," he finally said.

The mayor's daughter was silent. She released herself from their embrace and quietly filled the picnic basket. The mayor worried that his long silence had been the wrong thing to do as they made their way, hand in hand, out of the meadow.

After a long and quiet walk home, the mayor's daughter finally broke her silence once their house was in view.

"Dad," she said.

"Yes, sweetheart?"

"What was that parable you wanted to tell me?"

From the start, our conversation was meant to be an opening of possibilities rather than an instruction manual on how to live. This is not to discount the fact that instructions, guidelines, and formulas may work very well for us some of the time. But I believe this speaks to where we are at, more a measure of our state of readiness and awareness than of the method itself. A certain method, system or paradigm may work beautifully for *me*, but it does not mean that it will necessarily work for you in the same way. Many times I have handed someone a book that has changed my life and believed that it would do the same for them, only to see that they are not moved by the words and ideas in the same way as I had been. People have handed books to me with similar results.

And so it is with *Parables for the New Conversation*. If you have gotten this far, then I think it's safe to assume that you have gotten *something* out of it. But as I said earlier, it is yours to take as you will. You may not have always felt a part of the 'we' that I used so often in the book, and this is perfectly fine. This 'we' was often meant as a testament to the idea that in a most fundamental way we are all one, and we are all connected to the experiences and beliefs of one another, even if they do not all resonate with us personally.

Bring with you on your journey only those ideas in the book that appeal to you. Perhaps now is not the time for some ideas, and later you may decide to come back to them. What we need and what we are ready for naturally changes over the course of our lifetime. In the early stages of writing this book I went with my wife to India to study yoga. A few years earlier the idea might have seemed like folly to me. Some books that I left unread for years proved very influential to me later on when I finally did pick them up.

Like other books that delve into the world of spirit, this has been a conversation that attempts to point to an ultimate truth that is not only beyond words, in a way it resides beyond thought. Every spiritual tradition uses words and ideas and paradigms as pointers to the mysterious, to a place that seems familiar to us deep inside of ourselves, because the ultimate truth is indeed deep inside of ourselves. The very reason that I use parables is because they go a little bit beyond the limits of everyday language. They are more open to your interpretation. They can provide a more direct resonance with your experience. Your life itself endows you with an anthology of parables for you to reflect on, lived on the stage of a physical universe, which is itself merely a grand metaphor for the spectacular imagination of the Dao.

If any particular paradigm about the unseen is introduced to you as the absolute truth, as the final word on the subject of that which connects us all, I would recommend some caution. When someone promotes a truth that excludes other truths, and describes the One/Dao/God in a way that labels all other descriptions as illusion, then this view itself is deeply mired in illusion. If there is true unity in the One of many names, then there is also a unity in our different perceptions of it. While there may be differences in scope, complexity, and utility, to say one perception is 'right' and others 'wrong' is to miss the point entirely.

I marveled one time several years ago at a co-worker's insistence that his particular religious beliefs ruled out the possibility that anyone who was not a member of his religious order could have access to the truth about the spiritual world. He was a highly intelligent man, and so when I questioned the logic of his belief that his religion's relatively tiny membership was the only group of people who would actually be saved and go to heaven, he gave the solipsistic answer, "What would be my faith if I believed otherwise?"

A faith that *excludes* is necessarily a fragmented faith, by the very fact that it worships the All but does not encompass all. It is a mindset that promotes division and war, one that a growing number of people would like to disarm. The new conversation is an invitation to all people of all walks of life. Nobody is excluded. What is true for a single individual does not invalidate what is true for another. Each truth is an approximation, necessarily limited by perspective. But while it is limited, this does not make it untrue. As Khalil Gibran writes,

> Say not, "I have found the truth," but rather "I have found a truth."
> Say not, "I have found the path of the soul."
> Say rather "I have met the soul walking upon my path."
> For the soul walks upon all paths.

If the new conversation is really to be one that unifies rather than one that divides, then its guiding principle must be a deep and abiding respect for the way all others see the world. In so doing, it encourages each one of us to broaden our paradigm in a way that can eventually incorporate the paradigms of all others, even when—especially when—those views appear to be diametrically opposed. Our collective endeavor to be whole can only be fulfilled when the West sits down with the East, when science opens a dialogue with faith, when the mind welcomes the heart.

When I do *improv* theatre, one of the most important ways to bring a scene together is by employing the 'yes-and' form of dialogue. Players are advised not to negate 'offers' from other players but rather incorporate them in building the story on stage. The joy of having each other's ideas respected and included in the story is infectious, and unites not only the players on stage but the audience as well.

In life we are all together on the same stage. When the spotlight shines on us, our role is simply to be authentic, to live from a paradigm that makes possible the fulfillment of our unique desires. If the paradigm that you are currently using isn't working for you, why not latch on to a better one, one that strikes a chord with your being and your experience and helps make your life work? If you're worried that it's not right, that it's not true, that it's a fantasy or an illusion, stop worrying. At some level *all* that we experience here is an illusion, and *any* way that we structure our experience will be limited. It's up to each one of us to order and give meaning to our lives in the way that we see fit, in a way that best serves ourselves and others. That is how we are at choice, and ultimately responsible for everything that happens in our life— because we have chosen how we process and interpret every event.

What is an Ego Self? What is a Dao Self? They are simply constructions, concepts that I have used to try to facilitate the expression of my paradigm and the experience of my life in this book. These are neither the first nor the last words on the subject of who we are, but simply a part of the ongoing conversation. Previous paradigms put forth in ancient and modern texts, while different, hold common threads that bind us in our understanding of the human experience. If we continue to push our minds to the limits of what we can grasp, we can continue to create for ourselves a more refined language that can better accommodate our expanding consciousness and our growing hunger to communicate with each other.

If we are to experience Heaven on Earth, then we must help one another with the growing pains of this expansion. In the new conversation we are moving to fulfill our destiny as proper stewards of our planet by fathoming how we are the creators of it all, and then harnessing that creative power. It is when we start to manifest this power in the world from our highest selves that the assertion 'God made man in his own image' can have its fullest and most satisfying expression.

It is up to us what we do from this point on. We all have choice. We can do what we want. Our deepest experience of fulfillment is our guide. We need only reflect for a moment to notice if our lives are bliss and joy and rapture on a consistent basis, or are fraught with doubt, guilt and loneliness. Our Dao Self is patiently calling us, giving us guidance as to where we want to go. Are we listening to that voice and embracing it, or are we passing it off as unimportant? Are we even being still and quiet long enough to hear the voice, or are we running around all day chasing what we think we want and need? Paying attention to or ignoring that voice is our choice. But if we really knew that we were making a choice between Bliss and Suffering, between Love and Fear, between Unity and Isolation, which do you suppose we would choose?

Yes the path seems difficult sometimes. But let us not forget that we are here for each other. Literally. You are the fundamental reason that I am here and vice versa. If this were not the case, we would each have a planet all to ourselves. The universe is certainly big enough for it. So while we are here together and have created a language to communicate with each other, let's take advantage of it. Let us actively participate in the new conversation.

What does the new conversation really look like? Well, it could look like many things. A parent listening to what their child dreamt about the night before; a student and a teacher discussing a difference of opinion; a boss telling an employee a bit about his personal life; a group that meets on a regular basis to support each other on how to manifest in the world and fulfill their goals; or strangers who meet on an airplane, finding out that they share a passion.

The new conversation has as many appearances as there are ways for us to interact with each other. It is not what it looks like from the outside that defines the new conversation but rather how it is experienced by its participants on the inside. It is not what we know or even what we say—it is where we are coming from that makes all the difference. The new conversation is bound by a certain spirit that unites us, a spirit of respect, trust, acceptance, and openness. It is about listening with real curiosity. And it is grounded in speaking the truth as best we know it. As Neale Donald Walsch writes in *Conversations With God,*

> Ultimately, all real communication is about truth.
> And ultimately, the only real truth is love.
> That is why, when love is present, so is communication.
> And when communication is difficult, that is a sign that
> love is not fully present.

There is no better way to sum it up: the spirit that binds the new conversation is *love.* It is my hope that you feel that we have been engaging in such a conversation, you and I. And if so, my request is that you carry it forward, for the world awaits the mutual and collective energy of our voices. Let us dare to express our deepest desires and most intriguing visions. If you are not sure of what you will say, you are not alone. Anybody who thinks they know is fooling themselves. In the end it is a mystery for all of us. But we are not looking for experts anymore, just others who are willing to share in the inquiry with an open heart. We can no longer deny that we have something that needs to be said, for when we encourage each other to explore the depths of our being, we cannot help but be spellbound by its vastness, and dazzled by the endless possibilities it offers for our lives and for our world.

36. The Explorer

One day a large vessel from afar landed on the East beach. A world explorer emerged from the mists of the morning dew, a handsome figure decked in fine garments and gold jewelry. At the gates of the village he encountered the hermit who sat in rags with his beggar's bowl.

"What is this place, old man?"

"Allandon," the hermit replied.

"Allandon!" said the explorer with incredulous laughter. "This is the fabled island of Allandon?" His laughter verged on crying.

"Why do you laugh?" asked the hermit.

"It seems I have unceremoniously reached the pinnacle of my world travels," the explorer said. "I have voyaged at great expense to find Allandon, where they say life is harmonious and abundant. Instead the first thing I find is a pathetic old man who has been reduced to begging."

The explorer started walking back to his ship.

"I can understand your disappointment," the hermit said.

The explorer turned around. "Yes. I thought when I found Allandon I would finally find a place of true harmony. I have traveled the world to this end, but I am left to conclude that there is none."

"Ah, but there is such a place," the hermit said gently. "A place where only love and peace reside."

The explorer moved a few steps closer to the hermit, giving him a piercing stare. "Tell me where it is, and I will climb any peak to reach it."

"Alas, in that way you will never find it."

"Well then, must I charter the finest ship to cross the oceans to this place? If so I will do it."

"This place is deeper than the deepest ocean, and much higher than the highest mountain."

"Then I am lost," the explorer said.

"An excellent place to start your journey," the hermit said with a smile.

Afterword

Without the significant contribution of others who have nurtured the new conversation in recent years, my understanding of the diverse topics in this book—indeed, this book itself—would not have been possible. I feel as though I have already engaged in intimate conversations with many wonderful people at the forefront of the new conversation, though I have not formally met them but through their books and audio programs. Among those whose expression and insights have had a particularly profound impact on me are Wayne Dyer, Deepak Chopra, Neale Donald Walsch, Joseph Campbell, Eckhart Tolle, Marianne Williamson, Esther and Jerry Hicks, Shakti Gawain, Debbie Ford and Rupert Sheldrake.

If this book enters into the flow of the new conversation that has been circulating in our society, my intention will be fulfilled. I am especially hoping to continue the conversation with you, the reader. I would be interested in hearing your impressions, objections, insights, and questions. I invite you to continue this conversation with me through my website, www.daocoaching.com. Until then, take care.

Richard

ISBN 1425173982-5

9 781425 173982